THE DISCOUNT GUIDE FOR TRAVELERS OVER 55

THE DISCOUNT GUIDE FOR TRAVELERS OVER 55

FOURTH EDITION

CAROLINE & WALTER WEINTZ

Edited by John Melchert

E.P. Dutton New York

Published in the United States by E. P. Dutton, a division of NAL Penguin Inc., 2 Park Avenue, New York, N.Y. 10016.
Published simultaneously in Canada by Fitzhenry and Whiteside Limited, Toronto.

ISBN: 0-525-48358-6

W

Editor: Sandra W. Soule

10 9 8 7 6 5 4 3 2 1

Fourth Edition

THANK YOU

Our first thanks must go to Caroline and Clark Giles for their exhaustive and exhausting researching of senior discounts in Tennessee: Thank you!

Our particular thanks also go to John Melchert, able editor of this fourth edition, and to researchers Kathryn A. Buckley, Jennie Bucove, and Guy Zettler who checked and double-checked thousands of senior discounts.

In addition, we gratefully acknowledge the assistance of hundreds of state and area offices for the aging, chambers of commerce, and state and international tourism offices.

Special thanks go to the following for their great interest and help in gathering information for this book: Synetta Armstrong, Southwestern Bell Media; John J. Spaulding, Connecticut Department of Transportation; Shirley Condiff, Department for the Aging, Wichita, Kansas; Lawrence S. K. Lee, City and County of Honolulu; Roy R. Keen, Oklahoma Special Unit on Aging; Williamsburg Area Tourism and Conference Bureau; San Francisco Department of Public Health; Niagara Falls Convention and Visitors Bureau; Minneapolis Convention and Visitor Commission; Wake County Council on Aging.

Roberta Goldberg, Canadian Tourist Office; Anne Stocker, Metropolitan Toronto Convention and Visitors Association; Canada's Capital Visitors and Convention Bureau; Michel Harvey, Tourisme Québec; Elvira Quarin, Tourism, Vancouver.

Bedford Pace, British Tourist Authority; Danish Tourist Board; Minna Korhonen, Finnish Tourist Board; Irish Tourist Board; Italian Government Travel Office; Diana Willis, Jamaica Tourist Board; Norwegian Tourist Board; Evelyn Mariperisena, National Tourist Office of Spain; Swiss National Tourist Office; Yugoslav National Tourist Office.

Last but far from least, thanks to Sandy Soule and Rosanne McManus of Dutton, whose help made this edition possible.

With the help of all these people and many more from hotels, airlines, museums, theaters, and tourist attractions, we've done our best to put together the most accurate guide possible; however, opening hours, telephone numbers, and discount policies are subject to change and revocation without notice. So please help us to keep the *Discount Guide* up to date by bringing to our attention any corrections that should be made. Write to *The Discount Guide for Travelers Over 55*, E. P. Dutton, 2 Park Avenue, New York, NY 10016.

Contents

THE DISCOUNT GUIDE FOR TRAVELERS OVER 55

All About Discounts

Welcome to the fourth expanded and updated edition of *The Discount Guide for Travelers Over 55*. The hundreds of new discounts and scores of increased discounts in this latest edition prove that seniors who know where to look and who to ask can save more than ever before on plane and train travel, hotels and restaurants, entertainment, and tourist attractions.

So, if the phrase "senior citizen discount" makes you think of the corner drugstore, think again and think of *travel*. Senior citizen discounts will help you save money on vacations, business trips, visits to your children, weekends at the beach, European tours, journeys across the country, and trips across the state. *The Discount Guide for Travelers Over 55* names hundreds of travel discounts and shows you how to find thousands more.

Now that you've reached the age of 55, the travel industry treats you like a privileged person. Thousands of hotels will give you a 10% to 50% discount. Airlines may fly you for less. Automobile rental agencies will rent you a car at a substantial discount. In fact, trains, buses, museums, movie theaters—even bowling alleys—here and abroad offer you price breaks that you couldn't get when you were a year younger. Why? Because industry sees senior citizens as too old, too feeble, and too poor to pay full price? Not for a minute! The business world is waking up to the fact that people over 55 have money, the time to spend it, and a lifetime of experience in bargain hunting. Travel marketers know that seniors have the flexibility to travel during the middle of the week, during the middle of the day, when business travelers need to be at their appointments, when workers need to be at their jobs, and when students must be at their desks.

Traveling with senior discounts is a totally new concept that includes, but doesn't stop with, "budget" travel. So don't think that discount travel means that you'll have to give up comfort and quality or stay in a hotel miles from the beach or city center. Whether you want to spend $15 or $150 a day, you will find the discounts in the following pages helpful. If you've been saving for years for a lavish vacation and want to go first-class all the way, senior discounts will enable you to do it at a more moderate price. And senior discounts will stretch an expense account and make any business trip more fun. You can fly to your destination at a 50% discount, rent a large air-conditioned car at a 30% discount, and stay in one of the nicer rooms in a first-class hotel for a 25% discount. Or, if this doesn't fit your style or budget, you can take a bus to your destination for a 20% discount, stay at a budget hotel with a 10% discount, get around by local transportation at a 10% to 50% discount, and eat at a fast-food restaurant offering a 10% discount.

How young can you be to qualify for these senior discounts? It depends. Although 55, 60, 62, and 65 are all popular ages for defining senior citizen, anyone over 50 can ensure their senior status—and eligibility for senior discounts—by joining one of the national senior citizens' organizations. More about this in the section titled "Senior Citizens' Organizations."

What kind of identification do you need to claim your

senior discount? A driver's license, Medicare card, senior citizens' organization membership card, or passport are the chief forms of ID. Some hotels and restaurants issue their own senior IDs. Some of these are free—some aren't. See "Hotel, Transportation, and Sightseeing Discounts" for details.

Just because you're a senior citizen, don't expect to walk up to the airline ticket counter or hotel desk and hear the eager clerk exclaim, "And for you, sir, our 50% senior citizen discount!" In order to receive discounts anywhere, you must know about them and request them *before* you pay. To help you find these invisible discounts, *The Discount Guide for Travelers Over 55* identifies and explains the policies of companies and chains that offer senior citizen discounts. Study the company policies outlined in the next chapter, "Hotel, Transportation, and Sightseeing Discounts," before you start benefiting from the hundreds of discounts listed in "The Discounts: City-by-City Listings."

In addition to leading you to hundreds of regularly given senior discounts, the *Discount Guide* has enlisted the aid of many cooperative people to create special discounts only for the readers of *The Discount Guide for Travelers Over 55*. If the listing reads "10% discount with *Discount Guide*," you'll have to show your copy of this book, before you receive the discount.

And don't overlook the senior discounts in your own community. Keep an eye on your local newspaper and write to your area office for the aging for details of discount programs. If you can't find the address in the telephone directory, write to the state office for the aging—the addresses are given under the heading *Helpful Addresses* below each state name in "The Discounts: City-by-City Listings."

Knowing where to find senior discounts is only half the battle. You must understand how to take the best advantage of them. To get the most from senior citizen discounts, follow these three rules: (1) Plan ahead. (2) Join a major senior citizens' organization. (3) Take an active part in reminding the travel industry that senior discounts are important to you by asking for them wherever you go.

HOW TO USE THE *DISCOUNT GUIDE*

Rule Number One for discount travel is Plan Ahead—a deceptively short phrase that includes organizing all of the wheres, whens, and hows of your trip. You certainly won't want to plan every moment weeks in advance, but once you've decided where to go, hotel and transportation reservations will have to be made.

First, obtain all possible information about your destination. You'll find the addresses of the tourist information offices of the fifty states, Canada, Mexico, the Caribbean, and European countries in "The Discounts: City-by-City Listings." These offices are wonderful sources of colorful brochures and general information, but to get the most out of tourist offices, make a list of specific questions. Not just "Tell me what to see and do in Orlando, Florida," but "When won't Orlando be full of tourists? What is the weather like then? Are hotel and transportation prices lower? What special events happen at this time of year?" and "Do all of the major tourist attractions remain open in the off-season?" If you don't get complete or satisfactory answers to your questions, call the tourist information office and ask. Many of these offices now have toll-free numbers that are given in "The Discounts: City-by-City Listings."

Let's pretend that you've really written for information about Florida. The Florida Tourist Information office has suggested that you will find mild weather, not too many tourists, and special senior discounts in Florida from September to November. (If the tourist office forgets to tell you about "Senior Season" in Florida, check the details under Florida in "The Discounts: City-by-City Listings.") And since the weather, the prices, and your vacation dates all seem to point to Orlando, you've made up your mind.

Now that you've decided where and when to go, it's time to make the travel arrangements. The *Discount Guide* will steer you toward the most economical plans. For a quick summary of discount transportation, turn to the next chapter where there is advice on senior discounts offered by all forms of transport. You'll find that major airlines may give discounts to seniors flying to Florida, and that Amtrak, Trailways, and Greyhound give discounts to seniors traveling by train and bus. If you'd rather drive yourself, you can rent a car with a senior discount from Hertz, Avis, or National.

Where will you stay? "Hotels, Transportation, and Sightseeing" names and details the policies of hotel chains offering discounts of up to 25% to seniors. Be sure to read the paragraphs about each hotel chain very carefully. In many cases, seniors must meet specific requirements and make advance reservations to qualify for discounts.

Next turn to "The Discounts: City-by-City Listings" for specific names, addresses, and discounts. Look up Florida and turn to your destination city, Orlando. Here are over fifty hotels belonging to ten major chains that offer discounts to seniors. You'll also find the whereabouts of restaurants, tourist attractions, and museums that offer senior discounts. Telephone numbers and opening hours are included to make your planning as easy as possible.

TRAVEL AGENTS

If you hate to make plans, don't do it. Travel agents and package tours can arrange complete vacations *and* save you money.

A travel agent can plan your trip and buy your ticket, but a travel agent can't *think* for you. You must explain exactly where and when you want to go and how much you can spend. Only then can a good travel agent present you with all the brochures you can digest, a package of tickets and reservations, and a list of where to be when. And if you ask them to, travel agents will book you on cheap flights, into inexpensive hotels, and find you low-cost car rental; however, travel agents cannot always get you senior citizen discounts. Although some hotel chains offering senior discounts pay travel agents commissions, many do not. As travel agents are paid a commission by hotels for each reservation they make, many hotels feel they would lose money if they gave a 10% discount to the customer in addition to a 10% commission to the travel agent. A good travel agent, one who values a long-term relationship, will clearly explain where he or she can or cannot help.

While your travel agent plans your trip, check for possible discounts on transportation, hotel, and car rental in the *Discount Guide*. If the agent can't get these senior discounts for you, ask if you are eligible for rate reductions on some other basis (advance reservations, season, day of week, or fly/drive/hotel combinations, and so on).

800 NUMBERS ARE SUPER SAVERS!
See the first two chapters for the 800 numbers of all the major hotel, car rental, tour, and airline companies; 800 numbers are listed where available in the state-by-state listings for the state tourist offices. Use 800 numbers whenever possible to obtain information and make reservations. If no 800 number is provided, be sure to call 800 information at 1 (800) 555-1212, and ask—it's a free call too!

PACKAGE TOURS

Package tours are another alternative. There are almost no senior discounts available on these trips, but package tour buyers do take advantage of group rates for lodging, transportation, and meals. If you hate to make reservations, read time tables, and keep track of the vacation budget, a travel agent can find you a tour which arranges meals, tips, transportation, lodging, and takes care of virtually every arrangement and expense except sending souvenirs home to your relatives. You hardly need to take any cash at all if you pick one of these all-inclusive packages.

Be a smart consumer when selecting a package tour. Find out how long the company has been in business, and get the names of other travelers from your area; then call a few and ask them about their trip. When reading tour brochures, don't be misled by a cheap price in big type. It may be available on only one date, and may not include a 15% tax and service charge, which brings the real cost of a $1000 tour to $1150. When you see the phrase "you may wish to see . . ." connected to a description of sightseeing, that means it costs extra, so be clear on what really is and is not included. Pay attention to the details and ask questions; reputable companies are proud of the tours they present. Tours designed especially for seniors should offer a leisurely pace and an escort familiar with the desires of senior travelers. Ideally bus trips are kept short, and hotels are centrally located with a minimum of stairs.

The two best-known travel companies specializing in package tours for seniors for over twenty-five years are Saga International Holidays and Grand Circle Travel. Both offer coach tours and extended-stay vacations in the United States, Canada, Mexico, throughout Europe and the Mediterranean, plus Australia, New Zealand, Africa, and Asia. Neither are commissionable to travel agents.

Saga offers budget tours with accommodations in university dorms as well as more luxurious tours and cruises. Tours are open to anyone aged 60 and over, and their companions aged 50 to 59. Saga is a British-based and all European tours begin and end with a day or two in London. An attractive feature of the Saga tours is the option to add a week in London for about $500. Most Saga holidays run seventeen days and cost about $1400 to $2000. Tours can be combined quite cheaply. For example, the eighteen-night tour of Classical Europe can be combined with the fifteen-night coach tour of England and Scotland to form a thirty-three-day holiday for about $2400 (from Boston). For a copy of their clear and comprehensive brochure, call or write Saga International Holidays, Ltd., 120 Boylston St. Boston, MA 02116, or call toll-free (800) 343-0273 (except MA) or (800) 462-3322 (MA).

Catering to travelers 50 and over, Grand Circle Travel operates a wide variety of American, European, and Asian packages that range from Escorted Tours (ex., a nineteen-day Scandinavian tour from $2750), and Extended Vacations (two weeks or more in a hotel or apartment on the French, Spanish, Portuguese, or Yugoslavian coast, or in the Alps, London, Hawaii or Florida) to Countryside Tours (ex., a twenty-day Alpine tour from $1995) to the thirty-seven-day "Around the World" tour (from $9875). GCT produces an extensive series of brochures covering their many destinations, plus a helpful free brochure, "101 Tips for the Mature Traveler." Write Grand Circle Travel, 555 Madison Ave., New York, NY 10022, or call (212) 688-5900 or toll-free, (800) 221-2610.

The AARP Travel Service offers tours arranged by Olson-Travelworld, which has been in the tour business for fifty years. Budget trips, learning vacations, apartment stays, and luxury tours and cruises are offered, in the United States, Hawaii, Canada, Mexico, Eastern and Western Europe, and Asia. For information, AARP members should write or call: AARP Travel Service, P.O. Box 92337,

Los Angeles, CA 90009, (800) 227-7737. Have your membership number ready when calling.

The Gramercy Travel System, which has been arranging tours and cruises for singles for almost thirty years, has recently begun a new Caribbean cruise program for both married and single travelers over 45. For details, contact them at 444 Madison Ave., New York, NY 10022, (800) 223-6490 or (212) 758-2433.

Passages Unlimited recently began offering a variety of European tours to travelers over 55. All their flights are on Pan Am, and tours may be booked through travel agents. Passages works cooperatively with the Golden Circle program of Global of London, a thirty-five-year-old English tour operator. For more information, ask your travel agent or call or write Passages Unlimited, 48 Union St., Stamford, CT 06906, (800) 472-7724.

Tours for Seniors

Request information and tour schedules from your national senior citizens' organization and from *Saga International Holidays, Ltd.*, 120 Boylston St., Boston, MA 02116, (800) 343-0273 (except MA); *Grand Circle Travel*, 555 Madison Ave., New York, NY 10022, (800) 221-2610; AARP Travel Service, P.O. Box 92337, Los Angeles, CA 90009, (800) 227-7737; *Passages Unlimited*, 48 Union St., Stamford, CT 06906, (800) 472-7724; 50+ Young at Heart Program, *American Youth Hostels*, Travel Department, P.O. Box 37613, Washington, D.C. 20013, (202) 783-6161; *Interhostel*, Continuing Education, University of New Hampshire, Durham, NH 03824, (603) 862-1147.

In addition to these commercial tour operators, the National Council of Senior Citizens and Mature Outlook offer package tours specially tailored to their members. (More information about these organizations follow in the next section, "Senior Citizens' Organizations.")

Study-holidays are an increasingly popular alternative to traditional package tours. One- and two-week stays at U.S. and European universities are sponsored by Elderhostel and Interhostel. Turn to "Unusual Holidays for Seniors" for further information.

SENIOR CITIZENS' ORGANIZATIONS

The world of senior discounts is divided into MEMBERS and nonmembers. Without a senior citizens' organization membership card, even the most accommodating of merchants, innkeepers, and car renters will see you as just another elderly gentleman or little old lady asking for a few dollars off. However, the minute you flash your organization card you cease to be a mere individual. You become a member, one of millions of consumers whose business the company is eager to attract.

And anyone over 50 can become a member of one of the major senior citizens' organizations. It takes only five minutes and costs as little as five dollars. All you have to do is send your name and address and a small yearly membership fee to the organization of your choice. The major organizations are the American Association of Retired Persons and its sister organization, the National Retired Teachers Association (NRTA/AARP), the National Council of Senior Citizens (NCSC), Mature Outlook (formerly the National Association of Mature People), and Catholic Golden Age. And you don't have to be retired to join—just over 50 for the first two, over 40 for Mature Outlook.

In addition, many states have organized clubs and discount programs for their senior citizens. Although most of these clubs have state-oriented discount programs, the state of Ohio sponsors a nationally recognized discount program called the Golden Buckeye Club for Ohioans over 65. Members qualify for discounts at Ramada Inns and Hertz agencies across the country and abroad as well as receiving hundreds of discounts in Ohio.

The three major senior citizens' organizations and the state-sponsored programs are by no means the only organizations through which seniors can receive discounts. Religious and professional groups have retirement clubs with discount programs, *but* the size of the discount may vary with the size of the organization. You can be sure that the twenty-four million members of the NRTA/AARP get the biggest discounts of all.

Nonmembers can and do find hundreds of discounts; members will find that the discounts available through their organization are more numerous and more advantageous. For example, in "The Discounts: City-by-City Listings," the asterisks next to some discount listings indicate that these particular hotel chains and automobile rental firms give discounts only to the members of certain citizens' organizations. In order to determine if you are eligible for the discount, check the next chapter, "Hotel, Transportation, and Sightseeing Discounts," for information about individual hotel and car-rental chain policies.

One of the most important discount benefits offered by organizations is the opportunity for members to obtain discounts at age 50 that nonmembers are entitled to receive only after 55, 60, or 65. Many discount givers offer benefits to "senior citizens who are over 60 (or 65) *or* seniors who are members of a senior citizens' organization."

Don't, however, get the idea that senior citizens' organizations exist solely to help active seniors save money. These important organizations work on many levels to improve living conditions for mature Americans—for *you*. So become a *member*. The national addresses are listed below, but check to see if there's a local chapter in your town.

UNUSUAL VACATIONS FOR SENIORS

BED AND BREAKFAST

Bed and Breakfast accommodation is now a widespread alternative to staying in a hotel or motel. Some B&B reservation service organizations and individual B&Bs are listed in the city-by-city listing, but in many cases, B&B rates are too low to allow additional discounts for seniors. The best source of information on B&Bs is *Bed & Breakfast USA*, by Betty Rundback and Nancy Kramer (E. P. Dutton, $10.95). This annually revised guidebook gives the rates of specific B&Bs and notes when senior discounts are available.

ELDERHOSTEL

If studying volcanoes in Hawaii, learning how to cook in an authentic colonial kitchen, or going to college for a week or more appeal to you, write to Elderhostel.

THE AMERICAN ASSOCIATION OF RETIRED PERSONS and THE NATIONAL RETIRED TEACHERS ASSOCIATION, $7.50 yearly membership fee, 215 Long Beach Blvd., Long Beach, CA 90801, (800) 453-9600. THE NATIONAL COUNCIL OF SENIOR CITIZENS, $10 yearly membership fee includes spouse, 925 15th St., N.W., Washington, DC 20005, (202) 347-8800. MATURE OUTLOOK, $7.50 yearly membership fee includes spouse, P.O. Box 1209, Glenview, IL 60025, (800) 336-6336. CATHOLIC GOLDEN AGE, $7 yearly membership fee includes spouse, 400 Lackawanna Ave., Scranton, PA 18503.

Elderhostel is a network of over eight hundred colleges and universities in fifty states, Canada, Great Britain, Italy, Israel, Scandinavia, and Australia that offers special low-cost, one-week summer residential programs for people over 60. "Elderhostel," says the National Catalog, "combines the best traditions of education and hosteling. Inspired by youth hostels and folk schools of Europe, but guided by the needs of older citizens for intellectual stimulation and physical adventure, Elderhostel is for elder citizens on the move—not just in terms of travel but in the sense of reaching out to new experiences."

Thousands of liberal arts and science courses are taught by regular faculty members of the sponsoring colleges. Courses range from astronomy to oil painting, from computers to dance. There are no exams, no grades, and no required homework, and Elderhostel says the courses are suited to all levels of previous education.

Through the Elderhostel network, you can choose to spend one or more weeks on a single campus or you can schedule an ambitious summer of educational hosteling, traveling from one college campus to another.

Elderhostelers live in rooms in college dormitories and meals are eaten in the college cafeterias. Weekly fees for the U.S. programs are about $215.

Elderhostel catalogs are widely available in public libraries, or write: Elderhostel, 80 Boylston Street, Suite 200, Boston, MA 02116, or telephone (617) 426-8056.

INTERHOSTEL

If the Elderhostel philosophy excites you, Interhostel may be your answer to the Grand Tour. First held in the summer of 1980, Interhostels are two-week European travel/study programs developed for seniors over 50 by the University of New Hampshire, where the Elderhostel concept was founded. Seniors can attend lectures (in English) at a local university as well as sightsee. Accommodations and meals are provided either at the participating university or nearby hotels. Recent Interhostels were held in Austria, Greece, Great Britain, Ireland, Sweden, Switzerland, Spain, West Germany, and China. The two-week program costs $1095 ($1400 for China) plus transatlantic airfare.

For information, contact Division of Continuing Education, University of New Hampshire, Durham, NH 03824, telephone (603) 862-1147.

AYH 50+ YOUNG AT HEART PROGRAM

Youth Hostels aren't just for the young. The American Youth Hostel Association now sponsors 50+ Young at Heart van and bicycle tours of scenic and historic areas of the United States. Recent tours include a nine-day bicycle tour of New England ($290), a fourteen-day Fall Foliage Tour of New England by van ($585), a sixteen-day van tour of the Northwest US/Canadian border ($585), and a thirty-six-day train tour of European capitals ($2350 from Newark, NJ). For more information, write American Youth Hostels, Travel Department, P.O. Box 37613, Washington, DC 20013, or call (202) 783-6161.

And don't overlook Youth Hostels as a source of accommodation. The advantages of hosteling are impressive and probably the least important advantage is the low cost: most hostels charge less than $5 per night. If you've always wanted to stay in a Scottish castle, an Austrian *schloss*, an Italian villa, or an English half-timbered house, consider hosteling. In parts of Europe and Britain, hostels (often in historic buildings and scenic places) are quite close together so you can plan a vacation going from hostel to hostel—and you can make advance reservations. Possible disadvantages are the dormitory-style housing, the curfew (10:30 or 11:00), and the occasional absence of showers and hot water. To be eligible to stay at Youth Hostels, you must join the American or Canadian Youth Hostel Association for $10 annually for seniors 60 and over, $20 for other adults. Write American Youth Hostels, Inc. (see address above) or Canadian Hosteling Association, 130 Metcalf St., Suite 109, Ottawa, Ontario K2P 1P1.

SENIOR TRAVEL EXCHANGE PROGRAM

A nonprofit organization, S.T.E.P. has a new twist on the familiar student-exchange programs: senior exchange! S.T.E.P. arranges for seniors who open their own homes to European travelers to receive free bed and breakfast with European host families. S.T.E.P. also sponsors group tours to Europe. For information, send $1 to S.T.E.P., P.O. Box H, Santa Maria, CA 93456.

PARK VACATIONS

Looking for a scenic discount vacation? Consider staying in a state or national park. Seldom as spartan and rustic as you might think, some of these parks have elaborate lodges that definitely were not built for roughing it. Large recreation areas and restaurants are adjacent to many of these lodges, but don't envision picnic tables beside babbling brooks. Olympic-size swimming pools, tennis courts, and cafeterias rival park scenery in drawing visitors to state and national parks.

Entrance to all national parks is free to seniors 62 and over with a Golden Age Passport, obtainable free of charge from most National Park System areas that charge entrance fees. Driver's license, birth certificate, or written affidavits are acceptable proof of age. Thc Golden Age Passport also entitles the bearer and family to a 50% discount on the use of park facilities for camping, boating, parking, and other activities. And once away from the parks, this same Golden Age Passport gives seniors free admission to all national historical sites owned by the National Park Services.

If you're looking for a room with a view, try the Grand Canyon Lodge (South Rim, Grand Canyon, AZ 86023). Other favorites in the national parks are the Peaks of Otter Lodge on the Blue Ridge Parkway (Box 489, Bedford,

Virginia), the Glacier Park Lodge in Glacier National Park (East Glacier, Montana 59434), the Old Faithful Snow Lodge in Yellowstone, TW Services, Yellowstone Division, Yellowstone National Park, Wyoming 82190), and the Ahwahnee in Yosemite (Yosemite Park and Curry Co., Yosemite National Park, CA 95389). Reservations are imperative, especially in the summer and on the weekends year round. Check your bookstore or library for one of the several guidebooks to the national parks.

Some of the best state park vacationlands can be found in Arkansas, Georgia, Kentucky, Maryland, New Jersey, New York, Ohio, Oklahoma, South Carolina, Texas, and West Virginia. Most state park services offer discounts to senior citizens. For information, write to the state tourist offices listed in "The Discounts: City-by-City Listings."

SENIOR SKIING

Downhill and cross-country skiers over 62 can find special programs, discounts, and even free skiing at many resorts. The discounts are usually unadvertised, so contact

Rules for Savings on Car Rentals

1. Join a national senior citizens' organization and use its discount identification number.
2. Make advance reservations with the toll-free national reservation service.
3. Renting mid-week? A senior-citizen rate can save you money.
4. Renting for seven days or for the weekend? Senior discounts can save you another 5% to 10%.
5. Always ask, "Is this the cheapest rate you offer?"

See pages 32–34 for more information.

the individual ski areas to find out where discounts can be found.

Skiers over 70 can join the 70+ Ski Club, a nonprofit organization that sends to its members an eight-page list of free and discount skiing in the United States, Canada, Australia, Switzerland, and France. Only members of the 70+ Ski Club are eligible for these discounts. To join, send $5 for lifetime membership to the 70+ Ski Club, c/o Lloyd Lambert, 104 East Side Dr., Ballston Lake, NY 12019. All club profits go to the U.S. Ski Team Fund.

SENIOR SPORTS

The National Senior Sports Association (NSSA) arranges discounts, tournaments, and travel programs for golfers, tennis players, and bowlers age 50 and over. Bowlers get a 10% discount at any Brunswick Bowling Center, while golfers get a discount price on the "Gold Card," allowing them to play two times on 1200 U.S. courses with no greens fees. NSSA also conducts recreational and competitive tournaments at major resorts at reasonable package rates. For more information, contact NSSA at 317 Cameron St., Alexandria, VA 22314, (703) 549-6711.

Hotel, Transportation, and Sightseeing Discounts

HOTEL CHAINS AND HOTELS

Listed in the following pages are hundreds of hotels in the United States, Canada, Mexico, the Caribbean, and Europe that give discounts to seniors. Many of the listings include restrictions on season, day of week, and number of people occupying the room, so read them carefully.

Always ask for, but never count on receiving, senior discounts during what the hotel industry calls "High occupancy periods." Remember that hotels offer discounts to attract customers at times when their rooms would ordinarily not be filled. So don't expect to go to the beach for the Fourth of July or to Louisville on Kentucky Derby Day and receive a discount from your hotel.

Here are a few simple rules to prevent unpleasant surprises when you register or check out:

1. Make reservations as far in advance as possible and request the senior discount. Ask if any other discounts, such as weekend rates, are available.
2. When you register at the hotel, request the senior discount and present your senior citizen's organization membership card or other appropriate identification showing your age.
3. When you check out, remind the desk clerk of the discount—before he totals your bill.

This chapter explains the different rules and restrictions that hotel chains apply to the hundreds of individual discounts listed in the next chapter. Read these pages very carefully, and get to know which chains offer discounts at all their branches, which chains offer discounts every day of the year, which chains require advance reservations, and so on. *Unless otherwise noted, discounts are off the regular directory rate only, and may not be used in conjunction with other discounts or special promotions.* If you are traveling on a weekend, especially to a major city, you may find that the weekend rate offers greater savings.

The policies of individual hotels in a chain vary radically, so never completely trust discount information given to you by the central reservation service. If you want to be 100% certain that your discount is confirmed, call the hotel—the telephone numbers appear in the city-by-city discount listings. Many confusing chain-hotel policies will become clearer (if only slightly) when you understand that the parent companies outline only a general senior discount policy and then give the individual innkeepers considerable latitude as to how completely this policy will be followed. There are two reasons for this. One is that parent companies don't always own their hotels: they often franchise their name to hotels that they don't own. The other reason is that chain hotels spread all over the country in all types of communities naturally need to do business in ways appropriate to their own areas.

An asterisk appearing next to the discount listing of a chain hotel in "The Discounts: City-by-City Listings" means that it is the policy of the hotel chain to give discounts only to the members of certain senior citizens' organizations. Each chain caters to a different combination of organizations and the specifics are explained in a paragraph in this chapter about each of the major hotel chains. In addition, these brief explanations state whether chain-hotel discounts are extended by all branches or only by "Participating locations" of the hotel chain.

Be sure to follow quite strictly the advance reservation instructions given in this chapter; on the other hand, don't take the rules regarding "members only" and "participating locations only" as the final word on the subject. It never hurts to ask for a discount. If you are not a member of one of the senior citizens' organizations specified by the hotel chain, don't be completely discouraged. Ask the individual hotel reservationists (never the central reservation service) if you can have a discount by virtue of your advanced age alone, and you may find them surprisingly cooperative. And if the hotel where you want to stay is not listed here as a participating hotel, ask for a discount anyway.

ADAM'S MARK

Four Adam's Mark luxury hotels, located in Charlotte, NC; Clearwater Beach, FL; Kansas City, MO; Philadelphia, PA; offer senior discounts of 10% to 25% to AARP members. Toll-free reservation number: (800) 231-5858.

BEST WESTERN HOTELS AND MOTOR INNS

A large proportion of the 2,000 Best Western hotels and motor inns located throughout the United States and Canada offer 10% discounts to travelers over 55. The Best Western Travel Guide lists the senior discount plans of each property. Free copies are available at all Best Westerns or write Best Western, Box 10203, Phoenix, AZ 85064. Toll-free reservation numbers: United States and Canada, (800) 528-1234; hearing-impaired, (800) 528-2222.

DAYS INN

A $12 yearly membership in the Days Inn September Days Club entitles travelers over 55 (and their spouses) to receive a 10%–50% discount on rooms, meals, and even gifts at most of the over three hundred Days Inns and Lodges across the United States and Canada. In addition, membership in the September Days Club offers many other benefits: 25% to 40% discounts on Delta Airlines; discounts on Avis and Hertz rental cars; discounts at major theme parks, museums, and attractions; savings on travel and life insurance, records, vitamins, etc.; and a subscription to *American Traveler* magazine. Days Inn points out that with room, food, and gift discounts, the savings realized in just two nights can offset the annual fee. Travelers over 55 may join the September Days Club by requesting information and an application from (800) 241-5050 and sending a check or money order for $12 to the September Days Club, 2751 Buford Highway, N.E., Atlanta, GA 30324. Memberships can also be purchased at participating Days Inns and Lodges. AARP members also receive a 10% discount. Toll-free reservations numbers: (800) 325-2525; hearing-impaired, (800) 222-3297.

DOUBLETREE HOTELS

This small group of luxury properties offers a 15% discount at their hotels in Dallas; Denver; Houston; Kansas City; Anaheim, CA; Phoenix; Seattle; and Tucson. Toll-free reservations: (800) 528-0444.

ECONO-TRAVEL MOTOR HOTELS AND ECONOLODGES

Almost all Econo-Travel Motor Hotels and Econo-Lodges in the United States and Canada offer a 10%

discount to members of Econo-Travel's Senior Class or AARP members who present their cards when checking in. Seniors over 55 can join the Senior Class by requesting a free Senior Class card at their motel or by writing Econo-Lodges of America, Marketing Dept., P.O. Box 34626, Charlotte, NC 28234. Toll-free reservation number: (800) 446-7900.

EMBASSY SUITES

This chain of all-suite hotels offers members of AARP/NRTA and NCSC a 10% discount off regular rates. This discount does not apply to reservations made by travel agents. Rates are similar to the cost of a room at a luxury hotel, but you get a two-room suite with kitchenette, free breakfast, and free beverages. Toll-free reservations: (800)-EMBASSY.

HILTON

For a modest one-time membership fee, travelers over 62 can join Hilton's new senior discount program. Participating Hilton Hotels offer deep discounts. For more information and reservations, call toll-free (800) 445-8667.

HOLIDAY INNS

Over 75% of Holiday Inns throughout the United States, Canada, and forty-four other countries offer a 10% discount every day of the year to members of the National Retired Teachers Association/American Association of Retired Persons, and the National Council of Senior Citizens. This discount is not applicable to group or special rates and is not available through travel agents. To obtain the discount, present your current senior citizens' organization membership card when checking in. Travelers over 55 can join the Holiday Inn Travel Venture Club for greater savings. A $10 yearly membership fee entitles members to a 20% discount on room rates and a 10% discount on meals at participating Holiday Inns. Other special benefits include airfare discounts on Northwest, car-rental discounts at Hertz and National, and admission discounts at many theme parks and national attractions. Membership information is available from Holiday Inns or from (800) 654-6852, ext. 99. Holiday Inns' toll-free reservation number is (800) HOLIDAY.

HOWARD JOHNSON'S MOTOR LODGES

Most of the Howard Johnson's Motor Lodges in the United States, Canada, and Puerto Rico give 15% to 50% discounts to all travelers over 60 and to members of any national seniors organization. Howard Johnson's Road Rally program for seniors offers a 15% discount with no advance reservation requirements and a 50% discount with advance reservations. Participants also receive a Road Rally Savings Book worth hundreds of dollars in travel and merchandise. Toll-free reservation number for Road Rally: (800) 634-3464.

KNIGHTS INNS

Knights Inns offer a 10% discount to seniors at all of their 120 budget motels in the Southeast and Midwest. Contact their general offices at 6561 E. Livingston Ave., Reynoldsburg, OH 43068, (614) 866-1569 for a free directory.

LA QUINTA MOTOR INNS

La Quinta Motor Inns has over 150 locations in twenty-eight states, concentrated in the South, Midwest, and West. La Quinta offers a 20% discount to members of any bona fide retiree organization and to all senior citizens over 60 who present proper identification showing organization membership or age. Toll-free reservation number: (800) 531-5900.

LK MOTELS

LK Motels offer a 10% discount to seniors over 55 at their fifty-five budget properties in Ohio, Indiana, Kentucky, Michigan, Illinois, and Florida. To qualify, present the Golden Buckeye Card or proof of age when checking in. Toll-free reservations: (800) 848-5767; (800) 282-5711 in Ohio.

MARRIOTT HOTELS

Hotels and resorts participating in Marriott's Leisurelife Program give a wide range of discounts to travelers over 62. No membership fee or membership card is required to take advantage of the 50% lodging discount, 25% restaurant discount, or the 10% discount on gifts, jewelry, and clothing. Be sure to make advance reservations and to ask for the Leisurelife rates. Call toll-free from the United States and Canada: (800) 228–9290.

NENDEL'S

Nendel's offers 10% discounts to members of major senior citizens' organizations at their seventeen moderately priced motor inns in Washington, Oregon, Idaho, Nevada, and Utah. It also offers the discount to members of Vagabond's Club 55. Toll-free reservations: (800) 547-0106; (800) 452-0123 in Oregon.

QUALITY INNS

All of the nine hundred Quality Inns, Comfort Inns, and Clarion Hotels in the United States and abroad offer a 10% discount to seniors over 60 and to members of any senior citizens' organization. To receive the discount, present your membership card when checking in. The discount is not applicable to group or special rates and cannot be obtained through travel agents. Toll-free reservations numbers: Quality Inns, (800) 228–5151; Comfort Inns, (800) 228-5150; Clarion Hotels, (800) CLARION; hearing-impaired, (800) 228-3323.

RADISSON HOTELS

Radisson offers a 25% discount off regular rates to members of AARP/NRTA at their varied collection of inns, resorts, hotels, and plazas throughout the United States. There are six Radissons in the Minneapolis–St. Paul area, with others centered in Florida, Arizona, Georgia, and other cities in the Southeast and Midwest. Toll-free reservation number: (800) 228-9822.

RAMADA INNS

Almost five hundred Ramada Inns participating in Ramada's Best Years program offer 25% discounts to travelers over 60 or who are members of one of the following organizations: AARP/NRTA, NCSC, the Golden Buckeye Club, Mature Outlook, Retired Enlisted Association, National Association for Retired Credit Union People, Catholic Golden Age, and United Airlines Silver Wings Plus. The discount is not applicable to group or special rates and cannot be obtained through travel agents. To receive the discount, show your membership card when you check in. Toll-free reservation numbers: (800) 2-RAMADA; for Ramada Renaissance, (800) 228-9898; for hearing-impaired, (800) 228-3232.

RED LION INNS

All fifty-nine Red Lion Inns and Thunderbird Motor Inns offer a 20% discount on lodgings and a 15% discount on dining to the holders of AARP, Silver Passport, or Mature Outlook cards. Some restrictions and limitations apply. Toll-free reservations: (800) 547-8010.

RODEWAY INNS

All 150 Rodeway Inns in the United States, Canada, and Mexico offer a minimum discount of 10% to travelers over 55. Proof of age is required when checking in. Toll-free reservation number: (800) 228-2000; Nebraska, call collect (402) 571-2000.

SCOTTISH INNS/RED CARPET INNS/MASTER HOSTS INNS

Over 175 Master Host, Red Carpet, and Scottish Inns in twenty-five states and Canada offer 10% discounts to AARP members and to holders of their free Identicard. For information and reservations, call (800) 251-1962.

SHERATON HOTELS AND INNS

Sheraton Hotels and Inns participating in the Sheraton Retired Persons Room Rate Discount Program offer a 25% discount on room reservations in any but the minimum rate category to members of the AARP/NRTA, and to all seniors age 60 and over. Each Sheraton Hotel or Inn determines at what times the senior discount is available and may refuse to offer the discount during heavily booked periods. The discount does not apply to group rates or to the Sheraton Family Plan. This discount is available through travel agents. Present your organization membership card or proof of age at registration. Toll-free reservations: (800) 325-3535.

SONESTA HOTELS

Located in Boston; Key Biscayne and Orlando, Florida; New Orleans; Alexandria, Virginia; and Portland, Maine; in the United States, and abroad in Amsterdam; Eilat and Jerusalem; Cairo; and Bermuda, Sonesta hotels offer a 15% discount to AARP/NRTA members. Individual hotels may refuse to offer discounts during periods when they expect to be heavily booked. This discount is not applicable to group or special rates and is not available through travel agents. Present your organization card when you register. Toll-free reservation number: (800) 343-7170.

TRAVELODGE AND VISCOUNT HOTELS

Every one of the five hundred Travelodge and Viscount Hotels located throughout the United States and Canada offers a special senior rate to guests 55 years and older. Travelers must be members of Travelodge's free Golden Guest Club or members of a national seniors' organization. Advance reservations are recommended but not required. For information and reservations, call (800) 255-3050.

TREADWAY INNS

The eleven Treadway Inns and Resorts throughout the eastern states offer 10% to 15% discounts every day of the year to members of a recognized senior citizens' organization, such as AARP/NRTA or Catholic Golden Age. Ask for the senior discount when making reservations and present your identification card when checking in. This discount is not applicable to group or special rates and is not available through travel agents. Toll-free reservation number: (800) 631-0182; New Jersey, (201) 368-9624.

VAGABOND HOTELS

Concentrated in the West, the forty-three Vagabond hotels offer a special Club 55 rate to seniors. Prices vary from season to season and property to property, but represent about a 15% discount. Membership in Club 55 costs $10 and comes with a regular travel newsletter and a Club 55 Value Pack travel bag packed with gifts worth $39. Toll-free reservations and Club 55 application: (800) 522-1555.

HOTEL PRICES

The prices of the major hotel chains are quite close. Most of the hotels that offer senior discounts are in the medium price range, but beware—the "medium" price range varies considerably from city to city. Medium in a big city might go as high as $70 for a double-bedded room, while medium in a small city or resort will be under $35. Days Inn, Econo-Travel Motor Hotels, and Scottish Inns are the only budget chains that offer senior discounts, and their prices are consistently the lowest of the chain hotels listed in the *Discount Guide*.

Prices within the largest chains can also vary dramatically. Several have recently gone to a multitiered approach, offering different levels of comfort and luxury to attract different segments of the travel market. Quality Inns offer Comfort Inns at the budget level, Quality Inn at the moderate level, and Clarion Hotels at the luxury level. Holiday Inns set a similar pattern with their new Hampton Inns (budget), Holiday Inns (moderate), and Crown Plaza (luxury).

To help you understand the relative prices of hotels in the same city, here is a comparative listing of regular rates for double rooms in Atlanta, Georgia. You can expect prices in other cities to vary to the same degree.

To obtain the current rates for hotels, consult the free hotel chain directories. Better yet, dial the toll-free number of the reservation service and ask. *No* travel guide available in bookstores lists up-to-date prices.

COMPARATIVE HOTEL RATES: REGULAR DOUBLE ROOM

HOTEL	SR. DISC.	CEN-TRAL	SUB-URBAN	AIR-PORT
B & B	—	$30–65	$30–65	—
BEST WESTERN	10%	—	$44–57	—
DAYS INN	25%	$44–67	$28–35	$25–33
HOLIDAY INN	15%	$73–83	$46–60	$62–76
HOWARD JOHNSON'S	33%	—	$26–39	$42–53
LA QUINTA	20%	—	—	$38
QUALITY INN	10%	$44	—	—
RAMADA INN	25%	$44–53	$37	$73
RODEWAY INN	10%	$45–58	—	—

SAVE UP TO 50% BY ASKING FOR SPECIAL WEEKEND RATES.

PLANE, TRAIN, BUS, AND CAR RENTAL

AIRFARE DISCOUNTS

It often seems that nothing but the weather changes more quickly than airfares, so when planning a trip, use a good travel agent and keep asking, "Are you sure this is the best deal I can get?"

AMERICAN. Designed for travelers over 65 as well as younger companions, American's Senior SAAver Club gives a 10% discount off all domestic fares—including already discounted fares. Membership is $25 annually for travelers over 65 and $100 for younger companions.

BRANIFF. Travelers over 65 and their companions of any age are eligible for a 15% discount off any flight. There is no membership fee.

CONTINENTAL/NEW YORK AIR. For a one-time membership fee of $25, travelers over 65 can join the Golden Travelers Club and receive a 10% discount on any mainland fare.

DELTA. Members of Days Inns September Days Club receive 25% to 40% discounts on Delta flights and tours. Call (800) 241-5050 for information.

EASTERN. The Get Up & Go Passport provides a year of nearly unlimited travel for those 65 and older, plus 50% discounts at Holiday Inns, Hilton, Vista International, Dunfey, and Marriott Hotels. In 1987, Passports cost $1299 and included travel once a week, Monday to Thursday only, to ninety-five different cities within the United States. Foreign travel extensions are available for an extra charge. A second Passport may be purchased for one accompanying passenger, regardless of age. Call (800) 327-8376 for more information.

Or, for a $25 annual membership fee, travelers over 55 will receive a 10% discount on individual flights. The yearly membership fee for a companion of any age if $100.

PIEDMONT. Travelers over 60 who pay a one-time membership fee to join the Senior Class Travel Club earn a 10% discount for all flights plus double miles in the frequent-flyer plan. Members also receive special discounts at Hertz Rent A Car, Stouffer and Radisson hotels, and a newsletter featuring even more discounts and travel packages.

TWA. The VSP Senior Pass costs $1299 for domestic flights plus an additional $449 if you want to include a round-trip ticket to Europe or the Middle East. Purchasers must be over 65, with no age restrictions for one accompanying passenger. Travel is nearly unlimited, although each route may be traveled no more than three times round-trip. Peak travel times and dates may be blocked out.

Another TWA plan offers travelers over 62 a 10% discount on individual flights for a $25 one-time membership fee.

Package tour fans should look into the TWA Getaway Club, which offers tours specially designed for travelers over 60.

UNITED. Travelers over 65 can join the Silver Wings Club for an annual fee of $25 ($100 for a younger companion) and receive 10% off any published fare available in the United States, Canada, and Bahamas. Fringe benefits include discounts at Hertz Rent A Car and Westin and Ramada hotels. Travelers over 60 may join the Silver Wings Club and enjoy these fringe benefits, but only those over 65 receive airfare discounts.

USAIR. Passengers over 65—and one companion of any age—are eligible for a 10% discount. There is no membership fee.

Discounts are sometimes available on a handful of transatlantic and transpacific carriers, but again, they may not be the lowest fares available. KLM recently offered an Amsterdam fare to those aged 60 and over that cost no less than the APEX fare, but it did allow for a stay of up to one year. Senior discounts for air travel within Europe do exist, and you'll find them identified and explained under the listings for each country in the next section. Again, shop around to be sure that these discounts will best suit your travel needs.

DISCOUNT TRAIN TRAVEL

In the United States, Amtrak offers a 25% discount to seniors 65 and over on all round-trip journeys. This discount is valid on any day of the week and at any time of day except during heavy-travel holiday periods. Amtrak asks that you bring your driver's license or birth certificate as identification. When you call the local Amtrak office for further information, ask if you qualify for excursion tickets: in some cases an excursion round-trip ticket can save you more money than two one-way senior citizen tickets.

Canadian National Railways gives one-third off to seniors over 65, without any minimum-stay or price restrictions.

See "The Discounts: City-by-City Listings" for specific information on the many senior rail travel discounts offered in Europe. Austria, France, and Germany offer 30% to 50% discounts to men over 65 and women over 60 who purchase a senior ID card for a small fee. Greece offers the same to men and women over 65, and Swiss Railways offers its discount to men over 65 and women over 62. (Anyone able to explain that men/women age difference please write to the *Discount Guide*!) BritRail sells a pass that entitles seniors 65 and over to first-class travel for the same price as the second-class BritRail pass.

DISCOUNT BUS TRAVEL

Both of the major bus companies offer a 10% discount to seniors. Greyhound offers the discount to travelers over 55, and Trailways to travelers over 65. Be sure to ask about special promotional tickets; these may cost less than the senior discount fare. As do all transportation discounts, expect the details to change periodically; check with your local office.

CAR RENTAL DISCOUNTS

Never pay full price when renting a car. Hertz, Avis, and National offer a discounted flat-rate program to AARP members, plus 5% to 10% discounts on their less expensive weekly and weekend rates (see below). To get these special rates, cars must be returned to the original renting location. Mature Outlook and NCSC also offer similar, although not identical, programs to their members. When calling any of the car rental firms, be sure to supply your organization's assigned discount number to get accurate information.

AVIS. Participating Avis locations offer AARP members a flat rate starting at $35 daily. Although rates vary from one rental location to the next, these flat rates represent a savings of 25% to 40%. Avis also offers AARP members 5% discounts on their weekly and weekend rates. Discounts of 20% to 40% off daily rates depending on location are available in Canada. Some international Avis locations offer a 10% discount on normal time and mileage rates. AARP and other organization members should call (800) 331-1800 for information and reservations.

HERTZ. Hertz's AARP program in the United States is very similar to the Avis program described above. A 15% discount is given in Canada and a 25% discount on time and mileage rates is available at participating locations abroad. To reserve a car, call toll-free (800) 654-2200 or (800) 654-3001 from Alaska and Hawaii. The Hertz operator can reserve your car and arrange a senior discount when you give the Hertz Discount ID number of your senior organization. Confirm the discount at the rental desk.

NATIONAL. All travelers over 62 are eligible for National's Silver Opportunities program, which entitles them to a 12% discount off any domestic rate (including promotional specials!) in off-peak months and 10% off regular (nonpromotional) rates in peak months. The 12% off-peak discount is available from November through June; in Florida from May through November plus January. No club

Rules for Savings on Car Rentals

1. Join a national senior citizens' organization and use its discount identification number.
2. Make advance reservations with the toll-free national reservation service.
3. Renting mid-week? A senior-citizen rate can save you money.
4. Renting for seven days or for the weekend? Senior discounts can save you another 5% to 10%.
5. Always ask, "Is this the cheapest rate you offer?"

card is necessary, just a driver's license. Various domestic *and* international discounts are available to AARP/NRTA, Mature Outlook, and Catholic Golden Age members upon presentation of their membership cards and National Discount ID Number. Toll-free reservations for all plans: (800) CAR-RENT.

SAVING MONEY. Finding the cheapest rates can be very tricky. Rates offered by major firms such as Alamo, Ajaz, Budget, Dollar, Thrifty, and Tropical may be less than the discount rate offered by the big three, so shop around, and never reserve a rental car without asking for a discount or special rates.

One terrific money saver that has been offered each spring for the past several years is well worth investigating. At the end of the Florida season, just after Easter, all the majors need to move their fleets north for the summer. Typically, you can pick up a car from any of Florida's major airports between Easter and Memorial Day, and have seven days to drive it to any of thirty cities in the Northeast and Midwest. Although you have to pay for the gas and insurance, the car is free; sometimes the deal includes two airline tickets back to Florida, good until the end of June. When tickets are included, the total cost for two is still under $150. In the past, Avis, Hertz, and Budget have all offered this type of program; call them in early February to see what's available.

DISCOUNT TRAVEL FIRMS

If you are flexible enough to make last-minute travel plans (typically six weeks' notice), you can save from 15% to 60% on the cost of cruises, charter flights, and package tours. These discounts become available when airlines, cruise ships, and hotel companies realize that unless they discount the price, the space will remain unsold. Although no special discounts are offered to seniors, retirees are often in the best position to take advantage of such discounts. Most of these discounters require payment of an annual family membership fee of around $45 with various money-back guarantees. Some of these companies include Stand-buys, (800) 621-5839; Vacations to Go, (800) 624-7338; Discount Travel International, (800) 253-6200; and Encore Short-Notice Go-Card, (800) 638-8976. Two companies selling only cruises are South Florida Cruises, (800) 327-SHIP, and Spur of the Moment Cruises, (800) 343-1991.

DISCOUNT TRAVEL NEWSLETTER

Travelers who need to keep abreast of the latest developments and best discount plans may want to subscribe to *The Mature Traveler*, a monthly newsletter dedicated to aiding the vacation plans of older Americans. A year's subscription is $18 and is available from American Resource Publishing, P.O. Box 141, Pitman, NJ 08071.

THE SILVER PAGES

Since 1985, Southwestern Bell Media has provided anyone 60 or over a big money-saver, the "Silver Pages" discount book. The book, with pages of classified advertising from merchants and professionals who offer discounts, also contains a reference section with tips on health, finance, and travel. The company publishes a different version of the Silver Pages for each of its 92 "markets," but even if you don't live within the discount market area, you can still get the Silver Pages for only $5 (free to anyone in the specified market areas). And if you travel, ask about the "Silver Savers Passport" and use it anywhere you see the decal displayed. Call or write the Silver Pages, P.O. Box 31097, St. Louis, MO 63131, (800) 252-6060.

RESTAURANTS AND MUSEUMS

RESTAURANT DISCOUNTS

Restaurant discounts are probably the most invisible of all senior discounts, so get into the habit of asking for them before you order. These discounts may take the form of a percentage off the check, free beverage or dessert, or even a special senior menu. Some are available only midweek, whereas others are offered only during nonrush hours. Many restaurant chains now have senior discounts, discount clubs, or discount days, but the policies are up to the individual locations and vary so greatly within chains that it would be impossible to list their discount programs here. Watch for discounts at Big Boy, Burger King, Catfish Cabin, Friendly's, Hardee's, Long John Silver, McDonald's, Pizza Hut, Ponderosa Steak House, Roy Rogers, Sizzler Steak House, and Wendy's Hamburgers.

MUSEUM DISCOUNTS

In the following pages you will find a great variety of museums that offer discounts to seniors, from major art and natural history museums to local historical societies and very small wax museums. Please remember that this is a guide to *discounts*, and that although a listing in *The*

Discount Guide for Travelers Over 55 means that a museum welcomes seniors with its discount admission policy, the listing is not intended to imply anything about the quality of the establishment. By the same token, museums that do not offer senior discounts are not included. Free museums and attractions are noted under the "*Free!*" heading. For a complete listing of museums in any city, contact the appropriate tourist office.

Tours for Seniors

Request information and tour schedules from your national senior citizens' organization and from *Saga International Holidays, Ltd.*, 120 Boylston St., Boston, MA 02116, (800) 343-0273 (except MA); *Grand Circle Travel*, 555 Madison Ave., New York, NY 10022, (800) 221-2610; *AARP Travel Service*, P.O. Box 92337, Los Angeles, CA 90009, (800) 227-7737; *Passages Unlimited*, 48 Union St., Stamford, CT 06906, (800) 472-7724; 50+ Young at Heart Program, *American Youth Hostels*, Travel Department, P.O. Box 37613, Washington, D.C. 20013, (202) 783-6161; *Interhostel*, Continuing Education, University of New Hampshire, Durham, NH 03824, (603) 862-1147.

The Discounts: City-by-City Listings

In the following pages, you'll find hard, cold, money-saving evidence that those rarely advertised, nearly invisible discounts really do exist in the fifty states, Canada, Mexico, the Caribbean, and Europe. Here are hundreds of names, addresses, telephone numbers, and instructions for discount traveling.

To save you time and trouble, restrictions to the discounts have been listed. If the discount is valid only from 9:00 to 5:00 weekdays, the entry will tell you. When the discount is available only to seniors over 60 ("over 60" includes age 60) or 65, the listing says so, and when a discount entry reads simply "10% discount," the minimum age varies according to the local definition of senior citizen. (55, 60, 62, and 65 are all popular ages for discount minimums, but if you show any identification card that reads "senior citizen," the clerk will probably not quiz you on your age.) And when an asterisk (*) follows the entry, the discount is intended for members of senior citizens' organizations that anyone can join (see "Hotel Discounts" and "Car Rental Discounts").

As you read the discount listings, look for the phrases "with *Discount Guide*" and "for *Discount Guide* readers." This is your cue to whip out your copy of this book and ask for your special discount.

As for identification, any kind of senior citizens' identification card issued by the government, a senior citizens' organization, or even a drugstore will keep most vendors quite happy. For discounts on expensive items or travel, it's a good idea to be armed with driver's license or passport, a senior citizens' organization card, and your Medicare card. These should satisfy anyone. When taking advantage of the purchase privilege program of your senior citizens' organization, you must of course show your membership card.

There are many hundreds of discounts for traveling seniors that aren't listed here, so if your favorite senior discount does not appear in the *Discount Guide*, please send it in to be included in the next edition by filling in the contributor's form at the end of this book and mailing it to *The Discount Guide for Travelers Over 55*, E. P. Dutton, 2 Park Avenue, New York, NY 10016.

U.S.A.

ALABAMA

Helpful Addresses

ALABAMA BUREAU OF TOURISM AND TRAVEL
532 S. Perry St., Montgomery, AL 36104
(205) 261-4169, (800) 392-8096 (AL), (800) ALABAMA (except AL, AR, HI)

COMMISSION ON AGING
502 Washington Ave., Montgomery, AL 36130
(205) 261-5743

BIRMINGHAM

Hotels

DAYS INN: *50% discount with Days Inn September Days Club card.*
Airport, 5101 Airport Hwy., (205) 592-6110.

ECONO-TRAVEL MOTOR HOTEL: *10% discount with Econo Senior Class Card.*
Econo-Travel Motor Hotel, 103 Green Springs Hwy., (205) 942-1263.
Econo Lodge, 2224 5th Ave. N., (205) 324-6688.

HOLIDAY INN: *10–20% discount with Holiday Inn's Travel Venture Club Card.*
Airport, 5000 10th Ave., (205) 591-6900.
Airport, 7941 Crestwood Blvd., (205) 956-8211.
Medical Center, 420 S. 20th St., (205) 322-7000.

HOWARD JOHNSON'S: *15–50% discount with H.J.'s Road Rally Card.*
Vestavia Hills, 1485 Montgomery Hwy., (205) 823-4300.

LA QUINTA: *20% discount for over 60.*
905 11th Ct. W., (205) 324-4510.

QUALITY INN: *10% discount for over 60.*
South, I-65 & Oxmoor Rd., (205) 942-0110.

RAMADA INN: *25% discount for over 60.*
Airport, 5216 Airport Hwy., (205) 591-7900.
South, 1535 Montgomery Hwy., (205) 822-6030.
University, I-65 at Oxmoor Rd., (205) 942-2041.

RODEWAY INN: *10% discount.*
Airport, 5900 Airport Hwy., (205) 592-0061.

SHERATON: *25% discount for over 60.*
Perimeter Park, 8 Perimeter Dr., (205) 967-2700.

Car Rental

AVIS: *5–25% discount.**
Airport, (205) 592-8901.
2023 N. Fifth Ave., (205) 251-3223.

HERTZ: *5–25% discount.**
Airport, (205) 591-6090.

NATIONAL: *10%–12% discount for over 62.*
Airport, (205) 592-7259.
2315 N. Fifth Ave., (205) 252-6087.

Free!

Birmingham Botanical Gardens, Birmingham Museum of Art, Red Mountain Museum

---

MOBILE

Hotels

BEST WESTERN: *10% discount.*
Airport, 180 S. Beltline, (205) 343-9345.

HOLIDAY INN: *10–20% discount with Holiday Inn's Travel Venture Club Card.*
Airport Blvd. & I-65, (205) 342-3220.
6527 Hwy. 90 W. (Govt. Blvd.), (205) 666-5600.

**An asterisk indicates that the discount is intended for members of senior citizens' organizations that anyone can join. See "Hotel, Transportation, and Sightseeing Discounts."*

HOWARD JOHNSON'S: *15–50% discount with H.J.'s Road Rally Card.*
3132 Government Blvd., (205) 471-2402.

LA QUINTA: *20% discount*
816 Beltline Hwy., S., (205) 343-4051.

RAMADA: *25% discount for over 60.*
600 Beltline Hwy., (205) 344-8030.

RODEWAY INN: *10% discount.*
1724 Michigan Ave., (205) 478-3013.
9800 Battleship Pkwy., (205) 626-1081.

Car Rental

AVIS: *5%–25% discount.*
Airport, (205) 633-4743.

HERTZ: *5%–25% discount.**
Airport, (205) 633-4000.

NATIONAL: *10%–12% discount for over 62.*
Airport, (205) 633-4003.

Sights

BELLINGRATH GARDENS: *10% discount.*
Daily, 7 a.m. to sunset. (205) 973-2217.

OAKLEIGH: *30% off for over 65.*
350 Oakleigh Pl., (205) 432-1281.
Monday to Saturday, 10 a.m. to 4 p.m.; Sunday 2 p.m. to 4 p.m.
1830s antebellum home

Free!

Museum of the City of Mobile, Carlen House Museum, Fort Conde, Fine Arts Museum of the South, Phoenix Fire Museum

ALASKA

Helpful Addresses

ALASKA STATE DIVISION OF TOURISM
Dept. of Economic Development, Pouch E-445
Juneau, AK 99811.
(907) 465-2010

OLDER ALASKANS COMMISSION
Dept. of Administration, Pouch C
Mail Station 0209
Juneau, AK 99811
(907) 465-3250.

Package Tours for Seniors

Several cruises to Alaska are offered, from AARP's 7-day cruise (from $975) and Passages Unlimited's weeklong cruise (from $1500) to Saga's 13-night extravaganza (starting at $2475). See pages 7–10 for more about package tours.

ANCHORAGE

Hotels

HOLIDAY INN: *10%–20% discount with Holiday Inn's Travel Venture Club Card.*
239 W. 4th Ave., (907) 279-8671.

SHERATON: *25% discount for over 60.*
401 E. 6th Ave., (907) 276-8700.

TRAVELODGE: *Special senior rates for Travelodge's Golden Guest Club.*
115 E. 3rd St., (907) 272-7561.

Car Rental

AVIS: *5%–25% discount.**
Anchorage International Airport, (907) 243-2377
Downtown, 5th & B, (907) 277-4567.

HERTZ: *5%–25% discount.**
Airport, (907) 243-3308.

NATIONAL: *10%–12% discount for over 62.*
509 W. 3rd Ave., (907) 274-3695.

ARIZONA

Helpful Addresses

ARIZONA OFFICE OF TOURISM
1480 East Bethany Home Road, Phoenix, AZ 85014
(602) 255-3618

AGING AND ADULT ADMINISTRATION
Department of Economic Security
1400 W. Washington St., Phoenix, AZ 85007
(602) 255-3596

GOVERNOR'S ADVISORY COUNCIL ON AGING
P.O. Box 6123-008A
Phoenix, AZ 85005
(602) 255-4710

PHOENIX AND VALLEY OF THE SUN
CONVENTION & VISITORS BUREAU
505 N. 2nd St.,
Phoenix, AZ 85004
(602) 254-6500

PHOENIX

Hotels

BEST WESTERN: *10% discount.*
Bell Motel (May–December), 17211 N. Black Canyon Hwy., (602) 993-8300.
Central Plaza Inn, 4321 N. Central, (602) 277-6671.

DAYS INN: *10%–50% discount with Days Inn September Days Club card.*
2735 W. Sweetwater, (602) 993-7200.

DOUBLETREE: *15% discount.*
Scottsdale, 7353 E. Indian School Rd., (602) 994-9203.

EMBASSY SUITES: *10% discount. Reservations required.**
3210 N.W. Grand Ave., (602) 279-3211.
3211 E. Pinchot Ave., (602) 957-1350.
2333 E. Thomas Rd., (602) 957-1910.
1635 N. Scottsdale Rd., Tempe, (602) 947-3711.
2630 E. Camelback Rd., (602) 955-3992.

HOLIDAY INN: *10%–20% discount with Holiday Inn's Travel Venture Club Card.*
Airport, 2201 S. 24th St., (602) 267-0611.
Airport-East, 4300 E. Washington, (602) 273-7778.
3600 N. 2nd Ave., (602) 248-0222.
I–17 & W. Peoria Ave., (602) 943-2341.
Scottsdale, 5101 N. Scottsdale Rd., (602) 945-4392.

HOSPITALITY INN: *10% discount.*
409 N. Scottsdale Rd., Scottsdale, (602) 949-5115.

HOWARD JOHNSON'S MOTOR LODGE: *15%–50% discount with H.J.'s Road Rally Card.*
225 E. Apache Blvd., Tempe, (602) 967-9431.

KON TIKI HOTEL: *10% discount.*
2364 E. Van Buren, (602) 244-9361.

LA QUINTA: *20% discount.*
Airport, 911 S. 48th St., Tempe, (602) 967-4465.
Coliseum, 2725 N. Black Canyon Hwy., (602) 258-6271.

QUALITY INN: *10% discount for over 60.*
Airport, 1820 S. 7th St., (602) 254-9787.
Desert Sky, 3541 W. Van Buren Pkwy., (602) 273-7121.
Comfort Inn NW, 8617 N. Black Canyon Hwy., (602) 995-9500.
West, 2420 W. Thomas Rd., (602) 257-0801.

RAMADA INN: *25% discount for over 60.*
Airport, 3801 E. Van Buren, (602) 275-7878.
Valley Ho, 6850 Main St., Scottsdale, (602) 945-6321.
Scottsdale, Pima Golf Resort, 7330 N. Pima Rd., (602) 948-3800.

RED LION INN: *10% discount for over 50.**
La Posada, 4949 E. Lincoln Dr., (602) 952-0420.

RODEWAY INN: *10% discount.*
Airport, 1202 S. 24th St., (602) 273-1211.
Grand & Indian School, 3400 Grand Ave., (602) 264-9164.
Metro Center, 10402 N. Black Canyon Hwy., (602) 943-2371.
Scottsdale, 7110 E. Indian School Rd., (602) 946-3456.

ROYAL PALMS INN: *10% discount except February & March.*
5200 E. Camelback Rd., (602) 840-3610.

SHERATON: *25% discount for over 60.*
Airport, 2901 Sky Harbor Blvd., (602) 275-3634.
Greenway, 2510 W. Greenway Rd., (602) 993-0800.

SHERATON SCOTTSDALE REPORT: *40% discount January to mid-May; 24% discount mid-May to September; 37% discount September through December.*
7200 N. Scottsdale Rd., (602) 948-5000.

TRAVELODGE: *Special senior rates for Travelodge's Golden Guest Club.*
Airport, 2900 E. Van Buren, (602) 275-7651.
Convention Center, 965 E. Van Buren, (602) 252-6823.

TRAVELODGE—GRAND CANYON GATEWAY: *25% discount except June through August.*
430 E. Bill Williams Ave., Williams, (602) 635-2651.

VAGABOND HOTEL: *10% discount for Vagabond's Club 55.*
1221 E. Apache Blvd., Tempe, (602) 968-7793.

Public Transportation

PHOENIX TRANSIT SYSTEM: *55% discount for over 65; authorization cards available at local libraries.*
(602) 253-5000

Car Rental

AVIS: *5%–25% discount.**
1440 S. 23rd St., (602) 273-3200.

HERTZ: *5%–25% discount.**
Sky Harbor Airport, (602) 267-8822.

NATIONAL: *10%–12% discount for over 62.*
Sky Harbor Airport, (602) 275-4771.

THRIFTY RENT-A-CAR: *10% discount on daily and weekly rates to AARP.*
5001 N. Scottsdale Rd., (602) 990-9556.

Theaters

SCOTTSDALE CENTER FOR THE ARTS: *50% discount for over 65 one-half hour before most performances. Call box office for ticket availability. 50¢ discount on movie classics, Thurs.–Sat.*
7383 Scottsdale Mall, Scottsdale, (602) 994-ARTS.

Sights

AHWATUKEE'S HOUSE OF THE FUTURE: *25% discount*
5061 E. Elliot Rd., (602) 957-0800.
Tuesday to Sunday, 11 a.m. to 11:30 a.m.; 1 p.m. to 4:30 p.m. Tour reservations recommended.

BIG SURF: *$2.50 for over 65.*
1500 N. Hayden Rd., Tempe, (602) 947-7873.

COSANTI FOUNDATION: *33% discount.*
6433 Doubletree, Scottsdale, (602) 948-6145.
Daily, 9 a.m. to 5 p.m. Paolo Soleri's famous experiment in urban architecture.

DESERT BOTANICAL GARDEN: *20% discount.*
Galvin Parkway, Papago Park, (602) 941-1225.
Daily, 9 a.m. to sunset.

TURF SOARING SCHOOL: *10% discount on introductory glider ride with* Discount Guide.
8902 W. Carefree Hwy., (602) 439-3621.

Museums

HALL OF FLAME MUSEUM: *20% discount.*
6101 E. Van Buren, (602) 275-3473.
Daily, 9 a.m. to 5 p.m. Fire-fighting memorabilia.

THE HEARD MUSEUM: *25% discount for over 60.*
22 E. Monte Vista Rd., (602) 252-8848.
Monday to Saturday, 10 a.m. to 5 p.m.; Sunday 1 p.m. to 5 p.m.

ROYAL LONDON WAX MUSEUM: *20% discount for over 55.*
5555 E. Van Buren, (602) 273-1368.

Tour Operators

Many local tour operators offer 10% to 25% discounts for seniors. Be sure to ask when making reservations.

Free!

Arizona Mineral Museum, Bayless Museum, Central Arizona Museum, State Capitol, Valley Garden Center

TUCSON

Hotels

BEST WESTERN: *10% discount.*
Executive Inn, 333 W. Drachman St., (602) 791-7551.
Ghost Ranch Lodge, 801 W. Miracle Mile, (602) 791-7565.
Airport, 7060 S. Tucson Blvd., (602) 746-0271.

DAYS INN: *10%–50% discount with Days Inn September Days Club card.*
I-10 at Palo Verde & Irvington, (602) 571-1400.

EMBASSY SUITES: *10% discount.**
5335 E. Broadway, (602) 745-2700.
Airport, 7051 S. Tucson Blvd., (602) 573-0700.

HOLIDAY INN: *10%–20% discount with Holiday Inn's Travel Venture Club Card.*
Airport, 4550 Palo Verde Blvd., (602) 746-1161.
North, 1365 W. Grant Rd., (602) 622-7791.
181 W. Broadway, (602) 624-8711.

LA QUINTA: *20% discount.*
665 N. Freeway, (602) 622-6491.

QUALITY INN: *10% discount for over 60.*
6161 Benson Hwy., (602) 574-0191.
7007 E. Tanque Verde, (602) 298-2300.

RAMADA INN: *25% discount for over 60.*
404 N. Freeway, (602) 624-8341.

RODEWAY INN: *10% discount.*
Central, 950 N. Stone Ave., (602) 791-7503.
East, 6404 E. Broadway, (602) 747-1414.
810 E. Benson Hwy., (602) 884-5800.

SHERATON: *25% discount for over 60.*
350 S. Freeway, (602) 622-6611.
10000 N. Oracle Rd., (602) 629-2851.

TRAVELODGE: *Special senior rates for Travelodge's Golden Guest Club.*
Newton's, 222 S. Freeway, (602) 791-7511.
1136 N. Stone Ave., (602) 622-6714.
Viscount Suite, 4855 E. Broadway, (602) 745-6500.

**An asterisk indicates that the discount is intended for members of senior citizens' organizations that anyone can join. See "Hotel, Transportation, and Sightseeing Discounts."*

Car Rental

AVIS: *5%–25% discount.**
Tucson International Airport, (602) 294-1494.

HERTZ: *5%–25% discount.**
Tucson International Airport, (602) 294-7616.

NATIONAL: *10%–12% discount for over 62.*
Tucson International Airport, (602) 294-1451.

Free!

Arizona State Museum, Arizona Heritage Center, John C. Frémont Adobe, Fort Lowell Museum, Mineralogical Museum, Tucson Museum of Art.

ARKANSAS

Helpful Addresses

ARKANSAS STATE DEPARTMENT OF PARKS & TOURISM
1 Capitol Mall, Little Rock, AR 72201
(501) 371-1511, (800) 643-8383 (except AR), (800) 482-8999 (AR).

DIVISION OF AGING & ADULT SERVICES
Donaghey Bldg., Suite 1428, 7th & Main, Little Rock, AR 72201.
(501) 371-2441

HOT SPRINGS

Hotels

BEST WESTERN: *10% discount.*
1525 Central Ave., (501) 624-1258.
Hwy. 70 E. (501) 624-4436.

HOLIDAY INN: *10%–20% discount with Holiday Inn's Travel Venture Club Card.*
East, 1125 E. Grand, (501) 624-3321.
Lake Hamilton, Hwy. 7 South, Box 906, (501) 525-1391.

QUALITY INN: *10% discount for over 60.*
400 W. Grand, (501) 624-4441.

SHERATON: *25% discount for over 60.*
3501 Albert Pike, (501) 767-5511.

Car Rental

AVIS: *5%–25% discount.**
Memorial Field, (501) 623-3602.

HERTZ: *5%–25% discount.**
Memorial Field, (501) 623-7591.

Sights

MAGIC SPRINGS FAMILY THEME PARK: *30% discount.*
2201 Hwy. 70 E., (501) 624-5411.
Memorial Day to Labor Day: daily, 10 a.m. to 6 p.m. September: weekends only. Closed the rest of the year.

Museums

MID-AMERICA CENTER MUSEUM: *30% discount for 65 and over.*
400 Mid-America Blvd., (501) 767-3461.
Tuesday to Sunday, 10 a.m. to 5 p.m.

Free!

Dryden Potteries, Hot Springs National Park and Visitors Center with Grand Promenade past Bathhouse Row and open hot springs, Hot Springs Pottery

LITTLE ROCK

Hotels

BEST WESTERN: *10% discount.*
1 Gray Rd., North Little Rock, (501) 945-0141.
400 W. 29th St., (501) 758-5100.

DAYS INN: *10%–50% discount with Days Inn September Days Club card.*
3100 N. Main St., (501) 758-8110.
2508 Jacksonville Hwy., (501) 945-4167.

HOLIDAY INN: *10%–20% discount with Holiday Inn's Travel Venture Club Card.*
North, 111 W. Pershing Blvd., (501) 758–1440.
West, 201 S. Shackleford, (501) 223-3000.
Capitol Area, 617 S. Broadway, (501) 376-2071.
Airport East, I-440 exit #3, (501) 490-1000.
South, 11701 I-30, (501) 455-2300.

LA QUINTA: *20% discount.*
2401 W. 65th St., (501) 568-1030.
4100 McCain Blvd., (501) 945-0808.
200 Shackleford, (501) 224-0900.
901 Fairpark, (501) 664-7000.

RAMADA INN: *25% discount for over 60.*
120 W. Pershing St., N. Little Rock, (501) 758-1851.

Public Transportation

CENTRAL ARKANSAS TRANSIT: *50% discount for over 65. Take proof of age to the Information Center at 614 Center and apply for an Honored Citizen's ID Card which will be issued immediately.*
(501) 378-0361.

Car Rental

AVIS: *5%–25% discount.**
Airport, (501) 376-9151.
901 E. 8th St., (501) 376-9151.

HERTZ: *5%–25% discount.**
Airport, 3403 E. Roosevelt Rd., (501) 378-0777.

Restaurants

CHICKEN HUT: *10% discount for over 65.*
5010 West 65th St., (501) 565-9722.

EL CHICO RESTAURANT: *20% discount for over 65.*
1315 Breckenridge Dr., (501) 224-2550.

INTERNATIONAL HOUSE OF PANCAKES: *10% discount for over 65, except for specials, upon presentation of a "Golden Age" card available at the restaurant.*
101 N. University Ave., (501) 664-2014.

Theaters

ARKANSAS ARTS CENTER THEATER: *50¢ discount.*
MacArthur Park, (501) 372-4000.

ARKANSAS REPERTORY THEATER: *$1.00 less for over 60.*
6th & Main, (501) 378-0405.

ARKANSAS SYMPHONY ORCHESTRA: *Up to 50% discount on season ticket for over 60.*
2500 N. Tyler St., (501) 666-1761.

Sights

ARKANSAS TERRITORIAL RESTORATION: *25¢ discount for over 65.*
214 E. 3rd & Scott Sts., (501) 371-2348.
Monday through Saturday, 9 a.m. to 5 p.m.; Sunday, 1 to 5 p.m. Three homes restored to give an accurate picture of life in Arkansas from the 1820s through the 1850s.

Museums

ARKANSAS MUSEUM OF SCIENCE & HISTORY: *50% discount.*
MacArthur Park, 500 E. 9th St., (501) 371-3521.
Monday to Saturday, 9 a.m. to 4:30 p.m.; Sunday, 1 p.m. to 4:30 p.m. History of the state.

Free!

Arkansas Arts Center, the Old Mill, the Old State House, State Capitol.

Tours for Seniors
Request information and tour schedules from your national senior citizens' organization and from *Saga International Holidays, Ltd.*, 120 Boylston St., Boston, MA 02116, (800) 343-0273 (except MA); *Grand Circle Travel*, 555 Madison Ave., New York, NY 10022, (800) 221-2610; AARP Travel Service, P.O. Box 92337, Los Angeles, CA 90009, (800) 227-7737; *Passages Unlimited*, 48 Union St., Stamford, CT 06906, (800) 472-7724; 50+ Young at Heart Program, *American Youth Hostels*, Travel Department, P.O. Box 37613, Washington, D.C. 20013, (202) 783-6161; *Interhostel*, Continuing Education, University of New Hampshire, Durham, NH 03824, (603) 862-1147.

CALIFORNIA

Helpful Addresses

CALIFORNIA OFFICE OF TOURISM
1121 L St., Suite 103, Sacramento, CA 95814
(916) 322-1396

DEPARTMENT OF AGING
1600 K St., Sacramento, CA 95814
(916) 322-5290

LOS ANGELES

Helpful Address

GREATER LOS ANGELES VISITORS & CONVENTION BUREAU
515 S. Figueroa, Los Angeles 90071
(213) 624-7300

Bed & Breakfast Reservation Services

CALIFORNIA HOUSEGUESTS INTERNATIONAL: *10% discount for* Discount Guide *readers. 2-night minimum.*
18653 Ventura Blvd, #190B, Tarzana, CA 91356, (818) 344-7878.
Bed and breakfast accommodations statewide. Price range: $25 and up. Weekly, monthly rates available.

Hotels

BEST WESTERN: *10% discount.*
Anaheim, 1630 S. Harbor Blvd., (714) 774-1050.
Anaheim, 1201 W. Katella Ave., (714) 774-0211.
Anaheim, 1741 S. West St., (714) 772-9750.
Anaheim, 1717 S. Harbor Blvd., (714) 635-6550.
Anaheim, 1176 W. Katella Ave., (714) 776-0140.
Anaheim, 1057 W. Ball Rd., (714) 774-7600.

Hollywood, 6141 Franklin Ave., (213) 464-5181.
Downtown, 925 S. Figueroa, (213) 628-2222.
Sunset, 8400 Sunset Blvd., (213) 654-0750.

COCKATOO INN: *10% discount.*
Airport, 4334 W. Imperial Hwy., Hawthorne, (213) 679-2291, (800) 262-5286, (800) 458-2800 in CA.

DAYS INN: *10%–50% discount with Days Inn September Days Club card.*
5101 Century Blvd., Inglewood, (213) 419-1234.

EMBASSY SUITES: *10% discount.**
Buena Park, 7762 Beach Blvd., (714) 739-5600.
Airport, 1440 E. Imperial Ave., (213) 640-3600.

HACIENDA HOTEL: *10% discount.**
525 N. Sepulveda Blvd., (212) 615-0015; (800) 421-5900, (800) 262-1314 in CA.

HOLIDAY INN: *10%–20% discount with Holiday Inn's Travel Venture Club Card.*
Anaheim, 1850 S. Harbor Blvd., (714) 750-2801.
Buena Park, 7000 Beach Blvd., (714) 522-7000.
Burbank, 150 E. Angeleno, (818) 841-4770.
Convention Center, 1020 S. Figueroa St. & Olympic Blvd., (213) 748-1291.
Downtown, 750 Garland Ave., (213) 628-5242.
Hollywood, 1755 N. Highland, (213) 462-7181.
International Airport, 9901 La Cienega Blvd. at Century Blvd., (213) 649-5151.
Ontario Airport, 1801 E. G St., (714) 983-3604.

HOWARD JOHNSON's: *15%–50% discount with H.J.'s Road Rally Card.*
L.A. Airport, 5990 Green Valley Cir., Culver City, (213) 641-7740.

QUALITY INN: *10% discount for over 60.*
Anaheim Comfort Inn, 2200 S. Harbor Blvd., (714) 750-5211.

Anaheim/Buena Park, 7555 Beach Blvd., (714) 522-7360.
International Airport, 5249 W. Century Blvd., (213) 645-2200.

RAMADA INNS: *25% discount for over 60.*
Beverly Hills, 1150 S. Beverly Dr., (213) 553-6561.
Disneyland/Anaheim, 1331 E. Katella, (714) 978-8088.
International Airport, 9620 Airport Blvd. at Century, (213) 670-1600.

RODEWAY: *10% discount.*
Anaheim, 800 S. Beach Blvd., (714) 995-5700.
Downtown, 1903 W. Olympic Blvd., (213) 385-7141.

SHERATON: *25% discount for over 60.*
Anaheim, 1015 W. Ball Rd., (714) 778-1700.
North Hollywood, 333 Universal Terrace Pkwy., (213) 980-1212.
Wilshire Center, 2961 Wilshire Blvd., (213) 382-7171.

TRAVELODGE: *Special senior rates for Travelodge's Golden Guest Club. There are 58 Travelodge/Viscount Hotels in Los Angeles and Orange County*
Anaheim/Disneyland, 1166 W. Katella Ave., (714) 774-7817.
Anaheim at the Park, 1221 S. Harbor Blvd., (714) 758-0900.
Anaheim Harbor Inn, 2171 S. Harbor Blvd., (714) 750-3100.
Airport, 9750 Airport Blvd., (213) 645-4600.
West, 10740 Santa Monica Blvd., (213) 474-4576.

VAGABOND: *10% discount for Vagabond's Club 55.*
3101 S. Figueroa, (213) 746-1531.
1904 W. Olympic Blvd., (213) 380-9393.

Incredible deals!

Many hotels in the L.A. airport area offer one week of free parking for each night's stay; the Cockatoo and the Hacienda, listed above, are two examples. Combine these offers with the low fares available from Los Angeles and save hundreds of dollars.

Car Rental

AVIS: *5%–25% discount.**
Airport, (213) 646-5600.
1207 W. 3rd St., (213) 977-1450.
Anaheim, 200 W. Katella, (714) 635-5480.

HERTZ: *5%–25% discount.**
Airport, (213) 646-4861.
Anaheim, 221 W. Katella, (714) 772-0425.

NATIONAL: *10%–12% discount for over 62.*
Airport, (213) 670-4950.
Anaheim, 711 W. Katella, (714) 774-6250.

Tour Operators

Gray Line: *$2 discount for over 55.*

Gray Line of Los Angeles, 1207 W. 3rd St., Los Angeles, CA 90017, (213) 481-2121; (800) 528-5050 outside California.

Bus tours of Hollywood, Beverly Hills, Universal Studios, the Queen Mary, Disneyland.

Sights

DISNEYLAND: *25% discount, Thursday & Friday only.*
1313 Harbor Blvd., Anaheim, (714) 999-4000.
Mid-October to mid-March: Wednesday through Friday, 10 a.m. to 6 p.m.; weekends, 10 a.m. to 7 p.m. Mid-March to mid-October, daily with extended hours in the summer.

KNOTT'S BERRY FARM: *25% discount.*
8039 Beach Blvd., Buena Park, (714) 952-9400.
Memorial Day to Labor Day: Sunday to Thursday, 9 a.m. to midnight; Friday, Saturday, 9 a.m. to 1 a.m. Rest of year: Monday, Tuesday, Friday, 10 a.m. to 6 p.m.; Saturday, 10 a.m. to midnight; Sunday, 10 a.m. to 9 p.m.

LOS ANGELES ZOO: *65% discount.*
5333 Zoo Dr., (213) 666-4090.
April to September, 10 a.m. to 6 p.m.; rest of year, 10 a.m. to 5 p.m.

MOVIELAND: *25% discount for over 62.*
7711 Beach Blvd., Buena Park, (714) 522-1154.
Daily, 9 a.m. to 9 p.m. in summer; 10 a.m. to 8 p.m. in winter. Wax figures, memorabilia, and special effects.

UNIVERSAL STUDIOS TOUR: *$2 off regular admission.*
100 Universal City Plaza, Universal City, (818) 777-9600.
July to August, 8 a.m. to 6 p.m.; rest of year 9:30 a.m. to 3:30 p.m.

Museums

GEORGE C. PAGE MUSEUM OF LA BREA DISCOVERIES: *50% discount.*
5801 Wilshire Blvd., (213) 857-6311.
Tuesday to Sunday, 10 a.m. to 5 p.m. Free on second Tuesdays. Exhibits of fossils and prehistoric life.

**An asterisk indicates that the discount is intended for members of senior citizens' organizations that anyone can join. See "Hotel, Transportation, and Sightseeing Discounts."*

HOLLYHOCK HOUSE: *50% discount.*
4800 Hollywood Blvd., Griffith Park, (213) 662-7272.
Tuesday and Thursday, 10 a.m. to 1 p.m.; Saturday and first and third Sundays, noon to 3 p.m. Tours of this house designed by Frank Lloyd Wright begin on the hour.

HOLLYWOOD WAX MUSEUM: *30% discount.*
6767 Hollywood Blvd., (213) 462-8860.
Sunday to Thursday, 10 a.m. to midnight; Friday and Saturday, 10 a.m. to 2 a.m.

LOS ANGELES COUNTY MUSEUM OF ART: *50% discount.*
5905 Wilshire Blvd., (213) 857-6111.
Tuesday to Friday, 10 a.m. to 5 p.m.; Saturday and Sunday, 10 a.m. to 6 p.m.; second Tuesdays, free.

MUSEUM OF WORLD WARS: *20% discount.*
8700 S. Stanton Ave., (714) 952-1776.
Tuesday to Saturday, 10 a.m. to 8 p.m.; Sunday, noon to 7 p.m. Military displays and dioramas.

See a TV Show—Free!

Plan as far ahead as possible and send a stamped self-addressed envelope to:
ABC, Guest Relations and Ticket Office, 4151 Prospect Ave., Hollywood 90027, (213) 557-4103.

CBS, Ticket Division, 7800 Beverly Blvd., Los Angeles 90036, (213) 852-2624.

NBC, Tickets, 3000 W. Alameda Ave., Burbank 91523, (818) 840-3572.

Tickets can also be obtained in person from these addresses on a first-come, first-serve basis. Warning: the most popular shows may be booked up six months in advance.

Free!

Avila Adobe, California Museum of Science and Industry, Old Plaza Firehouse, Travel Town Transportation Museum, UCLA Botanical Gardens, Wells Fargo History Museum.

SAN DIEGO

Helpful Address

SAN DIEGO CONVENTION & VISITORS BUREAU
11 Horton Plaza
San Diego, CA 92101
(619) 263-1212

Discount Identification Card and Directory

As noted in the listings below, some senior discounts in San Diego are offered only to holders of a special identification card which may be purchased by anyone 50 years of age and over for $1 at the Senior Citizens' Services Office. Application for the card must be made in person at the Senior Citizens' Services Office, 202 "C" St., San Diego, CA 92101. The office is located in the lobby of the City Administration Building, telephone (619) 236-5765. Be sure to request a copy of the "Senior Citizen Discount Directory" along with your ID card. This invaluable directory lists senior discounts at dozens of beauty parlors, bowling alleys, dance studios, health clubs, restaurants, and movie and live theaters. There is a small charge for the directory.

Hotels

BEST WESTERN: *10% discount.*
5005 N. Harbor Dr., (619) 224-3254.
17065 W. Bernardo Dr., (619) 485-6530.
650 N. Mollison, (619) 442-0601.

710 E. St., (619) 420-5183.
655 W. San Ysidro Blvd., (619) 428-2204.

DAYS INN: *10%–50% discount with Days Inn September Days Club card.*
225 Bay Blvd., Chula Vista, (619) 425-8200.

HOLIDAY INN: *10%–20% discount with Holiday Inn's Travel Venture Club Card.*
Airport, 8110 Aero Dr., (619) 277-8888.
Embarcadero, 1355 N. Harbor Dr., (619) 232-3861.
Harbor View, 1617 First Ave., (619) 239-6171.

HOTEL SAN DIEGO: *10% discount.*
339 W. Broadway, (619) 234-0221.

HOWARD JOHNSON'S: *15%–50% discount with H.J.'s Road Rally Card.*
4545 Waring Rd., (619) 286-7000.

LA QUINTA: *20% discount.*
10185 Paseo Montril, (619) 484-8800.

PICKWICK HOTEL: *20% discount.*
132 W. Broadway, (619) 234-0141.

RAMADA INN: *25% discount for over 60.*
Bonita, 91 Bonita Rd., Chula Vista, (619) 425-9999.
Old Town, 2435 S. Jefferson St., (619) 260-8500.

SHERATON: *25% discount for over 60.*
Sheraton Inn-Airport, 1590 Harbor Island Dr., (619) 291-6400.
Sheraton Inn-Harbor Island Hotel, 1380 Harbor Island Dr., (619) 291-2900.

TRAVELODGE: *Special senior rates for Travelodge's Golden Guest Club. There are 36 Travelodge/Viscount Hotels in San Diego County.*
Airport, 2353 Pacific Hwy., (619) 232-8931.
Balboa Park, 840 Ash St., (619) 234-8277.

Cabrillo Central, 840 “A” St., (619) 234-8477.
Civic Center, 1505 Pacific Hwy., (619) 239-9185.
Downtown, 1345 Tenth Ave., (619) 234-6344.
Harbor, 1305 Pacific Hwy., (619) 233-0398.
Pacific Beach, 4760 Mission Blvd., (619) 483-6780.
Point Loma, 5102 N. Harbor Dr., (619) 223-8171.

VAGABOND: *10% discount.**
College, 6440 El Cajon Blvd., (619) 286-2040.
Mission Valley, 625 Hotel Circle St., (619) 297-1691.
Point Loma, 1325 Scott St., (619) 224-3371.

Public Transportation

SAN DIEGO TRANSIT: *50% discount for 62 and over.*
(619) 233-3004

Car Rental

AVIS: *5%–25% discount.**
International Airport, 3875 N. Harbor Blvd., (619) 231-7171

HERTZ: *5%–25% discount.**
International Airport, 3871 N. Harbor Blvd., (619) 231-7000.

NATIONAL: *10%–12% discount for over 62.*
International Airport, 3865 N. Harbor Blvd., (619) 231-7100.

Sights

SAN DIEGO HARBOR EXCURSION: *20% discount.*
Harbor Dr. & Broadway, (619) 233-6872.

SAN DIEGO "TIJUANA" TROLLEY: *75% discount.*
Kettner & C Sts., (619) 231-1466.

SEA WORLD: *25% discount for over 55 upon request.*
1720 S. Shores Rd., (619) 226-3901.
Open daily.

Museums

MARITIME MUSEUM ASSOCIATION: *30% discount.*
1306 N. Harbor Blvd., (619) 234-9153.
Daily, 9 a.m. to 8 p.m. Restored ships.

MISSION BASILICA SAN DIEGO DE ALCALA: *50% discount.*
10818 San Diego Mission Rd., (619) 283-7319.
Daily, 9 a.m. to 5 p.m. Mission built 1769.

REUBEN H. FLEET SPACE THEATER AND SCIENCE CENTER: *30% discount.*
Balboa Park, (619) 238-1168.
America's largest planetarium. Call for schedule.

SAN DIEGO MUSEUM OF ART: *15% discount.*
Laurel St. in Balboa Park, (619) 232-7931.
Tuesday to Sunday, 10 a.m. to 5 p.m.

SEELEY STABLES and CASA DE ESTADILLO: *50% discount.*
Calhoun St. in Old Town San Diego State Park, (619) 237-6770.
May to September, 10 a.m. to 6 p.m.; October to May, 10 a.m. to 5 p.m. Restored 1869 stables and 1825 adobe house.

WHALEY HOUSE: *25% discount.*
2482 San Diego Ave. & Harney St., (619) 298-2482.
Wednesday to Sunday, 10 a.m. to 4:30 p.m.
Restored 19th-century house and garden.

Free!

Cabrillo National Monument, San Diego Union Newspaper Museum, San Diego Historical Museum, Timkin Art Gallery, Villa Montezuma

SAN FRANCISCO

Helpful Address

SAN FRANCISCO CONVENTION & VISITORS BUREAU
P.O. Box 6977
San Francisco, CA 94101, (415) 974-6900

Join a National Senior Citizens' Organization
AARP/NRTA, $7.50 yearly, 215 Long Beach Blvd., Long Beach, CA 90801, (800) 453-9600; *National Council of Senior Citizens*, $10 yearly, 925 15th St., NW, Washington, DC 20005, (202) 347-8800; *Mature Outlook*, $7.50 yearly, P.O. Box 1209, Glenview, IL 60025, (800) 336-6226; *Catholic Golden Age*, $7 yearly, 400 Lackawanna Ave., Scranton, PA 18503. Avoid last-minute worry and disappointment by requesting your membership card four to six weeks before your trip.

Gold Card Discount Program

Senior residents of San Francisco can receive hundreds of discounts with a Senior Citizen Gold Card and a discount directory. Write San Francisco Department of Public Health, 1182 Market St., Rm. 212, San Francisco 94103.

Senior Citizens Travel Directory

Send $4.50 to H. H. Henry, 663 Carlston Ave., Oakland, CA 94610 for a directory and travel newsletter listing senior activities that range from outings to football games to trips to Alaska and Hawaii—often at senior discount prices.

Bed & Breakfast Reservation Services

CALIFORNIA HOUSEGUESTS INTERNATIONAL: *10% discount for* Discount Guide *readers. 2-night minimum.*
18653 Ventura Blvd., #190B Tarzana, CA 91356, (818) 344-7878. (L.A. telephone number.)

Hotels

BEST WESTERN: *10% discount.*
140 7th St., (415) 552-8600.
364 9th St., (415) 621-2826.
114 7th St., (415) 621-0701.
Sutter & Buchanan, (415) 921-4000.
Airport, 1100 El Camino Real, (415) 588-2912.

DAYS INN: *10%–50% discount with Days Inn September Days Club card.*
Airport, Hwy. 101 at Burlingame exit, (415) 342-7772.
Baybridge, 1603 Powell St., (415) 547-7888.

COMPARATIVE HOTEL RATES: REGULAR DOUBLE ROOM

HOTEL	SR. DISC.	
B & B	—	$40–90
BEST WESTERN	10%	$58–72
HOLIDAY INN	15%	$85–119
QUALITY INN	10%	$50–76
RAMADA INN	25%	$79–104
RODEWAY INN	10%	$50–52
SHERATON	25%	$132–203
VAGABOND	10%	$54–70

HOLIDAY INN: *10%–20% discount with Holiday Inn's Travel Venture Club Card.*
Financial District/Chinatown, 750 Kearny St., (415) 433-6600.
Fisherman's Wharf, 1300 Columbus, (415) 771-9000.
Golden Gateway, 1500 Van Ness, (415) 441-4000.
International Airport, 245 S. Airport Blvd., (415) 589-7200.
Union Square, 480 Sutter St., (415) 398-8900.

LA QUINTA: *20% discount.*
Airport, 20 Airport Blvd., (415) 483-2223.

QUALITY INN: *10% discount for over 60.*
Comfort Inn, 240 7th St., (415) 861-6469.
Downtown, 2775 Van Ness Ave., (415) 928-5000.

RAMADA INNS: *25% discount for over 60.*
Airport, 1250 Old Bayshore Hwy., Burlingame, (415) 347-2381.
Fisherman's Wharf, 590 Bay at Jones, (415) 885-4700.
Renaissance, 55 Cyril Magnin St., (415) 392-8000.

RODEWAY INN: *10% discount.*
Downtown, 895 Geary St., (415) 441-8220.

SHERATON: *25% discount for over 60.*
Airport, 1177 Airport Blvd., Burlingame, (415) 342-9200.
Fisherman's Wharf, 2500 Mason St. at Beach, (415) 362-5500.

TRAVELODGE: *Special senior rates for Travelodge's Golden Guest Club.*
Airport, 326 S. Airport Blvd., (415) 583-9600.
Bel Aire, 3201 Steiner St., (415) 921-5162.
Central, 1707 Market St., (415) 621-6775.
Downtown, 790 Ellis St., (415) 775-7612.
Fisherman's Wharf, 1201 Columbus Ave., (415) 776-7070.
Golden Gate, 2230 Lombard St., (415) 922-3900.
Presidio, 2755 Lombard St., (415) 931-8581.
Wharf, 250 Beach St., (415) 392-6700.

VAGABOND: *10% discount.**
Airport, 1640 Bayshore Ave., Burlingame, (415) 692-4040.
Downtown, 2550 Van Ness, (415) 776-7500.

Public Transportation

SAN FRANCISCO MUNICIPAL RAILWAY: *15¢ fare for over 65.* (415) 673-6864

Car Rental

AVIS: *5%–25% discount.**
San Francisco International Airport, Box 8021, (415) 877-6780.
675 Post St., (415) 885-5011.

HERTZ: *5%–25% discount.**
San Francisco International Airport, (415) 877-1600.
433 Mason St., (415) 771-2200.

NATIONAL: *10%–12% discount for over 62.*
Airport, (415) 877-4745.
550 O'Farrell, (415) 474-5300.

Sights

RIPLEY'S BELIEVE IT OR NOT MUSEUM: *30% discount for over 65.*
Fisherman's Wharf at Jefferson. (415) 771-6188.
Mid-June to mid-September: daily, 9 a.m. to midnight. Rest of year: Sunday to Thursday, 10 a.m. to 10 p.m.; Friday and Saturday, 10 a.m. to midnight.

SAN FRANCISCO ZOOLOGICAL GARDENS: *80% discount.*
Sloat Blvd. at the ocean, (415) 661-2023.
Daily 10 a.m. to 5 p.m.

Museums

ASIAN ART MUSEUM: *75% discount.*
Golden Gate Park, (415) 558-2993.
Daily, 10 a.m. to 5 p.m.

BALCLUTHA: *50% discount.*
National Maritime Museum, Pier 43, Fisherman's Wharf, (415) 673-0700.
Daily, 10 a.m. to 10 p.m. 1886 three-masted, square-rigged sailing vessel.

CALIFORNIA ACADEMY OF SCIENCES: *60% discount. Free on first Wednesdays.*
Golden Gate Park, (415) 221-5100.
Daily, 10 a.m. to 5 p.m. Natural history museum and Morrison Planetarium.

CALIFORNIA HISTORICAL SOCIETY: *50% discount.*
2090 Jackson St., (415) 567-1848.
Wednesday, Saturday, Sunday, 1 to 5 p.m.

CALIFORNIA PALACE OF THE LEGION OF HONOR: *60% discount.*
Lincoln Park, (415) 221-4811.
Wednesday to Sunday, 10 a.m. to 5 p.m. Fifteenth- through nineteenth-century French art.

EXPLORATORIUM: *50% discount.*
Lyon and Marina Ave., (415) 563-3200.
Wednesday to Friday, 1 p.m. to 5 p.m.; weekends, noon to 5 p.m. Hundreds of participatory science exhibits.

HAAS-LILLENTHAL HOUSE: *66% discount.*
2007 Franklin St., Eastlake, (415) 441-3004.
Wednesdays, noon to 4 p.m.; Sundays, 11 a.m. to 4:30 p.m. Restored Victorian house. Photographic exhibit.

M. H. DE YOUNG MEMORIAL MUSEUM: *65% discount.*
Golden Gate Park, (415) 221-4811.
Wednesday to Sunday, 10 a.m. to 5 p.m. African, American, European, Oceanic, Egyptian, Classical, and pre-Columbian art. In the west wing is the Asian Art Museum (see p. 69).

SAN FRANCISCO MUSEUM OF MODERN ART: *50% discount.*
Van Ness Ave. & McAllister St., (415) 863-8800.
Tuesday, Wednesday, Friday, 10 a.m. to 6 p.m.; Thursday, 10 a.m. to 10 p.m.; Saturday, Sunday, 10 a.m. to 5 p.m.

Bay Cruises

BLUE & GOLD FLEET: *50% discount.*
Pier 39, next to Fisherman's Wharf, (415) 781-7877.
Daily, summer, 10 a.m. to 6 p.m.; winter, until 4 p.m.

RED & WHITE FLEET: *50¢ to $5 off select trips.*
Pier 43½, (415) 546-2810.
Ticket booth at Pier 41 is open from 8 a.m. to 4 p.m. daily.

Free!

Acres of Orchids, Cable Car Barn and Museum, Chevron World of Oil, Chinese Historical Society of America, Hyde Street Pier Floating Museum, National Maritime Museum, Navy/Marine Corps/Coast Guard Museum, Old U.S. Mint, Palace of Fine Arts, Presidio Army Museum, Society of Pioneers Museum, Treasure Island Museum, Wells Fargo Bank Museum, Wine Museum of San Francisco

SOUTH LAKE TAHOE

Hotels

Note: Nearly all hotels in this area offer discounted rates from October through May, excluding holidays. Call (800) 822-5922 for reservations.

OLYMPIC MOTEL: *$2 discount except holidays.*
3901 Pioneer Tr., P.O. Box 5809, (916) 541-2119.

7-ELEVEN MOTEL: *Discount to AARP; varies by season.*
3640 Hwy. 50, P.O. Box 153, (916) 544-3640.

STARDUST: *10% discount except holidays.*
4061 Lake Tahoe Blvd., (916) 544-5211.

TAHOE VALLEY MOTEL: *10% discount.*
2241 Lake Tahoe Blvd., at Hwy. 50 & Tahoe Keys Blvd., P.O. Box 7702, (916) 541-0353.

TRAVELODGE: *Special senior rates for Travelodge's Golden Guest Club.*
3489 Hwy. 50, P.O. Box N, (916) 544-5266.
4003 U.S. 50 at Stateline, (916) 541-5000.
4011 U.S. 50 at Stateline, (916) 544-6000.

VAGABOND HOTEL: *10% discount.**
Hwy. 50, P.O. Box J, (916) 544-3476.

VILLA MONTREUX: *10% discount.*
971 Ski Run Blvd., (916) 544-3224.

Car Rental

AVIS: *5%–25% discount.**
Tahoe Valley Airport, (916) 541-7800.

HERTZ: *5%–25% discount.**
Tahoe Valley Airport, (916) 544-2327.

NATIONAL: *10%–12% discount for over 62.*
Tahoe Valley Airport, (916) 541-2277.

Tour Operators

GRAY LINE: *15% discount to AARP.*
Nevada Northern Grayline, 1675 Mill St., Reno, NV 89502, (702) 329-1147, (800) 822-6009.
Variety of Lake Tahoe tours, including sternwheeler trips and Heavenly Valley tram, all beginning in Reno, Nevada.

Rules for Savings on Car Rentals

1. Join a national senior citizens' organization and use its discount identification number.
2. Make advance reservations with the toll-free national reservation service.
3. Renting mid-week? A senior-citizen rate can save you money.
4. Renting for seven days or for the weekend? Senior discounts can save you another 5% to 10%.
5. Always ask, "Is this the cheapest rate you offer?"

See paged 32–34 for more information.

COLORADO

Helpful Addresses

COLORADO TOURISM BOARD
5500 S. Syracuse Circle, Suite 267,
Englewood, CO 80111
(303) 779-1067

AGING AND ADULT SERVICES DIVISION,
DEPARTMENT OF SOCIAL SERVICES
717 17th St., Denver, CO 80218
(303) 294-5913.

DENVER AND VICINITY

Hotels

BEST WESTERN: *10% discount.*
11 E. 84th Ave., (303) 428-5041.
401 E. 58th Ave., (303) 297-1717.
455 S. Colorado Blvd., (303) 388-5561.
3900 Elati St., (303) 458-0808.
7201 E. 49th Ave., Commerce City, (303) 287-7548.

DAYS INN: *10%–50% discount with Days Inn September Days Club card.*
36 E. 120th Ave., Northglenn, (303) 457-0688.
15059 W. Colfax, Golden, (303) 277-0200.

ECONOLODGE: *10% discount with Econo Senior Class Card.*
Bronco Stadium, 930 Valley Hwy., (303) 592-1555.

HOLIDAY INN: *10%–20% discount with Holiday Inn's Travel Venture Club Card.*
Airport, 4040 Quebec St., (303) 321-6666.
Colorado Blvd., 1475 S. Colorado Blvd., (303) 757-7731.

Downtown, 15th & Glenarm Place, (303) 573-1450.
Sports Center, 1975 Bryant, (303) 433-8331.

HOWARD JOHNSON'S: *15%–50% discount with H.J.'s Road Rally Card.*
South, 6300 E. Hampden Ave., (303) 758-2211.
West, 4765 Federal Blvd., (303) 433-8441.

LA QUINTA: *20% discount.*
Airport, 3975 Peoria Way, (303) 371-5640.
Central, 3500 Fox St., (303) 458-1222.
South, 1975 S. Colorado Blvd., (303) 758-8886.

QUALITY INN: *10% discount for over 60.*
1150 E. Colfax, (303) 831-7700.

RAMADA INN: 25% discount for over 60.
Airport, I-70 at Quebec St. exit, (303) 388-6161.
Foothills, 11595 W. 6th Ave., Lakewood, (303) 238-7751.
Wheatridge, 10101 I-70 Service Rd., N., (303) 422-7200.

RODEWAY INN: *10% discount.*
Airport, 4590 Quebec St., (303) 320-0260.

SHERATON: *25% discount for over 60.*
Airport, 3535 Quebec St., (303) 333-7711.
Denver Tech, 4900 DTC Pkwy., (303) 779-1100.
Thornton, 83 E. 120th Ave., (303) 451-1002.

TRAVELODGE: *Special senior rates for Travelodge's Golden Guest Club.*
Airport, 39th & Quentin, (800) 255-3050.
Central, I-25 & Speer Blvd., (303) 458-5454.
200 W. 48th Ave., (303) 296-4000.

Car Rental

AVIS: *5%–25% discount.**
Airport, 7511 E. 29th Way, (303) 398-3725.

HERTZ: *5%–25% discount.**
Airport, (303) 398-3990.
2001 Welton St., (303) 297-9400.

NATIONAL: *10%–12% discount for over 62.*
Airport, (303) 321-7990.
7070 Smith Rd., (303) 321-7990.

Sights

CHAMBERLIN OBSERVATORY: *50% discount.*
Observatory Park, 2930 E. Warren Ave., (303) 753-2070.
April through September: Tuesday and Thursday, 8:30 to 10 p.m. October through March: Tuesday and Thursday, 7 to 9 p.m. Reservations necessary.

DENVER BOTANIC GARDENS: *50% discount.*
1005 York St., (303) 575-2547.
Daily, 9 a.m. to 4:45 p.m.

DENVER ZOO: *60% discount.*
City Park, (303) 575-2552.
Daily, 10 a.m. to 5 p.m.; until 6 p.m. in summer.

Museums

COLORADO HISTORICAL SOCIETY: *65% discount.*
1300 Broadway, (303) 866-3682.
Tuesday to Saturday, 10 a.m .to 4:30 p.m.

DENVER ART MUSEUM: *30% discount.*
100 W. 14th Ave., (303) 575-2793.
Daily, 9 a.m. to 5 p.m.

DENVER MUSEUM OF NATURAL HISTORY: *50% discount.*
2001 Colorado Blvd., City Park, (303) 370-6363.
Daily, 9 a.m. to 5 p.m.

GRANT-HUMPHREYS MANSION: *50% discount.*
770 Pennsylvania St., (303) 866-3508.
Tuesday to Friday, 10 a.m. to 2 p.m.

MOLLY BROWN HOUSE: *50% discount over 60.*
1340 Pennsylvania St., (303) 832-4092.
Tuesday to Saturday, 10 a.m. to 3 p.m.; Sunday, noon to 3 p.m.; open until 4 p.m. in summer.

MUSEUM OF WESTERN ART: *50% discount.*
1727 Tremont Pl., (303) 296-1880.
Tuesday to Saturday, 10 a.m. to 6 p.m.; Sunday, Monday, 1 p.m. to 5 p.m.

Skiing Near Denver

Most Colorado ski resorts offer a sliding discount scale to seniors: in general, discounts increase starting from ages 60–64 to ages 65–69. Most resorts offer *free* skiing to those 70 and over.

BRECKENRIDGE: *Special senior discount.*
1 mi. W of CO 9, (303) 453-2368.

COPPER MOUNTAIN: *Special senior discount.*
Copper Mountain (75 miles west of Denver), (303) 968-2882; (800) 458-8386.

KEYSTONE & ARAPAHOE BASIN: *Special senior discount.*
Box 38, Keystone (75 miles west of Denver), (303) 468-2316.

VAIL/BEAVER CREEK: *Special senior discount.*
Vail (100 miles west of Denver), (303) 476-5677; (800) 525-3875.

WINTER PARK: *Special senior discount.*
2 mi. N.W. of U.S. 40, (303) 726-5514.

Free!

Arvada Arts Center, Colorado History Museum, Denver Art Museum, Denver Museum of Natural History, State Capitol, U.S. Mint

CONNECTICUT

Helpful Addresses

CONNECTICUT DEPARTMENT OF ECONOMIC DEVELOPMENT
Travel Director, 210 Washington St., Hartford, CT 06106
(203) 566-3385, (800) 243-1685 (east coast, except CT), (800) 842-7492 (CT)

DEPARTMENT ON AGING
175 Main St., Hartford, CT 06106
(203) 556-3238

Public Transportation

METRO-NORTH NEW HAVEN LINE: *50% discount for over 65; not available mornings before 9 a.m.*
New Haven, (203) 772-2093; Bridgeport, (203) 334-5052; Stamford, (203) 258-2559; (800) 223-6052 in CT. The New Haven Line services western Connecticut from New Haven to New York City (Grand Central Terminal). To obtain discount, present Medicare card or state-issued Elderly/Handicapped Transit ID card (applications at all Metro-North Ticket Offices, Connecticut Transit offices, agencies for the aging, and from the Department of Transportation).

ALL CONNECTICUT BUS SYSTEMS: *50% discount for over 65. Present Medicare card or Elderly/Handicapped Transit ID.*
Connecticut Dept. of Transportation, P.O. Drawer A, 24 Wolcott Hill Rd., Wethersfield, CT 06109, (203) 566-2336.

CONNECTICUT LIMOUSINE: *65 and over $3 discount for advance purchase.* Scheduled service to JFK, La Guardia, and Newark, (800) 242-2283.

CONNECTICUT COAST–OLD SAYBROOK TO MYSTIC

Hotels

DAYS INN: *10%–50% discount with Days Inn September Days Club card.*
Mystic, I-95 at Rte. 27 Interchange, (203) 572-0574.

HOLIDAY INN: *10%–20% discount with Holiday Inn's Travel Venture Club Card.*
New London, I-95 & Frontage Rd., (203) 442-0631.

HOWARD JOHNSON'S: *15%–50% discount with H.J.'s Road Rally Card.*
East Lyme, Flanders Rd., (203) 739-6921.
Mystic, I-95 & Rte. 27, (203) 536-2654.
Old Saybrook, 100 Essex Rd., (203) 388-5716.

QUALITY INN: *10% discount for over 60.*
Groton, 404 Bridge St., (203) 445-8141.

RAMADA INN: *25% discount for over 60.*
Mystic, I-95 & Rte. 27, (203) 536-4281.

TRAVELODGE: *Special senior rates for Travelodge's Golden Guest Club.*
Niantic, I-95, exit 74, (203) 739-5483.

Car Rental

AVIS: *5%–25% discount.**
Groton Airport, (203) 445-8585.
Hartford, Bradley International Airport, (203) 627-3500.

HERTZ: *5%–25% discount.**
Groton Airport, (203) 446-1200.
Hartford, Bradley International Airport, (203) 627-3850.

NATIONAL: *10%–12% discount for over 62.*
Groton Airport, (203) 445-7435.
Hartford, Bradley International Airport, (203) 627-3470.

Museums

JOSHUA HEMPSTEAD HOUSE: *25% discount.*
11 Hempstead St., New London, (203) 443-7949.
Mid-May to mid-October, daily except Monday, 1 p.m. to 5 p.m. Built 1678, Joshua Hempstead house has been faithfully restored and furnished.

NATHANIEL HEMPSTEAD HOUSE: *25% discount.*
11 Hempstead St., New London, (203) 247-8996.
Built 1759, one of only two surviving mid-18th-century cut-stone houses in Connecticut.

MYSTIC SEAPORT: *10% discount.*
Rte. 27, I-95, exit 90, (203) 572-0711.
Daily, 9 a.m. to 5 p.m. Winter, 9 a.m. to 4 p.m. Famous nineteenth-century maritime village "living museum."

**An asterisk indicates that the discount is intended for members of senior citizens' organizations that anyone can join. See "Hotel, Transportation, and Sightseeing Discounts."*

U.S.S. *CROAKER* SUBMARINE MEMORIAL: *33% discount.*
359 Thames St., Groton, (203) 448-1616.
Mid-April to mid-October, daily, 9 a.m. to 5 p.m.; rest of year, 9 a.m to 3 p.m. Restored World War II submarine.

Sights

MYSTIC MARINELIFE AQUARIUM: *10% discount.*
Coogan Blvd., I-95, exit 90, (203) 536-3323.
Mid-May to mid-September: daily, 9 a.m. to 7 p.m. Rest of year: 9 a.m. to 4:45 p.m.

Free!

Groton: Fort Griswold State Park and Museum. New London: Deshon-Allyn House, Lyman Allyn Museum, Herbert F. Moran Nature Center, Old Town Mill, U.S. Coast Guard Academy. Old Lyme: Florence Griswold Museum

DELAWARE

Helpful Addresses

DELAWARE STATE TRAVEL SERVICE
P.O. Box 1401, 99 Kings Hwy., Dover, DE 19901
(302) 736-4271, (800) 441-8846 (except DE), (800) 282-8667 (DE).

DIVISION ON AGING
1901 N. DuPont Hwy., New Castle, DE 19720
(302) 421-6791

WILMINGTON

Hotels

HOLIDAY INN: *10%–20% discount with Holiday Inn's Travel Venture Club Card.*
North, 4000 Concord Pike, (302) 478-2222.
Newark, 1203 Christiana Rd., (302) 737-2700.

SHERATON: *25% discount for over 60.*
U.S. 202, Concord Pike, (302) 478-6000.

Car Rental

AVIS: *5%–25% discount.**
903 Washington St., (302) 654-0380.

HERTZ: *5%–25% discount.**
Airport, (302) 328-5155.
1218 French St., (302) 658-7500.

NATIONAL: *10%–12% discount for over 62.*
Airport, (302) 328-5636.
1212 Washington St., (302) 655-7555.

Museums

BRANDYWINE BATTLEFIELD NATIONAL MUSEUM: *50% discount.*
U.S. 1, Chadds Ford, PA, (215) 388-1134.
April through October, 11 a.m. to 5 p.m.

BRANDYWINE RIVER MUSEUM: *50% discount for over 65.*
U.S. 1, Chadds Ford, PA, (215) 388-7601.
Daily, 9:30 a.m. to 4:30 p.m. Famous collection of works of American School artists N.C. Wyeth, Andrew Wyeth, Jamie Wyeth, and Howard Pyle.

DELAWARE MUSEUM OF NATURAL HISTORY: *30% discount.*
5 mi. NW on DE 52, Greenville, (302) 658-9111.

HAGLEY MUSEUM: *10% discount.*
3 mi. NW off DE 141, (302) 658-2400.
Tuesday to Saturday, 9:30 a.m. to 4:30 p.m.; Sunday, 1 to 5 p.m. Exhibits on industrial history.

WINTERTHUR MUSEUM AND GARDENS: *$1.50 off regular admission.*
Rte. 52, Winterthur, DE 19735, (302) 654-1548.
Closed Monday; hours vary. Collection of American decorative arts; landscaped gardens.

Free!

Wilmington: Delaware Art Museum, Hendrickson House, Holy Trinity (Old Swedes) Church, Old Town Hall. Nearby Pennsylvania: Brandywine Battlefield Park, Philips Mushroom Palace, Star Rose Gardens

Join a National Senior Citizens' Organization
AARP/NRTA, $7.50 yearly, 215 Long Beach Blvd., Long Beach, CA 90801, (800) 453-9600; *National Council of Senior Citizens*, $10 yearly, 925 15th St., NW, Washington, DC 20005, (202) 347-8800; *Mature Outlook*, $7.50 yearly, P.O. Box 1209, Glenview, IL 60025, (800) 336-6226; *Catholic Golden Age*, $7 yearly, 400 Lackawanna Ave., Scranton, PA 18503. Avoid last-minute worry and disappointment by requesting your membership card four to six weeks before your trip.

DISTRICT OF COLUMBIA

Helpful Addresses

WASHINGTON AREA CONVENTION & VISITORS ASSOCIATION
1575 I St. N.W., Washington, DC 20005, (202) 789-7000

OFFICE ON AGING
1424 K St. N.W., Washington, DC 20011
(202) 724-5626

GOLDEN WASHINGTONIAN CLUB
All Washington residents and visitors over 60 are eligible for discounts at the 1400 businesses listed in the Gold Mine directory sponsored by the D.C. Office on Aging. The 115-page listing of services, stores, and restaurants can be obtained by calling 466-GOLD, or visiting the Tourist Information Center, 14th St. and Pennsylvania Ave., N.W.

WASHINGTON, DC

Hotels

BEST WESTERN: *10% discount.*
1201 13th St., N.W., (202) 682-5300.
10 I St., S.W., (202) 488-7500.
Alexandria, VA, 625 First St., (703) 548-6300.
Arlington, VA, 2480 S. Glebe Rd., (703) 979-0400.

DAYS INN: *10%–50% discount with Days Inn September Days card.*
55 Hampton Pk. Blvd., Capitol Heights, MD, (301) 336-8900.
110 S. Bragg St., Alexandria, VA, (703) 354-4950.

HOLIDAY INN: *10%–20% discount with Holiday Inn's Travel Venture Club Card.*

Connecticut Ave., 1900 Connecticut Ave. N.W., (202) 332-9300.

Downtown, 1615 Rhode Island Ave. N.W., (202) 296-2100.

Dulles Airport, 1000 Sully Rd., Sterling, VA, (703) 471-7411.

2101 Wisconsin Ave. N.W., (202) 338-4600.

1501 Rhode Island Ave. N.W., (202) 483-2000.

Thomas Circle, Massachusetts Ave. at Thomas Cir. N.W., (202) 737-1200.

HOWARD JOHNSON'S: *15%–50% discount with H. J.'s Road Rally Card.*

Washington Plaza Hotel, 2505 Wisconsin Ave., N.W., (202) 337-7400.

National Airport, 2650 Jefferson Davis Hwy., Arlington, VA, (703) 684-7200.

QUALITY INN: *10% discount for over 60.*

Capitol Hill, 415 New Jersey Ave., N.W., (202) 638-1616.

Downtown, 1315 16th St. N.W., (202) 232-8000.

Pentagon City (National Airport), 300 Army-Navy Dr., (703) 892-4100.

RAMADA INN: *25% discount for over 60.*

Central, 1430 Rhode Island Ave. N.W., (202) 462-7777.

Renaissance, 1143 New Hampshire Ave. N.W., (202) 775-0800.

SHERATON: *25% discount for over 60.*

Connecticut Ave., 2660 Woodley Rd. & Connecticut Ave., (202) 328-2000.

Downtown, 923 16th St. N.W., (202) 638-2626.

Dulles Airport, 11810 Sunrise Valley Dr., Reston, VA, (703) 620-9000.

National Airport, Columbia Pike & Washington Blvd., Arlington, VA, (703) 521-1900.
National Airport, 1800 Jefferson Davis Hwy., (703) 486-1111.
New Jersey Ave. & F St. N.W., (202) 628-2100.

Restaurants

BABES TWO: *10% discount for over 60.*
4226 Wisconsin Ave., N.W., (202) 686-1000.

CASPIAN TEA ROOM: *10% discount for over 60.*
4801 Massachusetts Ave., (202) 244-6363.

CHARLIE CHIANG'S: *10% discount for over 60.*
1912 I St., N.W., (202) 293-6000.
4250 Connecticut Ave., N.W., (202) 966-1916.

CHEZ ARTISTE: *10% discount for over 60.*
1201 Pennsylvania Ave., N.W., (202) 737-7772.

CHINA VILLAGE: *20%–25% discount for over 60.*
521 G St., N.W., (202) 789-0083.

CLYDES OF GEORGETOWN: *10% discount for over 60.*
3236 M St., N.W., (202) 333-9180.

DAVID LEE'S: *20% discount for over 60.*
1875 Connecticut Ave., N.W., (202) 462-8110.
2661 Connecticut Ave., N.W., (202) 387-4477.

EL TORITO MEXICAN: *10% discount off food for over 60.*
Georgetown Park, 3222 M St., N.W., (202) 342-2290.

GAZEBO: *10% discount for over 60.*
2505 Wisconsin Ave., N.W., (202) 337-7230.

HUNAN ON CAPITOL HILL: *10% discount for over 60.*
201 D St., N.E., (202) 544-0102.

J. J. MELLON'S: *10% discount for over 60.*
1201 Pennsylvania Ave., N.E., (202) 737-5700.

KING ARTHUR'S: *20% discount for over 60.*
1819 M St., N.W., (202) 296-2191.

RED SEA RESTAURANT: *10% discount for over 60.*
2463 18th St., N.W., (202) 483-5000.

SAMURAI JAPANESE STEAK HOUSE: *Two for the price of one on some entrees, for over 60.*
Georgetown Park, 3222 M St., N.W., (202) 333-1001.

TAJ MAHAL: *10% discount for over 60.*
1327 Connecticut Ave., N.W., (202) 659-1544.

TUSCAN CANTINA: *15% discount off food for over 60.*
2605 Connecticut Ave., N.W., (202) 462-6410.

VITTORIO'S: *10% discount for over 60.*
Georgetown Park, 3222 M St., N.W., (202) 333-1145.

Car Rental

AVIS: *5%–25% discount.**
Dulles Airport, (703) 661-8874.
National Airport, (703) 379-4757.
1772 M St. N.W., (202) 467-6585.
Union Station, (202) 789-0742.

HERTZ: *5%–25% discount.**
Dulles Airport, (703) 471-6020.
National Airport, (703) 979-6300.

NATIONAL: *10%–12% discount for over 62.*
Dulles Airport, (703) 471-5278.
National Airport, (202) 783-1590.
1618 L St. N.W., (202) 347-4772.

Tour Operators

Gray Line: *10% discount to over 55.*
Gray Line of Washington, D.C., 333 E St., S.W., Washington, DC 20024, (202) 479-5900.
Bus tours highlighting the capital's historic monuments, public buildings, the Smithsonian, and Embassy Row.

Theater

ARENA STAGE: *35% discount for over 60 on weekdays.*
6th & Maine, S.W., (202) 488-3300.

FORD'S THEATRE: *Matinee discounts for over 55.*
511 10th St., N.W., (202) 347-6262.

JOHN F. KENNEDY CENTER FOR THE PERFORMING ARTS: *50% discount for over 65. Some Saturday evening performances are not discountable.*
Washington, DC, (202) 254-3774.
Seniors over 65 may purchase one ticket with a Medicare card or proof of age and buy one additional ticket for a friend with that person's Medicare card (a maximum of two tickets may be purchased). Tickets must be purchased at the Kennedy Center box office after securing a senior citizen's voucher from the Friends of the Kennedy Center office in the Hall of States. Call the Friends Volunteer office to verify that specially priced tickets have not sold out (telephone number above).

NATIONAL THEATRE: *50% discount for over 65.*
1321 Pennsylvania Ave., N.W., (202) 783-6854.

SHAKESPEARE THEATRE AT THE FOLGER: *20% discount in advance; 50% discount 30 minutes before curtain.*
301 E. Capitol St., S.E., (202) 546-4000.

TICKET PLACE: *Performing arts tickets for greater Washington events available to everyone at 50% discount. Available day of performance. Monday, 12:00–2:00 p.m.; Tuesday through Saturday, 11:00 a.m. to 6:00 p.m.*
13th and F Sts. N.W., (202) 842-5387.

Free! (With very few exceptions, all sights and museums in Washington are free.)

Corcoran Gallery of Art, D.A.R. Museum, the F.B.I., Folger Shakespeare Library, Ford's Theatre Museum, Jefferson Memorial, Library of Congress, Lincoln Memorial, Museum of African Art, Museum of Modern Art of Latin America, National Archives (Declaration of Independence and Bill of Rights), National Geographic Explorers Hall, Pierce Mill, U.S. Botanical Gardens and Conservatory, U.S. Capitol, U.S. Congress, U.S. Naval Observatory, U.S. Supreme Court, the White House

Free! The Smithsonian Museums

The "Castle," Freer Gallery of Art, Hirshhorn Museum and Sculpture Garden, National Air and Space Museum, National Gallery of Art, National Museum of American Art, National Museum of American History, National Museum of Arts and Industry, National Museum of Natural History, National Portrait Gallery, Renwick Gallery

Write to your Congressman before you go

Your Congressman can get you passes to the U.S. Congress Visitor's Gallery and tickets to special White House tours if you request them well before you visit Washington

FLORIDA

Helpful Addresses

FLORIDA DIVISION OF TOURISM
125 Van Buren St., Tallahassee, FL 32301
(904) 487-1462

PROGRAM OFFICE OF AGING AND ADULT SERVICES
1317 Winewood Blvd., Tallahassee, FL 32301
(904) 488-8922

Incredible Deal

You can get a free rental car to drive from any of several Florida cities to any of 30 cities from Dallas to Chicago to New York and Boston if you'll be going between Easter and Memorial Day. See Chapter 2, "Hotel, Transportation, and Sightseeing Discounts."

MIAMI

Hotels

BEST WESTERN: *10% discount.*
340 Biscayne Blvd., (305) 371-4400.

DAYS INN: *10%–50% discount with Days Inn September Days Club card.*
1050 N.W. 14th St., (305) 324-0200.
Airport, 3401 N.W. LeJeune Rd., (305) 871-4221.

HOLIDAY INN: *10%–20% discount with Holiday Inn's Travel Venture Club Card.*
Airport (Civic Center), 1170 N.W. 11th St., (305) 324-0800.
Airport (North), 1111 S. Poinciana Blvd., (305) 885-1941.
Biscayne Bay, 495 Brickell Ave., (305) 373-6000.

Convention Center, 2201 Collins Ave., Miami Beach, (305) 534-1511.
Golden Glades, 148 N.W. 167th St., N. Miami, (305) 949-1441.
Sports Center, 21485 N.W. 27th Ave., (305) 621–5801.

HOWARD JOHNSON'S: *15%–50% discount with H.J.'s Road Rally Card.*
Airport, 1980 N.W. LeJeune Rd., (305) 871-4370.
Bal Harbour, Biscayne Blvd. & 123rd St., (305) 891-7350.
Coral Gables, 1430 S. Dixie Hwy., (305) 665-7501.
Downtown Miami, 1100 Biscayne Blvd., (305) 358-3080.
Downtown Miami, 200 S.E. 2nd Ave., (305) 374-3000.
Golden Glades, 16500 N.W. 2nd Ave., (305) 945-2621.
Kendall, 10201 S. Dixie Hwy., (305) 666-2523.

LA QUINTA: *20% discount.*
Airport, 7401 N.W. 36th St., (305) 599-9902.

QUALITY INN: *10% discount for over 60.*
Airport, 1850 N.W. LeJeune Blvd., (305) 871-4350.
South, 14501 S. Dixie Ave., (305) 251-2000.

RAMADA INN: *25% discount for over 60.*
Airport, 3941 N.W. 22nd St., (305) 871-1700.
North, 16805 N.W. 12th Ave., (305) 624-8401.

SCOTTISH INN: *10% discount with Scottish Identicard.*
American Beach Resort, 15811 Collins Ave., (305) 940-0237.

SHERATON: *25% discount for over 60.*
Airport, 3900 N.W. 21st St., (305) 871-3800.
495 Brickell Ave., (305) 373-6000.
Bal Harbour, Oceanfront at 97th St., (305) 865-7511.
Hialeah Gardens, Palmetto Expwy. & N.W. 103rd, (305) 825-1000.

Key Biscayne, 555 Ocean Dr., (305) 361-5775.

TRAVELODGE: *Special senior rates for Travelodge's Golden Guest Club.*
Viscount Airport, 5301 N.W. 36th St., (305) 871-6000.

Car Rental

AVIS: *5%–25% discount.**
Airport, Bldg. 3014, (305) 526-3000.
Downtown, 255 N.E. 1st St., (305) 377-2531.
Miami Beach, 2318 Collins Ave., (305) 538-4441.

HERTZ: *5%–25% discount.**
Airport, (305) 526-5646.
666 Biscayne Blvd., (305) 377-4601.

NATIONAL: *10%–12% discount for over 62.*
Airport, (305) 526-5200.
Miami Beach, 17760 Collins Ave., (305) 931-7470.

Sights

ART DECO DISTRICT: *50% discount on tours.*
Miami Beach, (305) 672-1836 or 672-2014.
One square mile of restored 1920s and 1930s resort architecture. Boundaries are 6th St. to the south, 23rd St. to the north, Atlantic Ave. to the east, and Alton Rd. to the west.

MONKEY JUNGLE: *10% discount.*
14805 S.W. 216th St., (305) 235-1611.
Daily, 9:30 a.m. to 5 p.m.

WILDERNESS EXPERIENCES: *10% discount for over 65.*
P.O. Box 440474, Miami, FL 33144, (813) 695-3143.
Half-day to 3-day excursions through Big Cypress National Preserve, on a 12-foot-high "swamp machine."

Museums

CLOISTERS OF THE MONASTERY OF ST. BERNARD DE CLAIRVAUX: *30% discount.*
16711 W. Dixie Hwy., N. Miami Beach, (305) 945-1462.
Monday to Saturday, 10 a.m. to 5 p.m.; Sunday, noon to 5 p.m. Twelfth-century Spanish monastery that William Randolph Hearst brought to the U.S.

MUSEUM OF SCIENCE & SPACE TRANSIT PLANETARIUM: *20% discount.*
3280 S. Miami Ave., (305) 854-4247.
Sunday to Thursday, 10 a.m. to 6 p.m.; Friday, Saturday, 10 a.m. to 10 p.m. Slides, films, participatory exhibits; several planetarium shows daily.

Free!

Lummis Park, Sunspot Soaring Center.

ORLANDO AREA

Senior Season

Mid-September through mid-December is Senior Season in Central Florida. Hotels, attractions, restaurants, and stores offer substantial discounts to seniors over 55. In addition to discounts, a complete calendar of events is planned featuring the annual Golden Age Olympics. For information, write or call the Orlando Chamber of Commerce, 75 E. Ivanhoe Blvd., Orlando, FL 32802, (305) 425-1234. Brochures are not generally available until July.

Hotels

BEST WESTERN: *10% discount.*
3401 McLeod Rd., (305) 841-6450.

COMPARATIVE HOTEL RATES: REGULAR DOUBLE ROOM

HOTEL	SR. DISC.	
B & B	—	$35–75
BEST WESTERN	10%	$31–59
DAYS INN	25%	$26–43
ECONOLODGE	10%	$27–37
HOLIDAY INN	15%	$44–65
HOWARD JOHNSON'S	33%	$36–57
QUALITY INN	10%	$28–49
RAMADA INN	25%	$36–54
RODEWAY INN	10%	$27–46
SHERATON	25%	$53–70

DAYS INN: *10%–50% discount with Days Inn September Days Club card.*

Altamonte Springs, 450 N. Douglas Rd., (305) 862-7111.

I-4 & Rte. 436, 235 S. Wymore Rd., (305) 862-2800.

I-4 & Lee Rd., 650 Lee Rd., (305) 628-2727.

Beeline Expwy., 2323 McCoy Rd., (305) 859-6100.

US 441 & Sunshine St. Pkwy., 1221 W. Landstreet Rd., (305) 859-7700.

I-4 & SR 528A, 7335 Sandlake Rd., (305) 351-1900.

I-4 & US 192W, 7980 Spacecoast Pkwy., (305) 846-1000.

I-4 & US 192E, 5840 Spacecoast Pkwy., (305) 846-7969.

Kissimmee, 2095 Spacecoast Pkwy., (305) 846-7136.

I-4 & 33rd St., 2500 W. 33rd St., (305) 841-3731.

Florida Center, I-4 & 7200 International Dr., (305) 351-1200.

ECONOLODGE: *10% discount with Econo Senior Class Card.*

5870 Orange Blossom Tr., (305) 859-5410.

9401 Orange Blossom Tr., (305) 851-1050.
Maingate West, 8620 Hwy. 192 W., (305) 396-9300.
Orlando, 3300 W. Colonial Dr., (305) 293-7221.
Kissimmee, 4736 W. Spacecoast Pkwy., (305) 396-0400.

HOLIDAY INN: *10%–20% discount with Holiday Inn's Travel Venture Club Card.*
Airport, 7900 S. Orange Blossom Tr., (305) 859-7900.
Altamonte Springs, I-4 & SR 436, (305) 862-4455.
Disney World Area, 6515 International Dr., (305) 351-3500.
Disney World Main Gate, Rte. 192, (305) 396-7300.
Disney World Main Gate, I-4 & 192 E., (305) 396-4488.
Disney World Area, US 27 at I-4, (305) 424-2211.
Midtown, 929 W. Colonial Dr., (305) 843-1360.
Winter Park, 625 Lee Rd., (305) 645-5600.

HOWARD JOHNSON'S: *15%–50% discount with H.J.'s Road Rally Card.*
Circus World, I-4 & US 27, (813) 424-2311.
Executive Center/Downtown, I-4 & Colonial Dr., (305) 843-8700.
Florida Center, I-4 & Kirkman Rd., (305) 351-3333.
Disney World Main Gate, US 192 at SR 545, (305) 396-2500.
Disney World/Lake Buena Vista, Resort Hotel Plaza, (305) 828-8888.
Sea World, I-4 & SR 528A, (305) 351-1730.

KNIGHTS INN: *10% discount.*
South, I-4 at US 192, (305) 396-8186.
American Way at International Dr., (305) 351-6500.

LA QUINTA: *20% discount.*
Florida Mall, 8601 S. Orange Blossom Tr., (305) 859-4100.
Airport, 7931 Daetwyler Dr., (305) 857-9215.

QUALITY INN: *10% discount for over 60.*
International Dr., 5825 International Dr., (305) 351-4100 or (800) 327-1366.
International Dr., 7600 International Dr., (305) 351-1600.
Comfort Inn Main Gate, 7571 W. Spacecoast Pkwy., (305) 396-7500.
West, 3956 W. Colonial Dr., (305) 299-6710.
Winter Park, 901 N. Orlando Ave., (305) 644-8000.

RAMADA INN: *25% discount for over 60.*
Kissimmee, 2950 Reedy Creek, (305) 396-4466.
Airport, 8700 S. Orange Blossom Tr., (305) 851-2330.
Disney Area South, Spacecoast Pkwy. at U.S. 192 & U.S. 27, (813) 424-2621.
International, 8300 Jamaican Ct., (305) 351-1660.

RODEWAY INN: *10% discount.*
Convention Center, 9956 Hawaiian Ct., (305) 351-5100.
Eastgate, 5245 Spacecoast Pkwy., (305) 396-7700.
South, 4049 S. U.S. 441 & I-4, (305) 843-1350.
Central, 3200 W. Colonial Dr., (305) 295-5270.

SHERATON: *25% discount for over 60.*
Airport, 3835 Beeline Expwy. (305) 859-2711.
Disney World, Sheraton-Lakeside Inn, US 192 W., Kissimmee, (305) 828-8250.
Disney World, Sheraton Twin Towers, 5780 Major Blvd., (305) 351-1000.
Disney World, Sheraton World, Beeline Expwy. & International Dr., (305) 352-1100.

TRAVELODGE: *Special senior rates for Travelodge's Golden Guest Club.*
Disney World Village, 2000 Hotel Plaza, (305) 828-2424.
I-4 & SR 50, 409 N. Magnolia, (305) 423-1671.
Main Gate East, 5711 US #192, (305) 396-4222.
Main Gate West, 7785 W. US #192, (305) 396-1828.

Car Rental

AVIS: *5%–25% discount.**
Airport, 8445 Bear Rd., (305) 851-7600.
Walt Disney World, Royal Plaza, 1950 Preview Blvd., (305) 828-2828.

HERTZ: *5%–25% discount.**
Airport, 8425 Bear Rd., (305) 859-8400.

NATIONAL: *10%–12% discount for over 62.*
Airport, (305) 855-4170.
Disney World, Lake Buena Vista, (305) 824-3470.

Sights

SEA WORLD OF FLORIDA: *15% discount except Monday and Friday.*
7007 Sea World Dr., Orlando, FL 32821, (800) 432-1178 (FL), (800) 327-2420 (except FL). Daily 9 a.m. to 7 p.m. Aquarium & water-ski shows. Write for a free Dolphin Club card, providing 20% discount on Monday and Friday, plus 10% discount at Florida Festival restaurants and shops.

STARS HALL OF FAME WAX MUSEUM: *15% discount with free Silver Screen Society Card.*
I-4 & Rte. 528 near Disney World, (305) 351-1120. Daily, 10 a.m. to 10 p.m. Write for free Silver Screen card: 6825 Starway Dr., Orlando 32809.

WALT DISNEY WORLD: *Discount for advance tickets during Young at Heart Days.*

**An asterisk indicates that the discount is intended for members of senior citizens' organizations that anyone can join. See "Hotel, Transportation, and Sightseeing Discounts."*

Lake Buena Vista, (305) 824-4432.
October 1 through December 15 are "Young at Heart Days" when Florida residents over 55 enjoy unlimited use of Magic Kingdom/EPCOT Center attractions at a reduced price. For information write Walt Disney World Co., Regional Marketing, P.O. Box 40, Lake Buena Vista, FL 32830, Attn: Young at Heart Days.

Museums

ORLANDO SCIENCE CENTER: *25% discount.*
810 E. Rollins St., Loch Haven Park, (305) 896-7151
Daily; call for hours. Hands-on exhibits and planetarium shows.

Free!

Kennedy Space Center, Loch Haven Arts Center, Orange County Historical Museum, Slocum Water Gardens (Winter Haven).

TAMPA

Hotels

BEST WESTERN: *10% discount.*
1701 E. Busch Blvd., (813) 933-7681.

DAYS INN: *10%–50% discount with Days Inn September Days Club card.*
Busch Gardens, 2901 E. Busch Blvd., (813) 933-6471.
701 E. Fletcher Ave., (813) 977-1550.

ECONOLODGE: *10% discount with Econo's Senior Class card.*
11414 Central Ave., (813) 933-7831.
Busch Blvd. & 30th St., (813) 935-7855.

HOLIDAY INN: *10%–20% discount with Holiday Inn's Travel Venture Club Card.*
Central, 111 W. Fortune, (813) 223-1351.
International Airport, 4500 Cypress, (813) 879-4800.
Bearss Ave., I-275 & Bearss Ave., (813) 961-1000.
State Fair/I-4 E., 2708 N. 50th, (813) 621-2081.
West/Stadium, 4732 N. Dale Mabry Hwy., (813) 877-6061.

HOWARD JOHNSON'S: *15%–50% discount with H.J.'s Road Rally Card.*
Busch Gardens, 720 E. Fowler Ave., (813) 971-5150.
Airport, 700 N. West Shore Blvd., (813) 873-7900.

LA QUINTA: *20% discount.*
Airport, 4730 Spruce St., (813) 879-3970.
East, 2904 Melbourne Blvd., (813) 623-3591.

QUALITY INN: *10% discount for over 60.*
East, 2905 N. 50th St., (813) 621-3541.
North, 210 E. Fowler Ave., (813) 933-6487.

RAMADA INN: *25% discount for over 60.*
Airport, 5303 W. Kennedy Blvd., (813) 877-0534.
East, 9331 Adamo Dr., Hwys. 60 & 301, (813) 621-5511.
North, 820 E. Busch Blvd., (813) 933-4011.

RODEWAY INN: *10% discount.*
2520 N. 50th St., (813) 247-3941.

Car Rental

AVIS: *5%–25% discount.**
International Airport, (813) 883-3500.

HERTZ: *5%–25% discount.**
International Airport, (813) 883-3350.

NATIONAL: *10%–12% discount for over 62.*
International Airport, (813) 883-3782.

Sights

BUSCH GARDENS: *$3.50 off with discount coupon.*
P.O. Box 9158, Tampa, 33674, (813) 971-8282.

Free!

Tampa Museum, Pabst Brewery tours, Villazon & Co. Cigar Plant Tours

GEORGIA

Helpful Addresses

TOUR GEORGIA
Box 1776, Atlanta, GA 30301
(404) 656-3590

OFFICE OF AGING
878 Peachtree St. N.E., Rm. 632, Atlanta, GA 30309
(404) 894-5333

ATLANTA

Hotels

BEST WESTERN: *10% discount.*
Perimeter, 2001 Clearview Ave., (404) 455-1811.
Decatur, 1900 Glenfair Rd., (404) 288-7550.
West, 200 Six Flags Rd., (404) 491-2255.

DAYS INN: *10%–50% discount with Days Inn September Days Club card.*
2910 Clairmont Rd. & I-85, (404) 633-8411.
2768 Chamblee Tucker Rd. & I-85, (404) 458-8711.
4120 Fulton Industrial Blvd. & I-20, (404) 696-4690.
Frontage Rd. & I-75, Forest Park, (404) 363-0800.
2788 Forest Hills Dr. & I-75, (404) 768-7750.
Downtown, 300 Spring St., (404) 523-1144.

RADISSON HOTEL & CONFERENCE CENTER: *25% discount.**
1750 Commerce Dr., (404) 351-6100, (800) 824-8657.

HARLEY HOTEL: *10% discount.*
3601 N. Desert Dr., East Point, (404) 762-5141, (800) 321-2323.

HOLIDAY INN: *10%–20% discount with Holiday Inn's Travel Venture Club Card.*
Airport, 1380 Virginia Ave., (404) 762-8411.
Airport, 1900 Sullivan Rd., (404) 997-2770.
Downtown, 175 Piedmont Ave., (404) 659-2727.
Howell Mill Rd. & I-75 N., (404) 351-3831.
1944 Piedmont Cir. N.E. & I-85, (404) 875-3571.
Six Flags, 4225 Fulton Industrial Blvd., (404) 691-4100.

COMPARATIVE HOTEL RATES: REGULAR DOUBLE ROOM

HOTEL	SR. DISC.	CEN-TRAL	SUB-URBAN	AIR-PORT
B & B	—	$30–65	$30–65	—
BEST WESTERN	10%	—	$44–57	—
DAYS INN	25%	$44–67	$28–35	$25–33
HOLIDAY INN	15%	$73–83	$46–60	$62–76
HOWARD JOHNSON'S	33%	—	$26–39	$42–53
LA QUINTA	20%	—	—	$38
QUALITY INN	10%	$44	—	—
RAMADA INN	25%	$44–53	$37	$73
RODEWAY INN	10%	$45–58	—	—

SAVE UP TO 50% BY ASKING FOR SPECIAL WEEKEND RATES.

HOWARD JOHNSON'S: *15%–50% discount with H.J.'s Road Rally Card.*
Airport, 1377 Virginia Ave., (404) 762-5111.
Northeast, 2090 N. Druid Hills Rd., N.E., (404) 636-8631.

LA QUINTA: *20% discount.*
Airport, 4874 Old National Hwy., (404) 768-1241.

QUALITY INN: *10% discount for over 60.*
Comfort Inn, 120 North Ave. N.W., (404) 881-6788.

RAMADA INN: *25% discount for over 60.*
Airport, Renaissance, 4736 Best Rd., (404) 762-7676.
Central, 1630 Peachtree St. N.W., (404) 875-9711.
Northeast, 2960 N.E. Expwy. & Shallowford Rd., (404) 451-5231.

RODEWAY INN: *10% discount.*
330 W. Peachtree St., (404) 577-6970.

SCOTTISH INNS: *10% discount with Scottish Identicard.*
Airport, I-85 S. & Sylvan Rd., (404) 762-8801.
Midtown, I-75 N. at Howell Mill, (404) 351-1220.
Six Flags, 4430 Frederick Dr., (404) 691-6310.

SHERATON: *25% discount for over 60.*
Airport, 1325 Virginia Ave., (404) 768-6660.

TRAVELODGE: *Special senior rates for Travelodge's Golden Guest Club.*
Central, 311 Courtland St., N.E., (404) 659-4545
Peachtree, 1641 Peachtree St., N.E., (404) 873-5731.
Viscount, 2061 N. Druid Hils Rd. N.E., (404) 321-4174.

Car Rental

AVIS: *5%–25% discount.**
Airport, (404) 530-2700.
143 Courtland St. N.E., (404) 659-4814.

HERTZ: *5%–25% discount.**
Airport, Hangar One, (404) 765-1348.
202 Courtland St. N.E., (404) 659-3000.

NATIONAL: *10%–12% discount for over 62.*
Airport, (404) 530-2800.

Museums

ATLANTA HISTORICAL SOCIETY: *10% discount.*
3101 Andrews Dr. N.W., (404) 261-1837.
Monday to Saturday, 10:30 a.m. to 4:30 p.m.; Sunday, 12:30 p.m. to 4:30 p.m. Guided tours of three houses: Swann House (1928, Palladian inspired), Tullie Smith House Restoration (1840 farm), and McElreath Hall (library and historical exhibits).

Free!

Georgia State Museum of Science and Industry, M. L. King Birthplace

SAVANNAH

Hotels

BEST WESTERN: *10% discount.*
1 Gateway Blvd., (912) 925-2420.
Eisenhower at 204, (912) 355-1000.
412 W. Bay St., (912) 233-1011.

DAYS INN: *10%–50% discount with Days Inn September Days Club card.*
201 W. Bay St., (912) 236-4440.

ELIZA THOMPSON HOUSE: *10% discount.*
5 W. Jones St., (800) 447-4667 (GA), (800) 348-9378 (except GA).

HOLIDAY INN: *10%–20% discount with Holiday Inn's Travel Venture Club Card.*
Downtown, US 17-A at Talmadge Bridge, (912) 236-1355.
I-95 S., GA 204 & I-95, (912) 925-2770.
Midtown, 7100 Abercorn St., (912) 352-7100.

HOWARD JOHNSON'S: *15%–50% discount with H.J.'s Road Rally Card.*
Downtown, 121 W. Boundary St., (912) 236-1355.
Midtown, 7100 Abercorn St., (912) 352-7100.

LA QUINTA MOTOR INN: *20% discount.*
6805 S. Abercorn St., (912) 353-3004.

MULBERRY INN: *10% discount.*
601 E. Bay St., (912) 238-1200.

QUALITY INN: *10% discount for over 60.*
Airport, (912) 964-1421.
7 Gateway Blvd., I-95 & Hwy. 204, (912) 925-2280.
Downtown, 300 W. Bay St., (912) 236-6321.

RAMADA INN: *25% discount for over 60.*
Downtown, 201 W. Oglethorpe Ave., (912) 233-3531.

SHERATON: *25% discount for over 60.*
612 Wilmington Island Rd., (912) 897-1612.

TRAVELODGE SAVANNAH: *Special senior rates for Travelodge's Golden Guest Club.*
512 W. Oglethorpe Ave., (912) 233-9251.

Car Rental

AVIS: *5%–25% discount.**
Airport, (912) 964-1781.

BUDGET RENT-A-CAR: *AARP discount.*
Travis Field Airport, (912) 964-7111.

HERTZ: *5%–25% discount.**
Airport, (912) 964-9595.

NATIONAL: *10%–12% discount for over 62.*
Airport, Box 286-A, (912) 964-1771.

Restaurants

WESTERN STEER FAMILY STEAKHOUSE: *Free drinks for seniors.*
11512 Abercorn Extension, (912) 927-1603.

Sights

HARBOR BOAT TOURS: *15% discount.*
Cap'n Sam's Dock, Bull St., (912) 234-7248.

Museums

TELFAIR ACADEMY OF ARTS AND SCIENCES: *50% discount.*
121 Barnard St., (912) 232-1177.
Tuesday to Saturday, 10 a.m. to 4:30 p.m.; Sunday, 2 to 5 p.m.

HAWAII

Helpful Addresses

HAWAII VISITORS BUREAU
2270 Kalakaua Ave., Suite 801, Honolulu, HI 96815 (808) 923-1811.
441 Lexington Ave., Rm. 1407, New York, NY 10017, (212) 986-9203.

EXECUTIVE OFFICE ON AGING
335 Merchant St., #241, Honolulu, HI 96813
(808) 548-2593.

Bed & Breakfast Service

PACIFIC-HAWAII BED & BREAKFAST: *10% discount for* Discount Guide *readers. Minimum stay: 3 days. Double rooms: $25–60.*
19 Kai Nani Pl., Kailua, Oahu, HI 96734, (808) 262-6026.
Organizer Doris E. Epp writes, "Our rates here in Hawaii are most reasonable and we try to keep it this way so that everybody can afford to visit. My goal is to show visitors our *real* Hawaii." B&B is available on all of the Hawaiian Islands, Oahu, Maui, the island of Hawaii, and Molokai.

Transportation

HAWAIIAN AIRLINES: *Discount for 65 and over.*
P.O. Box 30008, Honolulu, HI 96820, (800) 367-5320 in U.S.; (800) 663-3389 in Canada.

Incredible Deal!

The late spring and early fall months are "off-season" in Hawaii. It's less crowded, and hotel rates drop as much as 50%!

HONOLULU

Senior Citizens' Information and Assistance Handbook

Senior citizens should request this invaluable sourcebook of information, addresses, and discounts from the Elderly Affairs Division, 650 S. King St., Honolulu, HI 96813, (808) 523-4545.

Hotels

BEST WESTERN: *10% discount.*
2045 Kalakaua Ave., (808) 955-6363.

HOLIDAY INN: *10%–20% discount with Holiday Inn's Travel Venture Club Card.*
Airport, 3401 Nimitz Hwy., (808) 836-0661.
Waikiki Beach, 2570 Kalakaua Ave., (808) 922-2511.

MIRAMAR HOTEL HAWAII: *10% discount for over 62.*
2345 Kuhio Ave., (808) 922-2077.

QUALITY INN: *10% discount for over 60.*
175 Paoakalani Ave., Waikiki, (808) 922-3861.

SHERATON: *25% discount for over 60.*
Moana Hotel, 2365 Kalakaua Ave., (808) 922-3111.
Princess Kaiulani Hotel, 120 Kaiulani Ave., (808) 922-5811.
Royal Hawaiian Hotel, 2259 Kalakaua Ave., (808) 923-7311.
Sheraton Waikiki Hotel, 2255 Kalakaua Ave., (808) 922-4422.
Surfrider Hotel, 2353 Kalakaua Ave., (808) 922-3111.

TRAVELODGE: *Special senior rates for Travelodge's Golden Guest Club.*
Waikiki Pacific Isle, 1850 Ala Moana Blvd., (808) 955-1567.

Public Transportation

M.T.L., Inc. (Bus): *Free to 65-and-over with bus pass. Annually renewable pass may be obtained by visitors from address below.*
725 Kapiolani Blvd., Honolulu, HI 96813, (808) 524-4626.

Car Rental

AVIS: *5%–25% discount.**
Airport, 417 Lele St., (808) 834-5564.
148 Kaiulani Ave., Waikiki, (808) 924–1688.

HERTZ: *5%–25% discount.**
Airport, P.O. Box 29240, (808) 836-2511.
Hyatt Regency, 2424 Kalakaua Ave., (808) 922-5344.

NATIONAL: *10%–12% discount for over 62.*
Airport, (808) 836-2655.
1778 Ala Moana Blvd., (808) 922-3331.

Restaurants

IDETA: *10% dinner discount for over 65.*
620 Kohou St., (808) 847-4844.

THE PLUSH PIPPIN: *10% discount for over 60 on weekdays from 2:30 to 5.*
108 Hekili St., (808) 261-7552.

SEIGETSU: *10% lunch and dinner discount for over 62.*
2155 Kalakaua Ave., (808) 922-8686.

TOKU SUSKI & RESTAURANT: *10% lunch and dinner discount for over 60. Mon. and Tues. only.*
735 Sheridan St., (808) 945-7747.

Tours

AIKANE CATAMARAN CRUISES: *10% discount for over 65.*
677 Ala Moana Blvd., Suite 918, (808) 538-3680.

Movie Theaters

KING THEATERS I & II: *$1.25 any time for 65 and over.*
59 S. King St., (808) 536-7738.

KUHIO THEATER: *$1.50 for 65 and over, matinees only.*
2095 Kuhio Ave., (808) 941-4422.

MARINA THEATERS I & II: *$2.50 for 65 and over any time.*
1765 Ala Moana, (808) 949-0188.

VARSITY THEATER: *$1.50 for 65 and over, matinees only.*
1106 University Ave., (808) 949-4144.

WAIKIKI THEATERS I & II: *$1.50 for 65 and over, matinees only.*
333 Seaside Ave., (808) 923-5353.

IDAHO

Helpful Addresses

IDAHO DIVISION OF TOURISM
State Capitol Building, Boise, ID 83720
(208) 334-2470, (800) 635-7820

OFFICE ON AGING
Room 114
State House, Boise, ID 83720
(208) 334-3833

BOISE

Hotels

BEST WESTERN: *10% discount.*
1070 Grove St., (208) 344-6556.

HOLIDAY INN: *10%–20% discount with Holiday Inn's Travel Venture Club Card.*
Airport, 3300 Vista Ave., (208) 344-8365.

NENDELS INN: *10% discount for Vagabond's Club 55.*
1025 S. Capital Blvd., (208) 344-7971, (800) 547-0106.

RED LION INN: *10% discount for over 50.**
Downtowner, 1800 Fairview, (208) 344-7691
2900 Chinden Blvd., (208) 343-1871

RODEWAY: *10% discount.*
1115 N. Curtis Rd., (208) 376-2700.

TRAVELODGE: *Special senior rates for Travelodge's Golden Guest Club.*
1314 Grove St., (208) 342-9351.

Car Rental

AVIS: *5%–25% discount.**
Airport, (208) 383-3350.

HERTZ: *5%–25% discount.**
Airport, (208) 383-3100.

NATIONAL: *10%–12% discount for over 62.*
Airport, (208) 383-3210.

Sights

BOISE TOUR TRAIN: *15% discount.*
Julia Davis Park, (208) 342-4796.

June–Labor Day: daily, 10:30 a.m., noon, and 3 p.m.; Friday and Saturday, also 7:30 p.m. One-and-a-half-hour guided tour of Capitol and historic sites.

Free!

Howard Platt Gardens, Idaho State Capitol, Idaho State Historical Society Museum

ILLINOIS

Helpful Addresses

ILLINOIS TRAVEL INFORMATION CENTER
310 S. Michigan Ave., Suite 108, Chicago, IL 60604
(312) 793-2094, (800) 252-8987 (IL), (800) 637-8560 (nearby states)

DEPARTMENT ON AGING
421 E. Capital Ave., Springfield, IL 62701
(217) 785-2870

CHICAGO

Save up to 50% on your hotel bill—ask the desk clerk about special weekend packages.

Hotels

BEST WESTERN: *10% discount.*
O'Hare Airport, 1750 S. Elmhurst Rd., Des Plaines, (312) 956-1700.
Airport, 10300 W. Higgins, (312) 296-4471.

HOLIDAY INN: *10%–20% discount with Holiday Inn's Travel Venture Club Card.*
City Center, 300 E. Ohio St., (312) 787-6100.
Mart Plaza–Financial District, 350 N. Orleans, (312) 836-5000.
Midway Airport, 7353 S. Cicero Ave., (312) 581-5300.
O'Hare Airport, Mannheim & Toohy Rd., (312) 296-8866.
O'Hare/Kennedy Expwy., 5440 N. River Rd., Rosemont, (312) 671-6350.

HOWARD JOHNSON'S: *15%–50% discount with H.J.'s Road Rally Card.*

COMPARATIVE HOTEL RATES: REGULAR DOUBLE ROOM

HOTEL	SR. DISC.	CENTRAL	AIRPORT
BEST WESTERN	10%	—	\$56–63
HOLIDAY INN	15%	\$92–116	\$64–81
HOWARD JOHNSON'S	33%	—	\$43–57
QUALITY INN	10%	\$69–85	—
RAMADA INN	25%	\$84–124	\$64–80
SHERATON	25%	—	\$75–105

SAVE UP TO 50% BY ASKING FOR SPECIAL WEEKEND RATES.

O'Hare/Kennedy Expwy., 8201 Higgins Rd., (312) 693-2323.
O'Hare/Schiller Park, Mannheim Rd. & Irving Park Rd., Schiller Park, (312) 671-6000.

QUALITY INN: *10% discount for over 60.*
One S. Halsted, (312) 829-5000.

RAMADA INN: *25% discount for over 60.*
O'Hare Airport, 6600 N. Mannheim Rd., (312) 827-5131.
Executive House, 71 E. Wacker Dr., (312) 346-7100.

RODEWAY INN: *10% discount.*
O'Hare, 3801 N. Mannheim, (312) 678-0670.
Downtown, 506 W. Harrison St., (312) 427-6969.

SHERATON: *25% discount for over 60.*
Sheraton-Homewood, 174th St. at Halsted, (312) 957-1600.
Sheraton North Shore, 933 Skokie Blvd., (312) 498-6500.
Sheraton-O'Hare, 6810 N. Mannheim Rd. (I-90 N. & 294), (312) 297-1234.
Sheraton-Plaza, 160 E. Huron, (312) 787-2900.

TRAVELODGE: *Special senior rates for Travelodge's Golden Guest Club.*
Airport, 3003 Mannheim Rd., Des Plaines, (312) 296-5541.
Downtown, 1240 S. Michigan, (312) 427-4111.

Car Rental

AVIS: *5%–25% discount.**
O'Hare Airport, Box 66041, (312) 694-5600.
Midway Airport, (312) 471-4495.

HERTZ: *5%–25% discount.**
O'Hare Airport, Box 66096, (312) 686-7272.

NATIONAL: *10%–12% discount for over 62.*
O'Hare Airport, (312) 694-4640.
Midway Airport, (312) 471-3450.
612 S. Wabash, (312) 922-2604.

Theaters

HOT TIX: *50% discount for all.*
State St. and Madison, (312) 977-1755. Tickets available for day of performance only.

Sights

ADLER PLANETARIUM: *Free for seniors.*
1300 S. Lake Shore Dr., (312) 322-0300.
Exhibits—Monday to Thursday, 9:30 a.m. to 4:30 p.m.; Friday, 9:30 a.m. to 9 p.m.; Saturday and Sunday, 9:30 a.m. to 5 p.m.
Sky shows: call for schedule.

BROOKFIELD ZOO: *65% discount.*
1st Ave. and 31st St., Brookfield, (312) 242-2630.
June to October: daily 9 a.m. to 6 p.m. Rest of the year: 10 a.m. to 5 p.m. One of the best.

CHICAGO BOTANICAL GARDENS: *50% discount on tram ride.*
½ mi. E. of I-94, Glencoe, (312) 835-5440.
Daily, 8 a.m. to dusk.

HERE'S CHICAGO: *45% discount.*
Water Tower Pumping Station, Chicago & Michigan Ave., (312) 467-7114.
Daily, 10 a.m. to 8 p.m.

JOHN G. SHEDD AQUARIUM: *50% discount.*
1200 S. Lakeshore Dr., (312) 939-2438.
May to August: Saturday to Thursday, 9 a.m. to 5 p.m. March to April, September to October: Saturday to Thursday, 10 a.m. to 5 p.m. November to February: Saturday to Thursday, 10 a.m. to 4 p.m. Friday all year: 10 a.m. to 9 p.m.

JOHN HANCOCK CENTER OBSERVATORY: *25% discount.*
875 N. Michigan Ave., (312) 751-3681
Daily, 9 a.m. to midnight. World's tallest residential-office skyscraper. Observatory is 1,030 ft. up.

Museums

ART INSTITUTE OF CHICAGO: *50% discount.*
Michigan Ave. at Adams St., (312) 443-3600.
Monday to Wednesday and Friday, 10:30 a.m. to 4:30 p.m.; Thursday, 10:30 a.m. to 8 p.m.; Saturday, 10 a.m. to 5 p.m.; Sunday, noon to 5 p.m.

BALZEKAS MUSEUM OF LITHUANIAN CULTURE: *50% discount.*
4012 S. Archer Ave., (312) 847-2441.
Daily, 1 to 4 p.m.

CHICAGO ACADEMY OF SCIENCE: *50% discount.*
2001 N. Clark St., Lincoln Park, (312) 549-0606.
Daily, 10 a.m. to 5 p.m.

CHICAGO HISTORICAL SOCIETY: *65% discount.*
N. Clark St. at North Ave., (312) 642-4600.
Historical exhibits and craft demonstrations. Monday to Saturday, 9:30 a.m. to 4:30 p.m.; Sunday, noon to 5 p.m.

DU SABLE MUSEUM OF AFRICAN-AMERICAN HISTORY: *50% discount.*
740 E. 56th Pl., (312) 947-0600.
Monday to Friday, 9 a.m. to 5 p.m.; Saturday and Sunday, noon to 5 p.m.

FIELD MUSEUM OF NATURAL HISTORY: *75% discount.*
Roosevelt Rd. at Lakeshore Dr., (312) 922-9410.
Daily, 9 a.m. to 5 p.m.

MUSEUM OF CONTEMPORARY ART: *50% discount.*
237 E. Ontario St., (312) 280-2660.
Tuesday to Saturday, 10 a.m. to 5 p.m.; Sunday, noon to 5 p.m.

OAK PARK TOUR CENTER: *50% discount.*
158 N. Forest Ave., Oak Park, (312) 848-1978.
Guided tours of the Frank Lloyd Wright Home and Studio, Unity Temple, and the Frank Lloyd Wright Historic District. Call for hours; open March to November.

PEACE MUSEUM: 65% discount.
364 W. Erie St., (312) 440-1860.
Tuesday to Sunday, noon to 5 p.m.

SPERTUS MUSEUM OF JUDAICA: *50% discount.*
618 S. Michigan Ave., (312) 922-9012.
Daily, call for hours.

PRAIRIE AVENUE HISTORIC DISTRICT: *50% discount.*
Prairie Ave., (312) 326-1393.
Tuesday and Thursday, 10 a.m. to 3 p.m.; Saturday and Sunday, 11 a.m. to 3:30 p.m. One-hour tours of famous restored houses of nineteenth-century millionaires.

Free!

Chicago Academy of Science, Chicago Board of Trade, Chicago Fire Academy, Chicago Mercantile Exchange, Chicago *Tribune* Freedom Center, Garfield Park Conservatory, Jane Addams's Hull House, Lincoln Park Conservatory, Museum of Science & Industry, Oriental Institute, Polish Museum, Telephony Museum, Weiss Museum of Judaica, and thirty-one free beaches.

SPRINGFIELD

Hotels

BEST WESTERN: *10% discount.*
1701 N. Walnut St., (217) 753-3446.
Capitol, 101 E. Adams, (217) 523-5661.

DAYS INN: *10%–50% discount with Days Inn September Days Club card.*
3000 Stevenson Dr., (217) 529-0171.

HOLIDAY INN: *10%–20% discount with Holiday Inn's Travel Venture Club Card.*
East, 3100 S. Dirksen Pkwy., (217) 529-7171.
South, 6th St. off I-55, (217) 529-7131.

HOWARD JOHNSON'S: *15%–50% discount with H.J.'s Road Rally Card.*
3190 Dirksen Pkwy., (217) 529-9100.

QUALITY INN: *10% discount for over 60.*
400 N. 9th St., (217) 522-7711.

SHERATON INN: *25% discount for over 60.*
3090 Stevenson Dr., (217) 529-6611.

Car Rental

AVIS: *5%–25% discount.**
Capitol Airport, N. Walnut, (217) 522-7728.

HERTZ: *5%–25% discount.**
Capitol Airport, (217) 525-8820.

NATIONAL: *10%–12% discount for over 62.*
Capitol Airport, (217) 544-6300.

Theaters

SPRINGFIELD MUNI OPERA: *Senior discount off general admission tickets.*
Box 2255, Springfield, 62705, (217) 522-3300.
Broadway shows in outdoor theater, June to August. Ticket office is at Roberts Brothers Clothing, 2 Old Capital Plaza, N.

GREAT AMERICAN PEOPLE SHOW: *$1 off admission.*
Box 401, Lincoln's New Salem State Park, Petersburg, IL 62675, (217) 632-7755 (summer), or 367-1900.
Nightly, except Monday, at 8 p.m., late June through August. Three plays cover Lincoln and his legacy.

**An asterisk indicates that the discount is intended for members of senior citizens' organizations that anyone can join. See "Hotel, Transportation, and Sightseeing Discounts."*

Free!

Abraham Lincoln Home and Tomb, Clayville Rural Life Museum, Dana Thomas House, Illinois State Museum, Lincoln Gardens, Old State Capitol, Parks Telephone Museum, State Capitol

INDIANA

Helpful Addresses

INDIANA TOURISM DEVELOPMENT DIVISION
One N. Capitol St., Suite 700, Indianapolis, IN 46204
(317) 232-8860, (800) 622-4464 (IN), (800) 858-8073 (nearby states)

DEPARTMENT OF AGING AND COMMUNITY SERVICES
251 N. Illinois St., Indianapolis, IN 46207
(317) 232-7006

INDIANAPOLIS

THE INDIANAPOLIS "500" IS HELD EVERY MEMORIAL DAY WEEKEND.
Visitors may find both discounts and hotel rooms hard to find during most of May. Make reservations early!

Hotels

BEST WESTERN: *10% discount.*
Airport, 5860 Fortune Circle, (317) 248-0621.

DAYS INN: *10% discount with Days Inn September Days Club card.*
I-465 at Emerson Rd., 5151 Elmwood Dr., (317) 783-5471.
I-465 at US 31 S., 450 Bixler Rd., (317) 788-0811.

EMBASSY SUITES: *10 discount.**
Downtown, 110 W. Washington St., (317) 635-1000.

HOLIDAY INN: *10% discount.**
East, I-70 at Shadeland Ave., (317) 359-5341.
North, 3850 DePauw Blvd., (317) 872-9790.
South, 520 E. Thompson Rd., (317) 787-8341.
Southeast, 5120 Victory Dr., (317) 783-7751.
Downtown, 123 W. Louisiana, (317) 631-2221.

HOWARD JOHNSON'S: *15%–50% discount with H.J.'s Road Rally Card.*
Downtown, 501 W. Washington St., (317) 635-4443.
East, 2141 N. Post Rd., (317) 897-2000.
Speedway, 2602 N. Highschool Rd., (317) 291-8800.

KNIGHTS INN: *10% discount.*
East, I-70 at 21st St., Shadeland, (317) 353-8484.
North, I-465 at S.R. 431, (317) 848-2423.

LA QUINTA: *20% discount.*
Airport, 5316 W. Southern Ave., (317) 247-4281.
East, 7304 E. 21st St., (317) 359-1021.

800 NUMBERS ARE SUPER SAVERS!
See the first two chapters for the 800 numbers of all the major hotel, car rental, tour, and airline companies, 800 numbers are listed where available in the state-by-state listings for the state tourist offices. Use 800 numbers whenever possible to obtain information and make reservations. If no 800 number is provided, be sure to call 800 information at 1 (800) 555-1212, and ask—it's a free call too!

RAMADA INN: *25% discount for over 60.*
South, 4514 S. Emerson Ave., (317) 787-3344.

RODEWAY INN: *10% discount.*
Airport, 3801 N. Mannheim, (312) 678-0670.
Downtown, 506 W. Harrison St., (312) 427-6969.

SHERATON: *25% discount for over 60.*
2820 N. Meridian, (317) 924-1241.
East, 7701 E. 42nd St., (317) 897-4000.

Car Rental

AVIS: *5%–25% discount.**
Airport, 2565 S. Highschool Rd., (317) 244-3307.

HERTZ: *5%–25% discount.**
Airport, (317) 244-2413.

NATIONAL: *10%–12% discount for over 60.*
Airport, (317) 243-7501.

Sights

INDIANAPOLIS ZOO: *45% discount.*
3120 E. 30th St., (317) 547-3577.
May to September: Monday to Friday, 10 a.m. to 5 p.m.; weekends, 10 a.m. to 6 p.m. Rest of year: daily, 10 a.m. to 4 p.m.

Free!

Children's Museum, Indianapolis Motor Speedway and Hall of Fame Museum (admission charged in May), Indiana State Museum, Indianapolis Museum of Art (Krannert Pavilion, Clowes Pavilion, Downtown Gallery, and IMA Columbus), Patrick Henry Sullivan Museum, State Capitol, and wine-tasting at Easley's Winery

IOWA

Helpful Addresses

IOWA DEVELOPMENT COMMISSION
Tourist Development Division, 600 Court Ave., Des Moines, IA 50309
(515) 281-3100

DEPARTMENT OF ELDER AFFAIRS
Suite 236, Jewett Bldg., 914 Grand Ave., Des Moines, IA 50319
(515) 281-5187

DES MOINES

Hotels

BEST WESTERN: *10% discount.*
1810 Army Post Rd., (515) 287-6464.
929 3rd St., (515) 282-5251.

HOLIDAY INN: *10%–20% discount with Holiday Inn's Travel Venture Club Card.*
Merle Hay, I-35 & I-80, (515) 278-0271.
West, 1800 50th St., (515) 223-1800.
Airport, 2101 Fleur Dr., (515) 283-1711.

HOWARD JOHNSON'S: *15%–50% discount with H.J.'s Road Rally Card.*
West, 4800 N. Merle Hay Rd., (515) 278-4755.

RAMADA INN: *25% discount for over 60.*
6215 Fleur Dr., (515) 285-1234.

RODEWAY INN: *10% discount.*
4995 Merle Hay Rd., (515) 278-2381.

SHERATON: *25% discount for over 60.*
11040 Hickman Rd., (515) 278-5575.

Public Transportation

METRO TRANSIT AUTHORITY (Bus): *30¢ fare for over 60.*
1100 MTA Ln., (515) 283-8111.
Register for ID card at Yonkers, 4th floor, 7th & Walnut St.
Card not valid during rush hours.

Car Rental

AVIS: *5%–25% discount.**
Des Moines Municipal Airport, (515) 245-2585.

HERTZ: *5%–25% discount.**
Des Moines Municipal Airport, (515) 285-9650.

NATIONAL: *10%–12% discount for over 62.*
Airport, (515) 285-3359.

Theater

INGERSOLL DINNER THEATRE: *$1–$3 discount.*
3711 Ingersoll, (515) 274-4686.

Museums

DES MOINES CENTER OF SCIENCE AND INDUSTRY: *75% discount.*
4500 Grand Ave., (515) 274-4138.
Monday to Saturday, 10 a.m. to 5 p.m.; Sunday, 1 to 5 p.m.

Sights

BOTANICAL CENTER: *50% discount.*
909 E. River Dr., (515) 283-4148.
Monday to Thursday, 10 a.m. to 6 p.m.; Friday, 10 a.m. to 9 p.m.; Weekends, 10 a.m. to 5 p.m.

LIVING HISTORY FARMS: *20% discount.*
2600 N.W. 111th St., (515) 278-5286.
Open mid-April through October. Monday to Saturday, 9 a.m. to 5 p.m.; Sunday, 12 p.m. to 6 p.m.

Free!

Des Moines Art Center, Iowa State Historical Museum, State Capitol

KANSAS

Helpful Addresses

KANSAS STATE DEPARTMENT OF ECONOMIC DEVELOPMENT
Tourist Division, 503 Kansas, Topeka, KS 66603
(913) 296-2009

DEPARTMENT ON AGING
610 W. 10th, Topeka, KS 66612
(913) 296-4986

TOPEKA

Hotels

BEST WESTERN: *10% discount.*
2950 S. Topeka Ave., (913) 267-1681.

HOLIDAY INN: *10%–20% discount with Holiday Inn's Travel Venture Club Card.*
914 Madison St., (913) 232-7721.
605 Fairlawn Rd., (913) 272-8040.

HOWARD JOHNSON'S: *15%–50% discount with H.J.'s Road Rally Card.*
3839 S. Topeka Blvd., (913) 266-4700.
Must be two people, two beds for discount.

RAMADA INN: *25% discount for over 60.*
South, 3847 S. Topeka Ave., (913) 267-1800.

Public Transportation

TOPEKA TRANSIT (Bus): *Half fare for over 65 upon presentation of Medicare card, or obtain senior citizens' card from Terminal.*
Terminal at 120 W. 6th, (913) 354-9571.

Car Rental

AVIS: *5%–25% discount.**
Forbes Field Airport, (913) 862-1803.

HERTZ: *5%–25% discount.**
Forbes Field Airport, (913) 862-1470.

NATIONAL: *10%–12% discount for over 62.*
Airport, (913) 862-0836.

Sights

TOPEKA ZOO: *75% discount for over 65.*
Gage Park, 6th & 10th Sts. entrance, (913) 272-5821.
Daily, 9 a.m. to 4:30 p.m.

Free!

Kansas Museum of History, Kansas State Historical Society, State Capitol

---

WICHITA

Hotels

BEST WESTERN: *10% discount.*
Airport, 600 S. Holland, (316) 722-8730.
9100 E. Kellogg, (316) 685-0371.

HOLIDAY INN: *10%–20% discount with Holiday Inn's Travel Venture Club Card.*
Downtown, 250 W. Douglas, (316) 264-1181.
East, 7335 E. Kellogg, (316) 685-1281.

HOWARD JOHNSON'S: *15%–50% discount with H.J.'s Road Rally Card.*
7300 E. Kellogg, (316) 684-0561.

LA QUINTA: *20% discount.*
7700 E. Kellogg, (316) 681-2881.

RAMADA AT BROADVIEW PLACE: *$2 discount for over 65 (excluding conventions).*
400 W. Douglas, (316) 262-5000.

RODEWAY INN: *10% discount.*
Central, 221 E. Kellogg, (316) 267-9281.

Public Transportation

METROPOLITAN TRANSIT AUTHORITY (Bus): *35¢ fare for over 65.*
1825 S. McLean Blvd., (316) 265-7221.

Car Rental

AVIS: *5%–25% discount.**
Mid-Continent Airport, (316) 946-4882.

HERTZ: *5%–25% discount.**
Mid-Continent Airport, (316) 943-3132.

NATIONAL: *10%–12% discount for over 62.*
Airport, (316) 943-0236.

**An asterisk indicates that the discount is intended for members of senior citizens' organizations that anyone can join. See "Hotel, Transportation, and Sightseeing Discounts."*

Restaurants

KINGS-X RESTAURANT: *10% discount for over 65.*
Several locations, (316) 838-7331.

SHOWCASE DINNER THEATRE: *Discount on Sunday brunch at the Loft restaurant for over 65.*
417 W. 37th, (913) 267-2558.

Theaters

CROWN-UPTOWN DINNER THEATRE: *$1 discount for over 65.*
3207 E. Douglas, (316) 681-1566.

DICKINSON THEATRE: *$2.50 discount for over 65.*
3825 East Harry, (316) 685-5386.

MUSIC THEATRE OF WICHITA, INC.: *$1 discount for over 65.*
Century II Theatre, 225 W. Douglas, (316) 265-3107.

Sights

MID-AMERICAN ALL-INDIAN MUSEUM: *75¢ discount for over 65.*
650 N. Seneca, (316) 262-5221.
Monday to Saturday, 10 a.m. to 5 p.m.; Sunday 1 p.m. to 5 p.m.

Free!

Wichita Art Association, Edwin A. Ulrich Museum of Art at Wichita State University

KENTUCKY

Helpful Addresses

KENTUCKY DEPARTMENT OF TRAVEL DEVELOPMENT
Capitol Plaza Tower, Frankfort, KY 40601
(502) 564-4930, (800) 372-2961 (KY), (800) 225-8747 (except KY)

DIVISION FOR AGING SERVICES
DHR Bldg., 6th Fl.
275 E. Main, Frankfort, KY 40601
(502) 564-6930

LOUISVILLE

During Kentucky Derby week (early May), be sure to make reservations well in advance for hotels and car rentals, and don't expect *any* discounts.

Hotels

BEST WESTERN: *10% discount.*
3315 Bardstown Rd., (512) 452-1501.

HOLIDAY INN: *10%–20% discount with Holiday Inn's Travel Venture Club Card.*
Downtown, 120 W. Broadway, (502) 582-2241.
Rivermont, I-71 & Zorn Ave., (502) 897-5101.
Shively S.W., 4110 Dixie Hwy., (502) 448-2020.
South/Airport, 3317 Fern Valley Rd. at I-65, (502) 964-3311.
Southeast, 3255 Bardstown Rd., at Watterson Expwy., (502) 454-0451.
Airport/East, 1465 Gardner Ln., (502) 452-6361.

HOWARD JOHNSON'S: *15%–50% discount with H.J.'s Road Rally Card.*
Downtown, 100 E. Jefferson St., (502) 582-2481.
4621 Shelbyville Rd., (502) 896-8871.

RAMADA INN: *25% discount for over 60.*
East, 9700 Bluegrass Pkwy., (502) 491-4830.

RODEWAY INN: *10% discount.*
101 E. Jefferson St., (502) 585-2200.

SEELBACH HOTEL: *25% discount.*
500 4th Ave., (502) 585-3200, (800) 626-2032.

SHERATON INN EAST: *25% discount for over 60.*
I-64 & Hurstbourne Ln., (502) 426-4500.

Public Transportation

TRANSIT AUTHORITY OF RIVER CITY: *Louisville residents 65 and over can obtain photo IDs which enable them to purchase discount commuter tickets.*
Union Station, 10th & Broadway, (502) 585-1234.

Car Rental

AVIS: *5%–25% discount.**
Standiford Field Airport, Lee Terminal, (502) 368-5851.

HERTZ: *5%–25% discount.**
Standiford Field Airport, (502) 361-1145.

NATIONAL: *12% discount for over 62.*
Standiford Field Airport, (502) 361-2515.

Restaurants

MASTERSON'S: *10% discount.*
1830 S. 3rd St., (502) 636-2511.

JEREMIAH SWEENEY'S: *10% discount.*
2800 Breckinridge, (502) 456-5050.

Movie Theaters

Almost all movie theaters give a discount, so be sure to ask at the box office.

Theaters

ACTORS THEATER OF LOUISVILLE: *50¢ discount during regular season. Special senior subscription also available.*
316 W. Main St., (502) 584-1205.

KENTUCKY CENTER FOR THE PERFORMING ARTS: *10%–50% discount, depending on date and performance.*
5 Riverfront Plaza, (502) 584-7777.
Houses Louisville Orchestra & Ballet, Kentucky Opera, Broadway Series and Children's Theatre.

LOUISVILLE PALACE: *Call for discount and performance information.*
625 4th Ave., (502) 589-0100.
Las Vegas–style entertainment.

Sights

BELLE OF LOUISVILLE: 10% discount.
Wharf, 4th St. & River Rd., (502) 582-2547.
Memorial Day to Labor Day. Stern-wheeler cruises.

KENTUCKY SHOW: *15% discount.*
651 4th Ave., (502) 585-4008.
Daily, 10 a.m. to 6 p.m. Multimedia portrait of Kentucky.

LOUISVILLE ZOOLOGICAL GARDENS: *65% discount for 60 and over.*
1100 Trevilian Way, (502) 459-2181.
Daily, 10 a.m. to 4 p.m.; longer hours in summer.

Museums

MUSEUM OF NATURAL HISTORY AND SCIENCE: *40% discount.*
727 W. Main St., (502) 587-3137.
Monday to Saturday, 9 a.m. to 5 p.m.; Sunday, 1 to 5 p.m.; Thursday, 9 a.m. to 9 p.m.

J. B. SPEED ART MUSEUM: *50% discount.*
2035 S. 3rd St., (502) 636-2893.
Tuesday to Saturday, 10 a.m. to 4 p.m.; Sunday, 2 p.m. to 6 p.m.

LOUISIANA

Helpful Addresses

LOUISIANA OFFICE OF TOURISM
Box 94291, Capitol Station, Baton Rouge, LA 70804
(504) 925-3850, (800) 231-4730 (except LA)

OFFICE OF ELDERLY AFFAIRS
P.O. Box 80374, Baton Rouge, LA 70898
(504) 925-1700

NEW ORLEANS

Bed & Breakfast Reservation Service

NEW ORLEANS BED & BREAKFAST: *10% discount for* Discount Guide *readers.*
P.O. Box 8163, New Orleans, LA 70182, (504) 822-5038; 822-5046.

Available all year (except Mardi Gras, Jazz Festival, Sugar Bowl); 3-night minimum stay required. Double room price range: $30 to $150.

Hotels

BEST WESTERN: *10% discount.*
French Quarter, 541 Bourbon St., (504) 524-7611.
2820 Tulane Ave., (504) 822-0200.

DAYS INN: *10%–50% discount with Days Inn September Days Club card.*
Airport, 1300 Veterans Blvd., Kenner, (504) 469-2531.
1630 Canal St., (504) 586-0110.

HOLIDAY INN: *10%–20% discount with Holiday Inn's Travel Venture Club Card.*
Convention Center, Poydras at S. Peters, (504) 525-9444.
Dauphine St., 301 Rue Dauphine, (504) 581-1303.
Royal St., 124 Royal, (504) 529-7211.

HOWARD JOHNSON'S: *15%–50% discount with H.J.'s Road Rally Card.*
Airport, 6401 Veterans Memorial Blvd., (504) 885-5700.
Downtown, 330 Loyola Ave., (504) 581-1600.
East, 4200 Old Gentilly Rd., (504) 944-0151.

LA QUINTA: *20% discount.*
Airport, 3100 I-10 Service Rd., (504) 835-8511
Airport, 5900 Veterans Memorial Blvd., (504) 456-0003.

QUALITY INN: *10% discount for over 60.*
Midtown, 3900 Tulane Ave., (504) 486-5541.

RAMADA INN: *25% discount for over 60.*
Airport, 2610 Williams Blvd., (504) 466-1401.
East, 10100 I-10 Service Rd., (504) 246-6000.

COMPARATIVE HOTEL RATES: REGULAR DOUBLE ROOM

HOTEL	SR. DISC.	CEN-TRAL	SUB-URBAN	AIR-PORT
B & B	—	$30–100	$30–100	—
BEST WESTERN	10%	$60–99	—	—
HOLIDAY INN	15%	$66–89	—	—
HOWARD JOHNSON'S	33%	$48–73	$30–53	$31–40
LA QUINTA	20%	—	—	$37
QUALITY INN	10%	$29–76	—	—
RAMADA INN	25%	—	$33–44	$40–44
RODEWAY INN	10%	—	$50–57	$38–43
SHERATON	25%	$97–128	—	$69–80

SAVE MORE BY ASKING ABOUT OFF-SEASON RATES.

Slidell, I-10 & I-12 at Gause Rd., (504) 643-9960.
Metairie, 2713 N. Causeway, (504) 835-4141.

RODEWAY INN: *10% discount.*
Airport, 851 Airline Hwy., Kenner, (504) 467-1391.
Kenner, 1700 I-10 Service Rd., (504) 467-1300.

SHERATON: *25% discount for over 60.*
Airport, 2150 Veterans Memorial Blvd., (504) 467-3111.
Downtown, 500 Canal St., (504) 525-2500.

SONESTA: *10% discount.**
300 Bourbon St., (504) 586-0300.

TRAVELODGE: *Special senior rates for Travelodge's Golden Guest Club.*
West, 2200 W. Bank Expwy., (504) 366-5311.

Car Rental

AVIS: *5%–25% discount.**
International Airport, (504) 464-9511.
2024 Canal St., (504) 523-4317.

HERTZ: *5%–25% discount.**
International Airport, (504) 468-3695.
1540 Canal St., (504) 568-1645.

NATIONAL: *10%–12% discount for over 62.*
International Airport, (504) 466-4335.
324 S. Rampart, (504) 525-0416.

Sights

AUDUBON PARK ZOO: *65% discount.*
Audubon Park, (504) 861-2537.
Monday to Friday, 9:30 a.m. to 5 p.m.; weekends, 9:30 a.m. to 6 p.m.

MUSÉE CONTI WAX MUSEUM: *50¢ discount over 62.*
917 Conti St., (504) 525-2605.
Daily, 10 a.m. to 5:30 p.m. Closed Christmas and Mardi Gras.

SUPERDOME TOURS: *50% discount.*
LaSalle and Poydras, (504) 587-3810.
Call for hours.

Incredible Deal!

Preservation Hall jazz concerts still cost only $2
726 St. Peter St., (504) 522-2238. Nightly, 8:30 p.m. to 12:30 a.m.

**An asterisk indicates that the discount is intended for members of senior citizens' organizations that anyone can join. See "Hotel, Transportation, and Sightseeing Discounts."*

Museums

BEAUREGARD-KEYES HOUSE: *senior discount.*
1113 Chartres St., (504) 523-7257.
Daily except Sunday, 10 a.m. to 4:30 p.m. Last tour 3 p.m. 1826 house of General P. G. T. Beauregard. Restored by author Frances Parkinson Keyes.

CONFEDERATE MUSEUM: *50% discount.*
929 Camp St., (504) 523-4522.
Monday to Saturday, 10 a.m. to 4 p.m.

GALLIER HOUSE: *20% discount.*
1118–32 Royal St., (504) 523-6722.
Daily except Sunday, 10 a.m. to 4:30 p.m. Last tour 3:45. Restored home of architect James Gallier, Jr. Tours of house, films on the Victorian era, and complimentary refreshments on the iron-lace balcony.

NEW ORLEANS MUSEUM OF ART: *50% discount.*
City Park, (504) 488-2631.
Daily except Monday, 10 a.m. to 5 p.m.

Free

Chalmette National Historical Park, Jean Lafitte National Historical Park.

MAINE

Helpful Addresses

MAINE PUBLICITY BUREAU
97 Winthrop St., Hallowell, ME 04347
(207) 289-2423

BUREAU OF MAINE'S ELDERLY
State House, Station #11, Augusta, ME 04333
(207) 289-2561
For more information, send a self-addressed stamped envelope requesting the *Resource Directory for Maine's Elderly* to P.O. Box 160, Carmel, ME 04419.

THE MAINE COAST

Hotels

BEST WESTERN: *10% discount.*
Bar Harbor, Rte. 1 (Hwy. 3), (207) 288-5823.

HOLIDAY INN: *10%–20% discount with Holiday Inn's Travel Venture Club Card.*
Portland, 88 Spring St., (207) 775-2311.
Ellsworth, US 1 & Bar Harbor Rd., (207) 667-9341.
Portland West, 81 Riverside St., (207) 774-5601.

HOWARD JOHNSON'S: *15%–50% discount with H.J.'s Road Rally Card.*
Portland, 155 Riverside St., (207) 774-5861.

QUALITY INN: *10% discount for over 60.*
South Portland, 738 Main St., (207) 774-5891.
Comfort Inn, Portland, 90 Maine Mall Rd., (207) 775-0409.

SAMOSET RESORT: *10% discount for AARP.*
Waldo Ave., Rockland, (207) 594-2511; (800) 341-1650.

SHERATON: *25% discount for over 60.*
Portland, 363 Maine Mall Rd., (207) 775-6161.

SONESTA: *10% discount.**
Portland, 157 High St., (207) 775-5411.

Car Rental

AVIS: *5%–25% discount.**
Bar Harbor Airport, (207) 667-5421.
Portland Airport, (207) 775-3168.

HERTZ: *5%–25% discount.**
Bar Harbor Airport, (207) 667-5017.
Portland International Jetport, (207) 774-4544.

NATIONAL: *10%–12% discount for over 62.*
Portland International Jetport, (207) 773-0036.
Rockland, Sheppard Chevrolet, (207) 594-8424.

Museums

MAINE MARITIME MUSEUM: *10% discount.*
963 Washington St., Bath, (207) 443-1316.
May through October, daily 10 a.m. to 5 p.m. Call for rest of year.

OWLS HEAD TRANSPORTATION MUSEUM: *33% discount.*
P.O. Box 277, Owls Head, (207) 594-9219.
Mid-May to mid-October: daily, 10 a.m. to 5 p.m.

WADSWORTH LONGFELLOW HOUSE: *35% discount.*
487 Congress St., Portland, (207) 772-1807.
June to September: Tuesday to Saturday, 10 a.m. to 4 p.m. Henry Wadsworth Longfellow's house. Built 1785.

Free!

Brunswick: Bowdoin Museum of Art, Peary-Macmillan Arctic Museum at Bowdoin College. Falmouth: Gilsland Farm (Maine Audubon Society). Lubec: Roosevelt Campobello Park. Mount Desert: Acadia National Park. Ogunquit: Marginal Way Walk. Rockland: Shore Village Museum, Ureneff's Sunken Garden of Tuberous Begonias. South Portland: Rachel Carson National Wildlife Park.

MARYLAND

Helpful Addresses

MARYLAND OFFICE OF TOURIST DEVELOPMENT
45 Calvert St., Annapolis, MD 21401
(301) 269-3517

OFFICE ON AGING
State Office Bldg., 301 W. Preston St., Room 1004, Baltimore, MD 21201
(301) 225-1100

BALTIMORE

Hotels

BEST WESTERN: *10% discount.*
Baltimore–Washington Airport, Rte. 176 & U.S. 1, (301) 796-3300.

DAYS INN: *10%–50% discount with Days Inn September Days card.*
100 Hopkins Place, (301) 576–1000.

HOLIDAY INN: *10%–20% discount with Holiday Inn's Travel Venture Club Card.*
Airport, 890 Elkridge Landing Rd., (301) 796-8400.
Downtown, 301 W. Lombard St., (301) 685-3500.
South, 6600 Ritchie Hwy., (301) 761-8300.
Moravia Rd., 6510 Frankford Ave., (301) 485-7900.

HOWARD JOHNSON'S: *15%–50% discount with H.J.'s Road Rally Card.*
Airport, 7253 Parkway Dr., Dorsey, (301) 796-1600.
Catonsville, 5701 Baltimore National Pike, (301) 747-8900.

QUALITY INN: *10% discount for over 60.*
Northwest, 10 Wooded Way, Pikesville, (301) 484-7700.
West, 5801 Baltimore National Pike, (301) 744-5000.

RAMADA INN: *25% discount for over 60.*
1701 Belmont Ave., (301) 265-1100.

SHERATON: *25% discount for over 60.*
400 N. Broadway, (301) 675-6800.

Car Rental

AVIS: *5%–25% discount.**
Airport, (301) 859-1680.
4 E. Lombard St., (301) 685-6000.

HERTZ: *5%–25% discount.**
Airport, (301) 859-3600.

NATIONAL: *10%–12% discount for over 62.*
Airport, (301) 859-8860.
300 W. Lombard, (301) 752-1127.

Sights

U.S. FRIGATE *CONSTELLATION: 40% discount.*
Pier 1, Pratt St., (301) 539-1797.
Daily, 10 a.m. to 4 p.m.; extended hours in summer.
First ship of U.S. Navy.

Museums

MARYLAND SCIENCE CENTER: *15% discount.*
601 Light St., (301) 685-5225.
End of June to Labor Day: Tuesday to Sunday, noon to 5 p.m. Rest of year: Tuesday to Thursday, 10 a.m. to 5 p.m.; Saturday, 10 a.m. to 10 p.m.; Sunday, noon to 6 p.m.

MOUNT CLARE MUSEUM: *50% discount.*
Washington Blvd. & Monroe St., (301) 837-3262.
Tuesday to Saturday, 11 a.m. to 4 p.m.; Sunday, 1 to 4 p.m. 1754 mansion with Colonial and Federal furniture.

MUSEUM OF INDUSTRY: *33% discount.*
1415 Key Hwy., (301) 727-4808.
Open weekends only. History of Baltimore manufacturing.

Tours for Seniors
Request information and tour schedules from your national senior citizens' organization and from *Saga International Holidays, Ltd.*, 120 Boylston St., Boston, MA 02116, (800) 343-0273 (except MA); *Grand Circle Travel*, 555 Madison Ave., New York, NY 10022, (800) 221-2610; AARP Travel Service, P.O. Box 92337, Los Angeles, CA 90009, (800) 227-7737; *Passages Unlimited*, 48 Union St., Stamford, CT 06906, (800) 472-7724; 50+ Young at Heart Program, *American Youth Hostels*, Travel Department, P.O. Box 37613, Washington, D.C. 20013, (202) 783-6161; *Interhostel*, Continuing Education, University of New Hampshire, Durham, NH 03824, (603) 862-1147.

MUSEUM OF MARYLAND HISTORY: *50% discount.*
201 W. Monument, (301) 685-3750.
Tuesday to Saturday, 11 a.m. to 4:30 p.m.

NATIONAL AQUARIUM: *20% discount.*
Pier 3, Pratt St., (301) 576-3810.
Daily, 10 a.m. to 5 p.m. Newest, most elaborate aquarium in the U.S.

STAR-SPANGLED BANNER FLAG HOUSE: *33% discount.*
844 E. Pratt St., (301) 837-1793.
Monday to Saturday, 10 a.m. to 4 p.m.; Sunday, 1 p.m. to 4 p.m. Restored 18th-century house and memorabilia.

Free!

Asbury House, Baltimore & Ohio Railroad Museum, Carroll Mansion, Fort McHenry, Lloyd St. Synagogue, Peale Museum, *Pride of Baltimore*, Walters Art Gallery

MASSACHUSETTS

Helpful Addresses

MASSACHUSETTS DIVISION OF TOURISM
Department of Commerce and Development, Leverett Saltonstall Building, 100 Cambridge St., Boston, MA 02202
(617) 727-3201

EXECUTIVE OFFICE OF ELDER AFFAIRS
38 Chauncy St., Boston, MA 02111
(617) 727-7750

New England Package Tours for Seniors

Saga Tours offers a 7-day tour of Cape Cod and Martha's Vineyard, and a 7-day fall foliage tour visiting

Massachusetts, Maine, New Hampshire, and Vermont. Prices start at $800. American Youth Hostels' 50+ program offers a 14-day fall foliage tour. Seniors travel by van and stay at hostels ($585 from Boston). See pages 7–10 for more about package tours.

BOSTON

Bed & Breakfast Reservation Service

NEW ENGLAND BED & BREAKFAST: *5% discount for* Discount Guide *readers.*
1045 Centre St., Newton Centre, MA 02159, (617) 244-2112 or 498-9819.
Request discount when you make your reservation. Double room: $40–57.

Hotels

BOSTON PARK PLAZA HOTEL (TREADWAY): *10% discount.**
50 Park Plaza, (617) 426-2000.

CHARLES HOTEL: *Discount to AARP.*
One Bennett at Eliot St., (617) 864-1200.

HOLIDAY INN: *10%–20% discount with Holiday Inn's Travel Venture Club Card.*
Somerville, 30 Washington St., (617) 628-1000.
Government Center, 5 Blossom St., (617) 742-7630.

HOWARD JOHNSON'S: *15%–50% discount with H.J.'s Road Rally Card.*
Cambridge, 777 Memorial Dr., (617) 492-7777.
Kenmore Square, 575 Commonwealth Ave., (617) 267-3100
Fenway, 1271 Boylston St., (617) 267-8300.

RAMADA INN: *25% discount for over 60.*
Woburn, 15 Middlesex Canal Park Rd., (617) 935-8760.

SHERATON: *25% discount for over 60.*
Sheraton-Boston, Prudential Center, (617) 236-2000.
Sheraton-Commander, 16 Garden St. (Harvard Sq.), Cambridge, (617) 547-4800.
Sheraton-Lexington, 727 Marrett Rd., Lexington, (617) 862-8700.

SONESTA HOTEL: *10% discount.**
5 Cambridge Pkwy., Cambridge, (617) 491-3600.

Car Rental

AVIS: *5%–25% discount.**
Airport, (617) 424-0800.
58 High St., (617) 482-6876.

HERTZ: *5%–25% discount.**
Airport, (617) 569-7272.
68 Eliot St., (617) 482-9102.

NATIONAL: *10%–12% discount for over 62.*
Airport, (617) 569-6700.
183 Dartmouth St., (617) 426-6830.

Sights

BAY STATE, SPRAY, AND PROVINCETOWN CRUISES: *15% discount Monday through Friday.*
20 Long Wharf, (617) 723-7800.
Provincetown and Boston Harbor cruises.

JOHN HANCOCK OBSERVATORY: *35% discount.*
Clarendon St. at Copley Sq. Tickets at St. James Ave. and Trinity Pl., (617) 247-1976.
Monday to Saturday, 9 a.m. to 11 p.m.
November to April: Sunday, noon to 11 p.m.
May to October: Sunday, 10 a.m. to 11 p.m.
The best view of Boston.

NEW ENGLAND AQUARIUM and *THE DISCOVERY: 20% discount.*

Central Wharf, (617) 742-8870.

Monday to Thursday, 9 a.m. to 5 p.m.; Friday, 9 a.m. to 9 p.m.; Saturday and Sunday, 9 a.m. to 6 p.m.

PRUDENTIAL CENTER: *50% discount.*

800 Boylston St., (617) 236-3318.

Daily, 9 a.m. to 11 p.m. Terrific view plus multimedia show.

"WHERE'S BOSTON?" *40% discount.*

Copley Place, 100 Huntington Ave., (617) 267-4949.

Monday to Saturday, 10 a.m. to 5 p.m.; Sunday, 1 p.m. to 5 p.m. Multimedia presentation using 40 projectors and 8 screens.

"WHITES OF THEIR EYES"; *30% discount.*

55 Constitution Rd., Bunker Hill, (617) 241-7575.

June to August, daily, 9 a.m. to 6 p.m.; September to May, daily, 9:30 a.m. to 4 p.m. Reenactment of Battle of Bunker Hill using life-sized figures.

Museums

BOSTON TEA PARTY SHIP AND MUSEUM: *20% discount.*

Congress St. Bridge, (617) 338-1773.

9 a.m. to dusk.

CHILDREN'S MUSEUM: *25% discount.*

Museum Wharf, 300 Congress St., (617) 426-8855.

Open daily, 10 a.m. to 5 p.m. in summer; closed Monday rest of year. Participatory exhibits.

CHINA TRADE MUSEUM: *50% discount.*
215 Adams St., Milton, (617) 696-1815.
Tuesday to Sunday, 1 p.m. to 4 p.m. Decorative arts museum.

FOGG ART MUSEUM: *50% discount.*
32 Quincy St., Cambridge, (617) 495-2387.
Monday to Saturday, 10 a.m. to 5 p.m.; Sunday, 1 p.m. to 5 p.m.

INSTITUTE OF CONTEMPORARY ART: *60% discount.*
955 Boylston St., (617) 266-5151
Wednesday to Sunday, 11 a.m. to 5 p.m.; Friday until 8 p.m.

LONGFELLOW NATIONAL HISTORIC SITE: *Free with Golden Eagle Passport.*
105 Brattle St., Cambridge, (617) 876-4491.
10 a.m. to 4:30 p.m.

MUSEUM OF FINE ARTS: *25% discount.*
465 Huntington Ave., (617) 267-9300.
Tuesday to Sunday, 10 a.m. to 5 p.m.; Wednesday, 10 a.m. to 9 p.m. Thursday, Friday, to 10 p.m., West Wing only.

MUSEUM OF SCIENCE: *40% discount.*
Science Park, Charles River Dam Bridge, (617) 589-0100 or 742-6088.
July to August: Monday to Saturday, 9 a.m. to 5 p.m.; Friday, 9 a.m. to 10 p.m.; Sunday, 10 a.m. to 5 p.m. September to June: Monday to Thursday, 9 a.m. to 4 p.m.

OLD STATE HOUSE: *30% discount.*
206 Washington St., (617) 242-5655.
April to October: daily, 9:30 a.m. to 5 p.m. November to March: Monday to Friday, 10 a.m. to 4 p.m.; Saturday, 9:30 a.m. to 5 p.m.; Sunday

11 a.m. to 5 p.m. Seat of the colonial legislature and site of the reading of the Declaration of Independence in 1776.

PAUL REVERE HOUSE: *60% discount.*
19 North Square, (617) 523-2338
April 15 to October 15; daily, 10 a.m. to 6 p.m. Rest of the year: 10 a.m. to 4 p.m. Oldest building in Boston.

U.S.S. *CONSTITUTION* MUSEUM: *50% discount.*
Boston National Historical Park, (617) 426-1812.
Daily, 9 a.m. to 6 p.m. Artifacts from the ship.

UNIVERSITY MUSEUM: *25% discount.*
24 Oxford St., Cambridge, (617) 495-2387.
Monday to Saturday, 9 a.m. to 4:30 p.m.; Sunday 1 p.m. to 4:30 p.m. Exhibits cover everything from archeology to zoology.

Free!

Arnold Arboretum, Bell Laboratory, Bunker Hill Monument and Museum, Faneuil Hall, Franklin Park Zoo, Hayden Gallery, MIT Museum, Old North Church, State House, U.S.S. *Constitution*

CAPE COD

Helpful Address

CAPE COD CHAMBER OF COMMERCE
U.S. Rte. 6 & Rte. 132, Hyannis, Cape Cod, MA 02601
(617) 362-3225

Incredible Deal!

Try the beach in May and September. You'll find fewer people and lower prices.

Hotels

HOLIDAY INN: *10%–20% discount with Holiday Inn's Travel Venture Club Card.*
Falmouth, 824 Main St. E., (617) 540-2500.
Hyannis, Rte. 132, (617) 775-6600.

ISAIAH B. HALL HOUSE: *10% discount off peak.*
152 Whig St., Dennis, (617) 383-9928.

SHERATON: *25% discount for over 60.*
Eastham, Sheraton Ocean-Park, Rte. 6 (617) 255-5000.
Falmouth, Sheraton Inn-Falmouth, 291 Jones Rd., (617) 540-2000.
Hyannis, Sheraton-Regal Inn, Rte. 132 & Bearses Way, (617) 771-3000.

Car Rental

AVIS: *5%–25% discount.**
Hyannis, Barnstable Airport, (617) 775-2888.

HERTZ: *5%–25% discount.**
Falmouth, Battles Pontiac, (617) 548-1923.
Hyannis, Barnstable Airport, (617) 775-5825.
Provincetown Airport, (617) 487-1245.

NATIONAL: *10%–12% discount for over 62.*
Falmouth, 50 Davis Straits, Rte. 28, (617) 548-1589.
Hyannis, Barnstable Airport, (617) 771-4353.

Sights

APTUCXET TRADING POST: *25% discount.*
24 Aptucxet Rd., Bourne, (617) 759-5379.
Mid-April to mid-October: Monday to Saturday, 10 a.m. to 5 p.m.; Sunday, 1 to 5 p.m.; closed Wednesdays until July. A re-creation of Pilgrim-Dutch trading post built in 1627.

AQUA CIRCUS OF CAPE COD: *15% discount.*
Rte. 28, West Yarmouth, (617) 775-8883.
Late June to Labor Day: daily, 9:30 a.m. to 9 p.m. March to late June and after Labor Day to mid-November: daily, 9:30 a.m. to 5 p.m.
Aquarium and zoo.

ASHUMET HOLLY RESERVATION: *50% discount.*
Currier Rd. & Ashumet Rd., Hatchville, E. Falmouth, (617) 563-6390.
Daylight hours year round..

PROVINCETOWN ART ASSOCIATION AND MUSEUM OF ART: *50% discount.*
460 Commercial St., Provincetown, (617) 487-1750.
Late May to Oct.: daily, 12 to 4 p.m., 7 to 10 p.m.

YESTERYEARS DOLL AND MINIATURE MUSEUM: *25% discount.*
Main & River Sts. in the Old First Parish Meeting House, Sandwich, (617) 888-1711.
May 1 to October 31: Monday to Saturday, 10 a.m. to 5 p.m.; Sunday, 1 to 5 p.m.

PIONEER VALLEY

Hotels

HOTEL NORTHAMPTON: *10% discount for AARP, depending on availability.*
36 King St., Northampton, (413) 584-3100.

HOWARD JOHNSON'S: *15%–50% discount with H.J.'s Road Rally Card.*
1150 Riverdale St., Springfield, (617) 739-7261.

QUALITY INN: *10% discount for over 60.*
296 Burnett Rd., (413) 592-7751.

Public Transportation

PIONEER VALLEY TRANSIT AUTHORITY: *50% discount; free bus within Amherst.*
1365 Main St., Springfield, (413) 781-7882; in Amherst and Northampton, (800) 586-5806.

Car Rental

NATIONAL: *10%–12% discount for over 62.*
72 King St., Northampton, (413) 586-1201.

Restaurants

JAMES McMANUS EATING PLACE: *20% discount, 2 to 5 p.m.; 10% other times.*
Camous Plaza, Rte. 9, Hadley.

Theater and Movies

FINE ARTS CONCERT HALL: *10% discount on concerts sponsored by Fine Arts Center.*
University of Massachusetts, Amherst.

HAMPSHIRE MALL MOVIE THEATERS: *50¢ off regular shows.*
Rte. 9, Hadley, (413) 545-1945.

Sights

MT. TOM SKI AREA: *Seniors ski at children's rates.*

WORCESTER

Hotels

BEST WESTERN: *10% discount.*
110 Summer St., (617) 757-0400.

HOWARD JOHNSON'S: *15%–50% discount with H.J.'s Road Rally Card.*
800 Southbridge St., Worcester, (617) 791-5501.
181 W. Boylston St., Worcester, (617) 835-4456.

MARRIOTT: *50% discount for Marriott Leisure Life members.*
10 Lincoln Square, Worcester, (617) 791-1600.

PUBLICK HOUSE COUNTRY MOTOR LODGE: *10% discount to AARP.*
Haynes St., Sturbridge, (617) 347-9555.

WESTBOROUGH PLAZA HOTEL: *50% discount to AARP, depending on availability.*
5 Turnpike Rd., Westborough, MA 01581, (617) 366-5511.

YANKEE DRUMMER INN: *10% discount with* Discount Guide *or AARP, NCSC membership.*
624 Southbridge St., Auburn, MA 01501, (617) 832-3221.

Public Transportation

WORCESTER REGIONAL TRANSIT AUTHORITY: *50% discount with senior ID.*

Car Rental

AVIS: *5%–25% discount.*
446 Lincoln St., Worcester, (617) 852-3080.

HERTZ: *5%–25% discount.*
Worcester Airport, (617) 753-7203.

Museums

WORCESTER SCIENCE CENTER: *25% discount.*
222 Harrington Way, (617) 791-9211.

WILLARD HOUSE & CLOCK MUSEUM: *25% discount.*
Willard St. Grafton.

Theaters and Exposition Halls

REDSTONE THEATRES/SHOWCASE CINEMAS: *$2.25 off regular admission for over 60.*
4 Southbridge St., Worcester.
50 Boston Turnpike, Shrewsbury.
Lincoln Plaza, Worcester.

MICHIGAN

Helpful Addresses

MICHIGAN TRAVEL BUREAU
Dept. of Commerce, P.O. Box 30226, Lansing, MI 48909
(517) 373-1195, (800) 292-2520 (MI), (800) 248-5700 (Northeast U.S.)

OFFICES OF SERVICES TO THE AGING
P.O. Box 30026, Lansing, MI 48909
(517) 373-8230

DETROIT AND VICINITY

Hotels

BEST WESTERN: *10% discount.*
25255 Grand River Ave., (313) 533-4020.

HOLIDAY INN: *10%–20% discount with Holiday Inn's Travel Venture Club Card.*
Airport, 31200 Industrial Expwy., (313) 728-2800.
Dearborn, 22900 Michigan, (313) 278-4800.
Hazel Park, 1 W. Nine Mile Rd., (313) 399-5800.

Troy, 2537 Rochester Ct., (313) 689-7500.
Warren, 32035 Van Dyke, (313) 264-0100.

KNIGHTS INN: *10% discount.*
Madison Heights, I-75 at 14-Mile Rd., (313) 583-7700.
Roseville, I-94 at Little Mack Rd., (313) 294-6140.
Warren, S.R. 53 at Chicago Rd., (313) 978-7500.

RAMADA INN: *25% discount for over 60.*
Airport, 8270 Wickham Rd., (313) 729-6300.
Southfield, 28225 Telegraph, (313) 355-2929.

RODEWAY INN: *10% discount.*
Airport, 8230 Merriman Rd., (313) 729-7600.

SHERATON: *25% discount for over 60.*
Airport, 8699 Merriman Rd., Romulus, (313) 728-7900.
Novi, 27000 Sheraton Dr., (313) 348-5000.

TRAVELODGE: *Special senior rates for Travelodge's Golden Guest Club.*
Dearborn, 23730 Michigan Ave., (313) 565-7250.

Public Transportation

WASHINGTON BLVD. TROLLEY CAR: *Free for seniors over 65.*
Department of Transportation ID card required.
1301 E. Warren Ave., Detroit, MI 48207, (313) 933-1300.

Car Rental

AVIS: *5%–25% discount.**
Airport, (313) 942-3450.

HERTZ: *5%–25% discount.**
Airport, (313) 729-5200.
1041 Washington Blvd., (313) 729-5200.

NATIONAL: *10%–12% discount for over 62.*
Airport, (313) 941-7000.

Sights

DETROIT ZOOLOGICAL PARK: *30% discount.*
8450 W. Ten Mile Rd., Royal Oak, (313) 398-0900.
Daily, 10 a.m. to 5 p.m. October to April, 10 a.m. to 4 p.m.

HISTORIC FORT WAYNE: *50% discount.**
6325 W. Jefferson Ave., (313) 297-9360.
May to November: Wednesday to Sunday, 9:30 a.m. to 5 p.m. 1843–48 fort.

Museums

DETROIT HISTORICAL MUSEUM: *50% discount.*
5401 Woodward Ave., (313) 833-1805.
Wednesday to Sunday, 9:30 a.m. to 5 p.m.

DETROIT SCIENCE CENTER: *50% discount.*
5020 John R. St., (313) 577-8400.
Tuesday to Friday, 9 a.m. to 4 p.m.; Saturday, 10 a.m. to 7 p.m.; Sunday, noon to 7 p.m. Films and hands-on exhibits.

HENRY FORD MUSEUM AND GREENFIELD VILLAGE: *15% discount.*
Oakwood Blvd., Dearborn, (313) 271-1620, (800) 835-2246.
Daily, 9 a.m. to 5 p.m. Incredible collection of cars, machines, and historic houses.

Free!

Aquarium, Children's Museum, Detroit Fire Department Museum, Money Museum

MINNESOTA

Helpful Addresses

MINNESOTA TRAVEL INFORMATION CENTER
240 Bremer Bldg., 419 North Robert Sts., St. Paul, MN 55101
(612) 296-5029, (800) 652-9747 (MN only), (800) 328-1461 (except MN).

BOARD ON AGING
Metro Square Bldg., Suite 204, 7th & Robert Sts., St. Paul, MN 55101
(612) 296-2544

MINNEAPOLIS–ST. PAUL

Hotels

BEST WESTERN: *10% discount.*
5225 Wayzata Blvd., (612) 545-0441.
3924 Excelsior Blvd., (612) 927-7731.
4820 Olson Memorial Hwy., (612) 588-0511.
41 N. 10th St., (612) 339-9311.
2201 E. 78th St., (612) 854-3411.
Airport, 8151 Bridge Rd., (612) 830-1300.

EMBASSY SUITES: *10% discount.**
Center, 425 S. 7th St., (612) 333-3111.
St. Paul, 175 E. 10th St., (612) 224-5400.

HOLIDAY INN: *10%–20% discount with Holiday Inn's Travel Venture Club Card.*
Minneapolis–St. Paul Int'l. Airport, Jct. I-494 & 34th Ave., (612) 854-9000.
Minneapolis Airport, 5401 Green Valley Dr. (I-494 & Hwy. 100), (612) 831-8000.
Minneapolis Downtown, 1313 Nicollet Mall, (612) 332-0371.
St. Paul North, 2540 N. Cleveland, (612) 636-4567.

St. Paul-State Capitol, 161 St. Anthony, (612) 227-8711.

St. Paul Downtown, 411 Minnesota St., (612) 291-8800.

HOWARD JOHNSON'S: *15%–50% discount with H.J.'s Road Rally Card.*

6003 Hudson Rd., (612) 739-7300.

QUALITY INN: *10% discount for over 60.*

St. Paul, 175 W. 7th St., (612) 292-8929.

RAMADA INN: *25% discount for over 60.*

Minneapolis Airport, 4200 W. 78th St., (612) 831-4200.

North, 2200 Freeway Blvd., (612) 566-8000.

RODEWAY INN: *10% discount.*

Airport, 1321 E. 78th St., Bloomington, (612) 854-3400.

THE SAINT PAUL HOTEL: *25% discount.*

350 Market St., (800) 457-9292.

SHERATON: *25% discount for over 60.*

Sheraton Airport Inn, 2525 E. 78th St., Bloomington, (612) 854-1771.

Sheraton Inn Northwest, I-94 and US 52, Brooklyn Park, (612) 566-8855.

Park Place, 555 Wayzata Blvd., (612) 542-8600.

TRAVELODGE: *Special senior rates for Travelodge's Golden Guest Club.*

St. Paul, 149 E. University Ave., (612) 227-8801.

Public Transportation

METROPOLITAN TRANSIT: *10¢ fare from 9 a.m. to 3:30 p.m. and after 6:30 p.m., Monday to Friday; all day Saturday, Sunday, and holidays. Riders 65 and over qualify with a Medicare card.*

Car Rental

AVIS: *5%–25% discount.**
Airport, (612) 726–1723.
829 3rd Ave. S., Minneapolis, (612) 332-6321.

HERTZ: *5%–25% discount.**
Airport, P.O. Box 1630, (612) 726-1600.

NATIONAL: *10%–12% discount for over 62.*
Airport, (612) 726-5600.
320 S. 10th St., (612) 338-8448.

Theaters

CHIMERA THEATRE: *$1 discount for over 65.*
30 E. 10th St., St. Paul, (612) 293-1043.

GUTHRIE THEATER: *50% discount or more for Sunday evening and matinee performances.*
Vineland Pl., (612) 377-2224.

MINNESOTA DANCE THEATER: *$1 discount.*
528 Hennepin Ave., Minneapolis, (612) 339-9150.

Rules for Savings on Car Rentals

1. Join a national senior citizens' organization and use its discount identification number.
2. Make advance reservations with the toll-free national reservation service.
3. Renting mid-week? A senior-citizen rate can save you money.
4. Renting for seven days or for the weekend? Senior discounts can save you another 5% to 10%.
5. Always ask, "Is this the cheapest rate you offer?"

See pages 32–34 for more information.

UNIVERSITY THEATER: *Discount rates.*
120 Rarig Center, University of Minnesota, (612) 625-4001. November to May.

Sights

MINNESOTA TWINS: *Discount on reserved grandstand seats and general admission seats on Thursdays during baseball season. 30% discount on Metrodome tours.*
Hubert H. Humphrey Metrodome, 900 S. 5th St., (612) 332-0386.

MINNESOTA ZOO: *50% discount for 62 and over.*
12101 Johnny Cake Rd., Apple Valley, (612) 432-9000. Winter, daily, 9:30 a.m. to 5 p.m.; summer, daily, 9:30 a.m. to 6 p.m.

VALLEY FAIR AMUSEMENT PARK: *30% discount.*
Hwy. 101, 3 mi. E. of Shakopee, (612) 445-6500. Daily, May to August; September weekends. Rides, shows, Imax theater.

Museums

AMERICAN SWEDISH INSTITUTE: *50% discount.*
2600 Park Ave. S., (612) 871-4907.
Tuesday to Saturday, 12 p.m. to 4 p.m.; Sunday, 1 to 4 p.m.

CHILDREN'S MUSEUM: *30% discount.*
1217 Bandana Blvd. N., St. Paul, (612) 644-3818.

GIBBS FARM MUSEUM: *15% discount.*
2097 W. Larpenteur, St. Paul, (612) 646-8629.
Mid-April to December: Tuesday to Friday, 10 a.m. to 5 p.m.; Sunday, noon to 4 p.m.

MINNEAPOLIS INSTITUTE OF ART: *Free for seniors.*
2400 3rd Ave. S., (612) 870-3131.
Tuesday to Saturday, 10 a.m. to 5 p.m.; Thursday, 10 a.m. to 9 p.m.; Sunday, noon to 5 p.m.

ST. PAUL ARTS AND SCIENCE CENTER OF MINNESOTA: *30% discount.*
30 E. 10th St., St. Paul, (612) 293-1043.
Tuesday to Saturday, 10 a.m. to 5 p.m., 6:30 to 9 p.m.; Sunday, 11 a.m. to 5 p.m., 6:30 to 9 p.m.

Free!

Bell Museum of Natural History, Como Park Conservatory, Hennepin County Museum, Minneapolis Grain Exchange Visitors' Gallery, Minnesota Historical Society, State Capitol, University Art Museum

MISSISSIPPI

Helpful Addresses

MISSISSIPPI DIVISION OF TOURISM
P.O. Box 849, Jackson, MS 39205
(601) 359-3414, (800) 962-2346 (MS), (800) 647-2290 (except MS)

COUNCIL ON AGING
301 W. Pearl St.,
Jackson, MS 39203
(601) 949-2070

Discounts

An unusually large number of merchants in Mississippi offer discounts to seniors. Travelers should ask wherever they shop, and state residents should write to their local agencies for the aging or to the Mississippi Council on Aging (address above) for complete information.

JACKSON AND VICKSBURG

Hotels

BEST WESTERN: *10% discount.*
Jackson, 5925 I-55 N., (601) 956-8000.
1520 Ellis Ave., (601) 355-7483.

DAYS INN: *10%–50% discount with Days Inn September Days Club card.*
616 Briarwood Dr., (601) 957-1741.
I-20, US 49 & US 80 E., (601) 939-8200.

HOLIDAY INN: *10%–20% discount with Holiday Inn's Travel Venture Club Card.*
Downtown, 200 E. Amite, (601) 969-5100.
Medical Center, 2375 N. State St., (601) 948-8650.
North, I-55 N. & Frontage Rd., (601) 366-9411.
Southwest, 2649 US 80 W., (601) 355-3472.
Vicksburg, US 8 & I-20, (601) 636-4551.

HOWARD JOHNSON'S: *15%–50% discount with H.J.'s Road Rally Card.*
I-20 & Rte. 55 S. at McDowell Rd., (601) 372-1006.

LA QUINTA: *20% discount.*
150 Angle St., (601) 373-6110.

RAMADA INN: *25% discount for over 60.*
Jackson Coliseum, 400 Greymont Ave., (601) 969-2141.
Jackson Metro, 1525 Ellis Ave., (601) 944-1150.
Vicksburg, 4137 I-20 & Frontage Rd., (601) 638-5811.

RODEWAY INN: *10% discount.*
3720 I-55 N., (601) 982-1122.

SCOTTISH INN: *10% discount with Scottish Identicard*
Jackson, 2263 Hwy. 80 W., (601) 969-1144.
Vicksburg, I-20 & Hwy. 80, (601) 638-5511.

SHERATON: *25% discount for over 60.*
I-55 N., exit 35, (601) 982-1044.
750 N. State St., (601) 948-8605.

Car Rental

AVIS: *5%–25% discount.**
Airport, (601) 939-5853.

HERTZ: *5%–25% discount.**
Airport, (601) 939-5312.

NATIONAL: *10%–12% discount for over 62.*
Airport, (601) 939-5713.

Sights

JACKSON ZOOLOGICAL PARK: *Free for over 65.*
2918 W. Capitol St., (601) 960-1575.
Summer: daily, 9 a.m. to 6 p.m. Rest of year: 9 a.m. to 5 p.m.

MISSISSIPPI PETRIFIED FOREST: *30% discount.*
MS 22 at Flora, (601) 879-8189.
Memorial Day to Labor Day, daily, 9 a.m. to 6 p.m. Rest of year, daily, 9 a.m. to 5 p.m.

MYNELLE GARDENS: *50% discount.*
4736 Clinton Blvd., (601) 960-1894.
Daily, 9 a.m. to 5 p.m.

**An asterisk indicates that the discount is intended for members of senior citizens' organizations that anyone can join. See "Hotel, Transportation, and Sightseeing Discounts."*

Free!

Governor's Mansion, Manship House, Museum of Natural Science, State Historical Museum, Vicksburg National Military Park

MISSOURI

Helpful Addresses

MISSOURI STATE DIVISION OF TOURISM
Box 1055, Jefferson City, MO 65102
(314) 751-4133

DIVISION ON AGING
P.O. Box 1337, 505 Missouri Blvd., Jefferson City, MO 65102
(314) 751-3082

KANSAS CITY

Hotels

BEST WESTERN: *10% discount.*
2620 N.E. 43rd St., (816) 453-6550.
Airport, I-29 & Exit 19, (816) 464-2300.
4309 Main St., (816) 561-9600.

EMBASSY SUITES: *10% discount.**
Country Club Plaza, 220 W. 43rd St., (816) 756-1720.

HOLIDAY INN: *10%–20% discount with Holiday Inn's Travel Venture Club Card.*
Downtown Towers, 424 Minnesota, (913) 342-6919.
International Airport, 11832 Plaza Circle, (816) 464-2345.
North, 7333 Parvin Rd., (816) 455-1060.
Sports Complex, I-70 at Blueridge, (816) 353-5300.

HOWARD JOHNSON'S: *15%–50% discount with H.J.'s Road Rally Card.*
610 Washington St., (816) 421-1800.
1600 N.E. Parvin Rd., (816) 453-5210.

RAMADA INN: *25% discount for over 60.*
South, 5701 Longview Rd., (816) 765-4100.
Southeast, 6101 E. 87th St., (816) 765-4331.

RODEWAY INN: *10% discount.*
1211 Armour Rd., (816) 471-3451.
5 E. Trafficway, (816) 842-6090.

SHERATON: *25% discount for over 60.*
Airport, 7301 N.W. Tiffany Springs Rd., (816) 741-9500.

TRAVELODGE: *Special senior rates for Travelodge's Golden Guest Club.*
Downtown, 921 Cherry St., (816) 471-1266.
3240 Broadway, (816) 531-9250.

Public Transportation

KANSAS CITY AREA TRANSPORTATION AUTHORITY: *Half fare for holders of a "Metro Senior Citizens" card or Medicare card.*
(816) 346-0200.

Car Rental

AVIS: *5%–25% discount.**
International Airport, (816) 243-5760.

HERTZ: *5%–25% discount.**
International Airport, (816) 243-5765.
1217 Wyandotte, (816) 421-0300.

NATIONAL: *10%–12% discount for over 62.*
International Airport, (816) 243-5770.

Free!

Board of Trade, Hallmark Visitor Center, Kansas City Art Institute, Liberty Museum, Livestock Exchange & Stockyard

ST. LOUIS

Hotels

BEST WESTERN: *10% discount.*
Airport, 4530 N. Lindbergh, Bridgeton, (314) 731-3800.
Six Flags, 10709 Hwy. 366, (314) 821-6600.
I-270 & Dorsett Rd., (314) 291-8700.
1351 Dunn Rd., (314) 868-1111.

DAYS INN: *10%–50% discount with Days Inn September Days Club card.*
Airport, 4545 Woodson Rd., (314) 423-6770.

EMBASSY SUITES: *10% discount.**
Downtown, 901 N. 1st St., (314) 241-4200.

HARLEY HOTEL: *10% discount.*
3400 Rider Tr. S., Earth City, (314) 291-6800, (800) 321-2323.

HOLIDAY INN: *10%–20% discount with Holiday Inn's Travel Venture Club Card.*
Airport, 4545 N. Lindbergh, Bridgeton, (314) 731-2100.
Airport, I-270 at St. Charles Rock Rd., Bridgeton, (314) 291-5100.
Clayton Plaza, 7730 Bonhomme, (314) 863-0400.
Market St., 2211 Market, (314) 231-3232.
Riverfront, 4th & Pine, (314) 621-8200.

HOWARD JOHNSON'S: *15%–50% discount with H.J.'s Road Rally Card.*

Airport North, 9075 Dunn Rd., Hazelwood, (314) 895-3366.

Airport West, 1425 S. 5th St., St. Charles, (314) 946-6936.

Hampton Ave., 5915 Wilson Ave., (314) 645-0700.

Southwest, 1200 S. Kirkwood, (314) 821-3950.

LA QUINTA: *20% discount.*

Airport, 5781 Campus Ct., Hazelwood, (314) 731-3881.

MARRIOTT PAVILION: *50% discount for Marriott Leisure Life members.*

1 Broadway, (314) 421-1776.

QUALITY INN: *10% discount for over 60.*

Comfort Inn, 3730 S. Lindbergh Blvd., (314) 842-1200.

RAMADA INN: *25% discount for over 60.*

Airport, 9636 Natural Bridge Rd., (314) 426-4700.

Westport, 12031 Lackland, (314) 878-1400.

South, 6926 S. Lindbergh at I-55, (314) 894-0600.

RODEWAY INN: *10% discount.*

Airport, 10232 Natural Bridge Rd., Woodson Terrace, (314) 427-5955.

South, 3660 S. Lindbergh, (314) 821-3000.

SHERATON: *25% discount for over 60.*

Airport, 4201 N. Lindbergh Blvd., (314) 731-3600.

Convention Plaza, 910 N. 7th St., (314) 231-5100.

Car Rental

AVIS: *5%–25% discount.**

Airport, P.O. Box 10005, (314) 426-7766.

911 Washington St., (314) 241-5780.

HERTZ: *5%–25% discount.**

Airport, P.O. Box 10014, (314) 426-7555.

400 N. Tucker, (314) 421-3131.

NATIONAL: *10%-12% discount for over 62.*
Airport, (314) 426-6272.
900 Washington Ave., (314) 621-0060.

Theater

GOLDENROD SHOW BOAT: *$2 discount on Sunday matinee dinner show.*
St. Louis Riverfront, (314) 621-3311.

Sights

MISSOURI BOTANICAL GARDEN: *Free for seniors.*
4344 Shaw Blvd., (314) 577-5100.
9 a.m. to 4:30 p.m.; until 7:30 p.m. in summer.

ST. LOUIS CARDINALS: *Discount for over 65.*
Busch Memorial Stadium, (314) 421-3060.
Call for schedule and discount information.

SIX FLAGS OVER MID-AMERICA: *Senior discount.*
Allenton Rd., Eureka, (314) 938-4800 or (800) 325-3187.
June through August; daily, 10 a.m. to 10 p.m., closed Monday. September, October, April, May: weekends only.

Museums

NATIONAL MUSEUM OF TRANSPORT: *50% discount.*
3015 Barrett Station Rd., (314) 965-7998.
Daily, 9 a.m. to 5 p.m.

Free!

Anheuser-Busch Brewery Tours, Grant's Farm, Jefferson Barracks Historical Park, Medical Museum and National Museum of Quackery, Missouri Historical Society,

Museum of Science and Natural History, Museum of Westward Expansion, Old Courthouse, St. Louis Art Museum, St. Louis Cathedral, St. Louis Zoological Park, Soldiers Memorial Military Museum, Washington University Gallery of Art

MONTANA

Helpful Addresses

TRAVEL MONTANA
Department of Commerce, 1424 9th Ave., Helena, MT 59620
(406) 444-2654 or (800) 548-3390

COMMUNITY SERVICES DIVISION
P.O. Box 4210, Helena, MT 59604
(406) 444-3865

Package Tour for Seniors

Covering six states, Saga's 14-night National Park Holiday includes Yellowstone, Mt. Rushmore, Grand Teton National Park, as well as Rocky Mountain State Park, Zion National Park, and the Black Hills of South Dakota (from $1300). See pages 7–10 for more information on package tours.

BILLINGS

Hotels

BEST WESTERN: *10% discount.*
Broadway at 1st Ave., (406) 245-5121.
2511 1st Ave., (406) 259-5511.

HOLIDAY INN: *10%–20% discount with Holiday Inn's Travel Venture Club Card.*
West, I-90 & Mullowney Ln., (406) 248-7701.

RAMADA INN: *25% discount for over 60.*
I-90 & Mullowney St., (406) 248-7151.

SHERATON: *25% discount for over 60.*
27 N. 27th St., (406) 252-7400.

TRAVELODGE: *Special senior rates for Travelodge's Golden Guest Club.*
3311 2nd Ave., (406) 245-6345.

Car Rental

AVIS: *5%–25% discount.**
Logan Airport, (406) 252-8007.

HERTZ: *5%–25% discount.**
Logan Airport, (406) 248-9151.

NATIONAL: *10%–12% discount for over 62.*
Logan Airport, (406) 252-7626.

Sights

POMPEY'S PILLAR: *15% discount.*
Off US 10, (406) 259-8426.

Memorial Day to Labor Day: daily, 8 a.m. to 6 p.m. Rock formation used by Indians for smoke signals. Named by explorer George Rogers Clark.

Free!

Indian Caves, Western Heritage Center, Yellowstone Art Center, Yellowstone County Museum

NEBRASKA

Helpful Addresses

NEBRASKA DIVISION OF TRAVEL & TOURISM
Department of Economic Development,
P.O. Box 94666,
301 Centennial Mall South,
Lincoln, NB 68509
(402) 471-3111 or (800) 222-4307

DEPARTMENT ON AGING
P.O. Box 95044,
301 Centennial Mall S.
Lincoln, NB 68509
(402) 471-2306

LINCOLN

Hotels

BEST WESTERN: *10% discount.*
5200 O St., (402) 464-9111.
Airport, 1200 W. Cornhusker Hwy., (402) 475-9541.

HOLIDAY INN: *10%–20% discount with Holiday Inn's Travel Venture Club Card.*
Airport, 1101 Bond St., (402) 475-4971.
Northeast, 5250 Cornhusker Hwy., (402) 464-3171.

RAMADA INN: *25% discount for over 60.*
2310 N.W. 12th St., (402) 475-5911.

Car Rental

AVIS: *5%–25% discount.**
Airport, (402) 472-1202.

HERTZ: *5%–25% discount.**
Airport, (402) 474-4079.
2100 N St., (402) 474-4079.

NATIONAL: *10%–12% discount for over 62.*
Airport, (402) 474-4301.

Free!

Sheldon Memorial Art Gallery & Sculpture Garden, State Capitol, State Historical Society Museum, University of Nebraska State Museum, William Jennings Bryan House

OMAHA

Hotels

BEST WESTERN: *10% discount.*
Airport, (402) 348-0222.
6901 N. 72nd St., (402) 571-6161.
7764 Dodge St., (402) 393-5500.

EMBASSY SUITES: *10% discount.**
7270 Cedar St., (402) 397-5141.

HOLIDAY INN: *10%–20% discount with Holiday's Inn's Travel Venture Club Card.*
Central, 3321 S. 72nd St., (402) 393-3950.
Northwest, 655 N. 108th Ave., (402) 496-0850.

HOWARD JOHNSON'S: *15%–50% discount with H.J.'s Road Rally Card.*
3650 S. 72nd St., (402) 397-3700.

LA QUINTA: *20% discount.*
3330 N. 104th Ave., (402) 493-1900.

RAMADA INN: *25% discount for over 60.*
Central, 7007 Grove, (402) 397-7030.

SHERATON: *25% discount for over 60.*
Southwest, 4888 S. 118th St., (402) 895-1000.

TRAVELODGE: *Special senior rates for Travelodge's Golden Guest Club.*
3902 Dodge St., (402) 558-4000.

Car Rental

AVIS: *5%–25% discount.**
1409 Dodge St., (402) 384-0621.
Eppley Airfield, (402) 422-6480.

HERTZ: *5%–25% discount.**
Eppley Airfield, (402) 422-6870.
202 N. 19th St., (402) 341-2200.

NATIONAL: *10%–12% discount for over 62.*
Eppley Airfield, (402) 422-6565.

Museums

GREAT PLAINS BLACK MUSEUM: *25% discount.*
2213 Lake St., (402) 345-2212.
Monday to Friday, 8 a.m. to 5 p.m.

JOSLYN ART MUSEUM: *50% discount.*
2200 Dodge St., (402) 342-3300.
Tuesday to Saturday, 10 a.m. to 5 p.m.; Sunday, 1 p.m. to 5 p.m.

Free!

Boys Town, Union Pacific Museum

NEVADA

Helpful Addresses

NEVADA COMMISSION ON TOURISM
Capitol Complex, 600 E. Williams, Carson City, NV 89710
(702) 885-4322, (800) 992-0900 (in NV).

DIVISION ON AGING
505 E. King St., Carson City, NV 89710
(702) 885-4210

LAS VEGAS

Visit Las Vegas from September to March

Sydell Pearson, director of the Las Vegas Senior Citizens Center, writes, "Summer is the tourist season, therefore it is more crowded; hence easier to get reservations and better rates between September and March. The weather is also more moderate. Better rates apply in the middle of the week too." Seniors are invited to visit the Senior Citizens Center at 450 E. Bonanza Rd.

Hotels

BEST WESTERN: *10% discount.*
3500 Paradise Rd., (702) 731-2020 or (800) 634-6501.
1322 E. Fremont, (702) 385-1150.
5330 E. Craig Rd., (702) 643-6111.
905 Las Vegas Blvd., (702) 385-1213.
99 Convention Center Dr., (702) 735-6117.
1150 Las Vegas Blvd. S., (702) 382-6001.
4970 Paradise Rd., (702) 798-5530.

HOLIDAY INN: *10%–20% discount with Holiday Inn's Travel Venture Club Card.*
Center Strip, 3475 Las Vegas Blvd. S., (702) 369-5000.

LA QUINTA: *20% discount.*
3782 Las Vegas Ave. S., (702) 739-7457.

RAMADA INN: *25% discount for over 60.*
Tropicana, 3801 Las Vegas Blvd., (702) 739-2222.

RODEWAY INN: 10% discount.
3786 Las Vegas Blvd. S., (702) 736-1434.

COMPARATIVE HOTEL RATES*: REGULAR DOUBLE ROOM

Hotel	Sr. Disc.	
BEST WESTERN	10%	$35–52
HOLIDAY INN	15%	$47–67
LA QUINTA	20%	$32–48
RAMADA INN	25%	$49–94
RODEWAY INN	10%	$35–37
VAGABOND	10%	$41–57

*SAVE MORE ON MIDWEEK RATES.

TRAVELODGE: *Special senior rates for Travelodge's Golden Guest Club.*
Downtown, 2028 E. Fremont St., (702) 384-7540.
Strip, 2830 Las Vegas Blvd., (702) 735-4222.
Strip, 3419 Las Vegas Blvd., (702) 734-6801.
Strip, 3735 Las Vegas Blvd. S., (702) 736-3443.
Tropicana, 3111 W. Tropicana Ave., (702) 798-1111.
Viscount, 3740 Las Vegas Blvd. S., (702) 735-1167.

VAGABOND: *10% discount for Vagabond's Club 55.*
Strip, 3688 Las Vegas Blvd. S., (702) 736-0991.

Public Transportation

LAS VEGAS TRANSIT (bus): *40% discount on 10-ride ticket.*
Phone for routes and schedules, (702) 384-3540.

Car Rental

AVIS: *5%–25% discount.**
McCarran Airport, (702) 739-5595.
Caesar's Palace Hotel, 3570 Las Vegas Blvd. S., (702) 731-7790.
Las Vegas Hilton, 3000 Paradise Rd., (702) 734-8011.

HERTZ: *5%–25% discount.**
Las Vegas Strip, (702) 735-4597.
McCarran Airport, (702) 736-4900.

NATIONAL: *10%–12% discount for over 62.*
McCarran Airport, (702) 739-5391.
Strip, (702) 739-5391.

Sights

BONNIE SPRINGS OLD NEVADA: *25% discount.*
20 mi. W. on Charleston Blvd., (702) 875-4191.
Daily, 10:30 a.m. to 6 p.m. Western mining town with entertainment.

Theater

JUDY BAYLEY THEATER: *30% discount.*
University of Nevada, (702) 739-3801.

Museum

LIBERACE MUSEUM: *50¢ discount.*
1775 E. Tropicana Ave., (702) 798-5595.
Daily, 10 a.m. to 5 p.m., Sunday 1 p.m. to 5 p.m.

Free!

Art Museum of Las Vegas, Museum of Natural History. Many free casino tours.

Incredible Deals—Meals and Entertainment

Many Las Vegas hotels have 24-hour buffets where you can get a great meal for as little as $2.95 to $8.95. And many hotel lounges feature entertainment for little or no cover charge and/or a two-drink minimum. Get complete information from the Greater Las Vegas Chamber of Commerce, 2301 E. Sahara Ave., Las Vegas, NV 89104.

NEW HAMPSHIRE

Helpful Addresses

NEW HAMPSHIRE VACATION CENTER
P.O. Box 856,
Concord, NH 03301
(603) 271-2343 or (800) 258-3608 (Northeast except NH)

COUNCIL ON AGING
105 Loudon Rd., Bldg. #3, Concord, NH 03301
(603) 271-2751

The New Hampshire Division of Parks grants free admission to parks, historic sites, beaches, and ski areas to seniors with proper identification.

Package Tours for Seniors

New Hampshire is often included in New England Fall Foliage Tours. See "Massachusetts" for more tour information.

Hotels

BEST WESTERN: *10% discount.*
Nashua, 220 Daniel Webster Hwy. S., (603) 888-1200.
Seabrook, Rte. 107 & Stard Rd., (603) 474-3078.

HOLIDAY INN: *10%–20% discount with Holiday Inn's Travel Venture Club Card.*
Manchester, 21 Front St., (603) 669-2660.
Manchester, 700 Elm St., (603) 625-1000.
Nashua, North East Blvd., (603) 888-1551.

HOWARD JOHNSON'S: *15%–50% discount with H.J.'s Road Rally Card.*
Nashua, Everett Tpk. & Rte. 111, (603) 889-0173.

RAMADA INN: *25% discount for over 60.*
Concord, 172 N. Main, (603) 224-9534.
Keene, 401 Winchester St., (603) 357-3038.

SHERATON: *25% discount for over 60.*
Lebanon/Hanover, Airport Rd., (603) 298-5906.
Manchester, I-293 & US 3, (603) 622-3766.

Car Rental

AVIS: *5%–25% discount.**
Concord, New Hampshire Hwy., (603) 225-5652.
Keene, 250 Marlboro, (603) 352-8525.
Manchester Airport, (603) 624-4000.
Nashua Holiday Inn, Northeastern Blvd., (603) 888-1000.
Portsmouth, 54 Barlett St., (603) 431-8600.

HERTZ: *5%–25% discount.**
Keene, 465 West St., (603) 352-0800.
Lebanon Airport, (603) 298-8927.
Nashua, 254 Main St., (603) 883-4023.

NATIONAL: *10%–12% discount for over 62.*
Keene, 600 Main St., (603) 357-4045.
Lebanon Airport, (603) 298-5701.
Portsmouth, 155 Mirona Rd., (603) 431-4707.

Museums

FROST PLACE: *25% discount.*
Ridge Rd., Rte. 116, Franconia, (603) 823-5510.
Tuesday to Sunday, 1 p.m. to 5 p.m.; July and August. Home of poet Robert Frost.

NEW ENGLAND SKI MUSEUM: *50% discount.*
Rte. 18, Franconia, (603) 823-7177.
Daily in summer and winter, 10 a.m. to 4 p.m. Exhibits and films.

STRAWBERY BANKE: *20% discount.*
Hancock & Marcy Sts., Portsmouth, (603) 433-1100.
May to October: daily, 9:30 a.m. to 4:30 p.m.
Restoration of the original Portsmouth settlement.

WENTWORTH-COOLIDGE MANSION: *Free for seniors.*
Little Harbour Rd., Portsmouth, (603) 436-6607.
Mid-June to September, daily, 10 a.m. to 5 p.m.
Forty-room mansion. Built 1695.

WENTWORTH GARDNER HOUSE: *25% discount.*
Mechanic & Gardner Sts., Portsmouth, (603) 436-4406.
Mid-May to mid-October: Tuesday to Saturday, 10 a.m. to 5 p.m.; Sunday, 2 p.m. to 5 p.m.
Restored 1760 home.

Free!

Concord: New Hampshire Historical Society. Hampton Beach: Tuck Memorial Museum. Jaffrey: Cathedral of the Pines. Nashua: Clydesdale Hamlet, tours of Anheuser-Busch Brewery. Manchester: Currier Gallery of Art. Portsmouth: Ft. Constitution.

NEW JERSEY

Helpful Addresses

NEW JERSEY DIVISION OF TRAVEL AND TOURISM
CN-286, Trenton, NJ 08625
(609) 292-2470

DIVISION ON AGING
P.O. Box 2768, 363 W. State St., Trenton, NJ 08625
(609) 292-4833

NEW JERSEY SHORE

Incredible Deal—May and September at the beach. You'll find fewer people and lower prices.

Hotels

CORDOVA GUEST HOUSE: *10% discount for over 55.*
26 Webb Ave., Ocean Grove, (212) 751-9577 or (201) 774-3084.

HOLIDAY INN: *10%–20% discount with Holiday Inn's Travel Venture Club Card.*
Tom's River, 290 Hwy. 37 E., (201) 244-4000.

HOWARD JOHNSON'S MOTOR LODGE: *15%–50% discount with H.J.'s Road Rally Card.*
Asbury Park, Asbury Park Cir., Neptune, (201) 776-9000.
Tom's River, Rte. 37 & Hooper Ave., (201) 244-1000.

QUALITY INN: *10% discount for over 60.*
W. Atlantic City, Comfort Inn West, Black Horse Pike, (609) 645-1818.

Join a National Senior Citizens' Organization *AARP/NRTA*, $7.50 yearly, 215 Long Beach Blvd., Long Beach, CA 90801, (800) 453-9600; *National Council of Senior Citizens*, $10 yearly, 925 15th St., NW, Washington, DC 20005, (202) 347-8800; *Mature Outlook*, $7.50 yearly, P.O. Box 1209, Glenview, IL 60025, (800) 336-6226; *Catholic Golden Age*, $7 yearly, 400 Lackawanna Ave., Scranton, PA 18503. Avoid last-minute worry and disappointment by requesting your membership card four to six weeks before your trip.

RAMADA INN: *25% discount for over 60.*
W. Long Branch, Monmouth Park, Rte. 36, (201) 229-9000.

TRAVELODGE: *Special senior rates for Travelodge's Golden Guest Club.*
Neptune/Belmar, Hwy. 35 & New York Ave., (201) 988-8750.
Tom's River, 5 W. Water St., (201) 244-0800.

Car Rental

AVIS: *5%–25% discount.**
Asbury Park, A&B Texaco Servicenter, Main St. & 6th Ave., (201) 776-6444
Atlantic City, 114 S. New York, (609) 345-3246.

HERTZ: *5%–25% discount.**
Asbury Park, 1415 Main St., (201) 775-1515
Atlantic City, 1400 Albany Blvd., (60) 646-1212.

Free!

Atlantic City piers, Ocean City Historical Museum

NEW MEXICO

Helpful Addresses

NEW MEXICO TRAVEL DIVISION
Commerce & Industry Dept., Bataan Memorial Building, Santa Fe, NM 87503
(505) 827-6230 or (800) 545-2040

STATE AGENCY ON AGING
224 E. Palace Ave., 4th Floor, Santa Fe, NM 87501
(505) 827-7640

ALBUQUERQUE

Hotels

BEST WESTERN: *10% discount.*
Old Town, 1015 Rio Grande Blvd., (505) 843-9500.
2400 Yale Blvd., (505) 242-7022.
18 Winrock Ctr. N.E., (505) 883-5252.

HOLIDAY INN: *10%–20% discount with Holiday Inn's Travel Venture Club Card.*
Midtown, 2020 Menaul N.E., (505) 884-2511.

HOWARD JOHNSON'S: *15%–50% discount with H.J.'s Road Rally Card.*
East, 15 Hotel Cir. N.E. (505) 296-4852.

LA QUINTA: *20% discount*
2424 San Mateo Blvd., (505) 884-3591.
2116 Yale Blvd. S.E., (505) 243-5500
5241 San Antonio Dr., (505) 821-9000.

QUALITY INN: *10% discount for over 60.*
Comfort Inn, 13031 Central N.E., (505) 294-1800.

RAMADA INN: *25% discount for over 60.*
East, 25 Hotel Cir. N.E., (505) 296-5472.
6815 Menaul N.E., (505) 881-0000.

SHERATON: *25% discount for over 60.*
800 Rio Grande Blvd., N.W., (505) 843-6300.

TRAVELODGE: *Special senior rates for Travelodge's Golden Guest Club.*
East, 3711 Central Ave., N.E., (505) 265-6961.

Car Rental

AVIS: *5%–25% discount.**
Airport, P.O. Box 9086, (505) 842-4080.

HERTZ: *5%–25% discount.**
Airport, P.O. Box 9032, (505) 842-4235.

NATIONAL: *10%–12% discount for over 62.*
Airport, (505) 842-4222.

Sights

INDIAN PUEBLO CULTURAL CENTER: *25% discount.*
2401 12th St. N.W., (505) 843-7270.
Monday to Saturday, 9:30 a.m. to 5:30 p.m.; open Sunday in summer. Indian crafts and dance demonstrations.

SANDIA PEAK AERIAL TRAMWAY: *10% discount.*
I-25 & Tramway Rd., (505) 298-8518.
Summer: daily except Wednesday, 10:30 a.m. to 10 p.m. Ski season: noon to 9 p.m. Rest of year: 5 to 9 p.m.

RIO GRANDE ZOO: *50% discount.*
903 10th St. S.W., (505) 843-7413.
Daily, 9 a.m. to 5 p.m.

Museums

ALBUQUERQUE MUSEUM: *Free to seniors.*
2000 Mountain Rd., (505) 243-7255
Tuesday to Friday, 10 a.m. to 5 p.m.; Weekends, 1 p.m. to 5 p.m.

Free!

Fine Arts Center, Indian Petroglyph State Park, Maxwell Museum of Anthropology, Meteoritics Museum, National Atomic Museum, Rio Grande Nature Center, Telephone Pioneer Museum

SANTA FE

Hotels

BEST WESTERN: *10% discount.*
2405 Cerrillos Rd., (505) 471-8000.

LA QUINTA: *20% discount.*
4298 Cerrillos Rd., (505) 471-1142.

QUALITY INN: *10% discount for over 60.*
Comfort Inn, 3011 Cerrillos Rd., (505) 471-1211.

RAMADA INN: *25% discount for over 60.*
2907 Cerrillos Rd., (505) 471-3000.

RODEWAY INN: *10% discount.*
2900 Cerrillos Rd., (505) 471-8072.

SHERATON: *25% discount for over 60.*
750 N. St. Francis Dr., (505) 982-5591.

TRAVELODGE: *Special senior rates for Travelodge's Golden Guest Club.*
646 Cerrillos Rd., (505) 982-3551.

Car Rental

AVIS: *5%–25% discount.**
Inn of the Governors, 234 Don Gaspar, (505) 982-4361.

HERTZ: *5%–25% discount.**
Airport, (505) 982-1844.
855 Cerrillos Rd., (505) 982-1844.

NATIONAL: *10%–12% discount for over 62.*
Airport, (505) 983-2232.

Free!

Hall of the Southwest Indian, Institute of American Indian Arts, Museum of Fine Arts, Museum of International Folk Art, Oldest House, Palace of the Governors, Pecos National Monument, San Miguel Mission

NEW YORK

Helpful Addresses

NEW YORK STATE DEPT. OF TOURISM
One Commerce Plaza, Albany, NY 12245
(518) 474-4116; (800) CALL NYS (Northeast U.S.)

OFFICE FOR THE AGING
Agency Building #2, New York State Plaza, Albany, NY 12223
(518) 474-4425.

NY CONVENTION & VISITORS BUREAU
2 Columbus Circle, New York, NY 10019, (212) 397-8222.

NEW YORK CITY

The New York City Department for the Aging states that "there are numerous discounts available to senior citizens within the city and throughout New York State. Discounts can be found at movie theaters and at state parks, to give two examples." For any specific problems encountered while visiting the city, call the Department at (212) 577-0800.

Hotels

BEST WESTERN: *10% discount*
Barbizon Plaza, 106 Central Park S., (212) 247-7000.
Milford Plaza, 8th Ave. & 45th St., (212) 869-3600.
Airport, 108-25 Horace Harding Expwy., (718) 699-4400.

HOLIDAY INN: *10%–20% discount with Holiday Inn's Travel Venture Club Card.*

JFK Airport, 144-02 135th Ave., (718) 659-0200.
LaGuardia Airport, 100-15 Ditmars Blvd., E. Elmhurst, (718) 898-1225.

HOWARD JOHNSON'S: *15%–50% discount with H.J.'s Road Rally Card.*
West Side, 851 8th Ave., (212) 581-4100.

QUALITY INN: *10% discount for over 60.*
Lexington Hotel, 511 Lexington Ave., (212) 755-4400.

SHERATON: *25% discount for over 60.*
St. Regis-Sheraton, 2 E. 55th St., (212) 753-4500.
Sheraton Centre, 811 7th Ave., (212) 581-1000.
Sheraton City Squire, 790 7th Ave., (212) 581-3300.
Sheraton Inn at LaGuardia, 90-10 Grand Central Pkwy., E. Elmhurst, (212) 446-4800.
Sheraton Inn-Newark Airport, 901 Spring St., Elizabeth, NJ, (201) 527-1600.
Sheraton-Russell, 45 Park Ave., (212) 685-7676.

Public Transportation

METROPOLITAN TRANSPORTATION AUTHORITY: *50% discount for 65 and over with Medicare card.*

Car Rental

AVIS: *5%–25% discount.**
310 E. 64th St., (212) 593-8363.
Kennedy International Airport, (718) 656-5266.
LaGuardia Airport, (718) 507-3600.
Newark (NJ) International Airport, (201) 961-4300.

HERTZ: *5%–25% discount.**
310 E. 48th St., (800) 654-3131.
Kennedy International Airport, (718) 656-7600.
LaGuardia Airport, (718) 478-5300.
Newark (NJ) International Airport, (201) 621-2000.

NATIONAL: *10%–12% discount for over 62.*
305 E. 80th St., (212) 476-5876.
Kennedy International Airport, (718) 632-8300.
La Guardia Airport, (718) 476-1033.
Newark (NJ) International Airport, (201) 622-1270.

Broadway Theaters

TKTS: *Half-price tickets for everyone.*
(212) 354-5800.
Broadway & 47th St. in the heart of the theater district.
No. 2 World Trade Center in the Wall St. area.
Both offices sell tickets for that day's Broadway shows at half price plus a small service charge ($1.50). The Broadway office is open from 10 a.m. to 2 p.m. for matinee tickets and from 3 p.m. to 8 p.m. for evening performances. Lines may start forming over an hour before the office opens, so go prepared to stand in line. If you're feeling daring, go about 15 minutes before curtain time; there probably won't be any line at all, and there should be four or five shows left to choose from. At the Broadway office, the line forms outside the office in the open air. You may find the World Trade Center office more convenient; it's open from 11 a.m. to 5:30 p.m., Monday through Friday; 11 a.m. to 3:30 p.m. Saturday; the lines are often shorter and they are *inside*. Note: don't count on being able to get tickets for the most current popular shows from TKTS.

MUSIC AND DANCE BOOTH: *Half-price tickets for everyone.* (212) 382-2323.
Bryant Park, 42nd St. & Ave. of the Americas.
Tickets for that day's performances.

"TWOFERS": *Approx. 30% discount.*

Twofers are coupons which allow the bearer to buy one or two tickets to a Broadway and off-Broadway performance at about a 30% discount. Twofers can be obtained at the New York Convention and Visitors Bureau's information centers, located at Times Square or 2 Columbus Circle, at many stores and hotels, and by mail from Hit Shows Club (send a stamped, self-addressed envelope to 300 W. 43rd St., NY, NY 10036). With twofers you can buy tickets in advance and choose your seat location—something you can't do with tickets from TKTS.

TV Shows: Write as far in advance as possible.

WABC: *Free tickets for live TV shows.*
Guest Relations, 36A W. 66th St., NY, NY 10023, (212) 887-3537.

WCBS: *Free tickets for live TV shows.*
CBS Tickets, 524 W. 57th St., NY, NY 10019, (212) 975-2476.

WNBC: *Free tickets for live TV shows.*
30 Rockefeller Plaza, NY, NY 10112, (212) 664-3055.

Movies

Nearly all movie theaters in New York City offer senior discounts to those over 60. Discounts are most frequently available weekdays before 5 p.m.; tickets usually cost between $2 and $3. Some theaters require you to buy a special senior ID for $1 or $2, but this will usually pay for itself the first time you use it. Theater chains offering discounts include Century, Cinema 5, Interboro, Loews, RKO, Walter Reade, and United Artists; see newspapers for details.

Sights

BRONX ZOO: *Free for over 65.*
Bronx Park, Fordham Rd. & Pelham Pkwy., (212) 367-1010.
March to October: daily, 10 a.m. to 5 p.m. Rest of year: 10 a.m. to 4:30 p.m.

LINCOLN CENTER TOUR: *10% discount.*
Leaves from Metropolitan Opera House, (212) 877-1800.
Daily, 10 a.m. to 5 p.m. One-and-a-half-hour tour covers Metropolitan Opera House, New York State Theater, Alice Tully Hall, Vivian Beaumont Theater, and the Juilliard School.

NEW YORK AQUARIUM: *Free over 65. Weekdays after 2 p.m.*
Daily, 10 a.m. to 6 p.m. in summer, until 5 p.m. rest of year.

NEW YORK BOTANICAL GARDEN CONSERVATORY: *50% discount.*
Bronx Park, entrance at Southern Blvd., (212) 220-8700.
Tuesday to Sunday, 10 a.m. to 5 p.m.

ROCKEFELLER CENTER OBSERVATION ROOF: *15% discount.*
70th floor of RCA Bldg., 30 Rockefeller Plaza, (212) 489-2947.
April to September: daily, 10 a.m. to 9 p.m. Rest of year: daily, 11 a.m. to 7 p.m.

ROCKEFELLER CENTER TOUR: *10% discount.*
Leaves from RCA Bldg. lounge, (212) 489–2947.
Monday to Saturday, every 30 to 45 minutes. Tour includes RCA Bldg. and Observation Roof, and Radio City Music Hall backstage.

STATEN ISLAND FERRY: *10¢ for seniors.*
Battery Park, South Ferry, (212) 248-8097. Fabulous views of New York Harbor.

WAVE HILL ENVIRONMENTAL CENTER: *50% discount on weekends.*
249th St. & Independence Ave., Bronx, (212) 549-2055.
Gardens, restored mansions, outdoor sculpture. Overlooking Hudson River. Special events in summer.

WORLD TRADE CENTER OBSERVATION DECK: *50% discount.*
Liberty & West Sts., (212) 466-7397.
Daily, 9 a.m. to 9 p.m.

Museums

Note: Virtually every museum in New York is closed on Monday.

AMERICAN CRAFTS MUSEUM: *50% discount.*
77 W. 45th St., (212) 391-8770.
Monday to Saturday, 10 a.m. to 5 p.m.; Sunday, 11 a.m. to 5 p.m.

AMERICAN MUSEUM OF NATURAL HISTORY: *Seniors pay what they wish ($1.50 suggested).*
Central Park W. & 79th St., (212) 873-4225.
Monday, Tuesday, Thursday, Sunday, 10 a.m. to 6 p.m.; Wednesday, Friday, Saturday, 10 a.m. to 9 p.m.

BROOKLYN MUSEUM: *50% discount.*
Washington Ave. & Eastern Pkwy., (718) 638-5000.
Wednesday to Saturday, 10 a.m. to 5 p.m.; Sunday, noon to 5 p.m. Major collection of Oriental, American, and Middle Eastern art.

THE CLOISTERS: *50% discount.*
Ft. Tryon Park, (212) 923-3700.
Tuesday to Saturday, 10 a.m. to 4:45 p.m.; Sunday noon to 4:45 p.m. Medieval art housed in a building constructed from five medieval cloisters.

COOPER-HEWITT MUSEUM, NATIONAL MUSEUM OF DESIGN: *50% discount.*
2 E. 91st St., (212) 860-6868.
Wednesday to Saturday, 10 a.m. to 5 p.m.; Tuesday, 10 a.m. to 9 p.m.; Sunday, noon to 5 p.m. Free on Tuesday evening.

FRICK COLLECTION: *50% discount.*
1 E. 70th St., (212) 288-0700.
Wednesday to Saturday, 10 a.m. to 6 p.m. Sunday, 1 p.m. to 6 p.m. Fourteenth- to nineteenth-century art displayed in former house of Henry Clay Frick.

GUGGENHEIM MUSEUM: *35% discount.*
1071 5th Ave., (212) 360-3500.
Wednesday to Sunday, 11 a.m. to 5 p.m.; Tuesday, 11 a.m. to 8 p.m. Nineteenth- and twentieth-century art displayed in an unusual building designed by Frank Lloyd Wright.

INTERNATIONAL CENTER OF PHOTOGRAPHY: *50% discount.*
1130 5th Ave., (212) 860-1777.
Tuesday to Friday, noon to 5 p.m.; Saturday, Sunday, 11 a.m. to 6 p.m.

JEWISH MUSEUM: *30% discount.*
1109 5th Ave., (212) 860-1888.
Monday to Thursday, noon to 5 p.m.; Sunday, 11 a.m. to 6 p.m.

METROPOLITAN MUSEUM OF ART: *50% discount.*
Fifth Ave. & 82nd St., (212) 535-7710.
Wednesday to Saturday, 10 a.m. to 4:45 p.m.; Tuesday, 10 a.m. to 8:45 p.m.; Sunday, 11 a.m. to 4:45 p.m. The most comprehensive art collection in America.

MUSEUM OF AMERICAN FOLK ART: *50% discount.*
125 W. 55th St., (212) 851-2474.
Tuesday to Sunday, 10:30 a.m. to 5:30 p.m.

MUSEUM OF THE AMERICAN INDIAN: *50% discount.*
Broadway & W. 155th, (212) 283-2420.
Tuesday to Saturday, 10 a.m. to 5 p.m.; Sunday, 1 to 5 p.m.

MUSEUM OF HOLOGRAPHY: *45% discount.*
11 Mercer St., (212) 925-0526.
Wednesday to Sunday, noon to 6 p.m. Laser art.

MUSEUM OF MODERN ART: *60% discount.*
11 W. 53rd St., (212) 708-9480.
Tuesday to Saturday, 11 a.m. to 6 p.m.; Thursday, 11 a.m .to 9 p.m.; Sunday, noon to 6 p.m.

SOUTH ST. SEAPORT MUSEUM: *60% discount.*
Fulton & South Sts., (212) 669-9400.
Daily. Restored ships and shops.

STUDIO MUSEUM IN HARLEM: *65% discount.*
144 W. 125 St., (212) 864-4500.
Wednesday to Friday, 10 a.m. to 6 p.m.; Saturday, Sunday, 1 p.m. to 6 p.m.

THEATRE MUSEUM: *50% discount.**
Minskoff Arcade, 44th St. near Broadway, (212) 944-7161.
Wednesday to Saturday, noon to 8 p.m.; Sunday, 1 p.m. to 5 p.m.

WHITNEY MUSEUM OF AMERICAN ART: *50% discount for over 62.*
945 Madison Ave., (212) 570-3676.
Wednesday to Saturday, 11 a.m. to 6 p.m.; Tuesday 11 a.m. to 8 p.m.; Sunday and holidays, noon to 6 p.m.

Free!

American Stock Exchange, Brooklyn Botanical Garden, Brooklyn Children's Museum, Fraunces Tavern Museum, Museum of the City of New York, New York Botanical Garden, New York Public Library, New York Shakespeare Festival, New York Stock Exchange, Police Museum

800 NUMBERS ARE SUPER SAVERS!
See the first two chapters for the 800 numbers of all the major hotel, car rental, tour, and airline companies; 800 numbers are listed where available in the state-by-state listings for the state tourist offices. Use 800 numbers whenever possible to obtain information and make reservations. If no 800 number is provided, be sure to call 800 information at 1 (800) 555-1212, and ask—it's a free call too!

NIAGARA FALLS (U.S. and Canadian)

Helpful Address

NIAGARA FALLS CONVENTION & VISITORS BUREAU
345 3rd St., Niagara Falls, NY 14303
(716) 278-8010.

Hotels

BEST WESTERN: *10% discount.*
New York, 7001 Buffalo Ave., (716) 283-7612.

HOLIDAY INN/HOLIDOME: *10%–20% discount with Holiday Inn's Travel Venture Club Card.*
114 Buffalo Ave., (716) 285-2521.

HOWARD JOHNSON'S: *15%–50% discount with H.J.'s Road Rally Card.*
New York, 454 Main St., (716) 285-5261.
New York, 6505 Niagara Falls Blvd., (716) 283-8791.

QUALITY INN: *10% discount for over 60.*
New York, 443 Main St., (716) 284-8801.
Ontario, 4946 Clifton Hill, (416) 358-3601.
Ontario, Comfort Inn, (416) 356-2461.

RAMADA INN: *25% discount for over 60.*
New York, 401 Buffalo Ave., (716) 285-2541.

SHARON AAA MOTEL: *10% discount after first night.*
New York, 7560 Niagara Falls Blvd., (716) 283-5646.

SUMMIT MOTOR INN: *10% discount.*
New York, 9500 Niagara Falls Blvd., (716) 297-5050.

SUMMIT PARK COURT MOTEL: *10% discount.*
New York, 2305 Niagara Falls Blvd., (716) 731-5336.

TRAVELODGE: *Special senior rates for Travelodge's Golden Guest Club.*
New York, 200 Rainbow Blvd., (716) 285-7316.
Ontario, 5591 Victoria Ave., (416) 357-1626, (800) 263-2552.

WALDORF NIAGARA MOTOR LODGE: *15% discount; reservations required.*
795 Rainbow Blvd., (716) 284-9778.

Camping

NORTON'S MOTEL & CAMPSITE: *$1 discount for over 62 with* Discount Guide.
2405 Niagara Falls Blvd., Niagara Falls, NY 14304.

Restaurants

MOM'S FAMILY RESTAURANT: *10% discount for 65 and over.*
US 62, Mil-Pine Shopping Center, (716) 297-6031.

THE RED COACH INN RESTAURANT: *10% discount for over 65.*
2 Buffalo Ave., (716) 282-1459.

Sights

AQUARIUM OF NIAGARA FALLS: *30% discount.*
701 Whirlpool St., (716) 285-3575.
Daily, 9 a.m. to 7 p.m. in summer; 9 a.m. to 5 p.m. rest of year.

OLD FORT NIAGARA: *30% discount.*
Moses Parkway, Youngstown, NY, (716) 745-7611.
Summer, daily, 9 a.m. to 7:30 p.m.; winter, 9 a.m. to 4:30 p.m.

GRAY LINE OF BUFFALO: *10% discount.*
5355 Junction Rd., Lockport, NY 14094, (716) 625-9211.
Year-round tours of the falls.

SKYLON TOWER: *50% discount.*
5200 Robinson St., Ontario, (416) 356-2651.
Views of Canadian and American falls.

Museums

NATIVE AMERICAN CENTER FOR THE LIVING ARTS (THE TURTLE): *33% discount.*
25 Rainbow Mall, NY, (716) 284-2427.
Summer, daily, 10 a.m. to 8 p.m. Call for rest of year.

NIAGARA FALLS MUSEUM: *30% discount.*
5651 River Rd., Ontario, (416) 356-2151.
Daily, summer, 8:30 a.m. to midnight; rest of year, 9 a.m. to 6 p.m.

NIAGARA WAX MUSEUM: *30% discount.*
301 Prospect St., (716) 285-1271.
Summer, daily, 9 a.m. to 11 p.m.; rest of year, 9 a.m. to 5 p.m. Closed in winter.

Free!

The annual Niagara Summer Experience festival (July to August), the annual Niagara Falls Festival of Lights (Thanksgiving to New Year), Niagara Wine Cellars, New York State Power Vista and Visitor Center, Our Lady of Fatima Shrine, Schoellkopf Geological Museum, the Wintergarden at Rainbow Mall.

NORTH CAROLINA

Helpful Addresses

NORTH CAROLINA TRAVEL AND TOURISM DIVISION
P.O. Box 25249, 430 N. Salisbury St., Raleigh, NC 27611
(919) 733-4171, (800) 438-4404 (except NC), (800) 847-4862 (NC)

DIVISION ON AGING
1985 Umpstead Dr., Kirby Bldg., Raleigh, NC 27603
(919) 733-3983

Senior Tarheel Discount Program

The North Carolina Division on Aging and the State of North Carolina sponsor an extensive state-wide discount program for state residents over 60. Write to the local county councils on aging for further information about this program.

RALEIGH

Helpful Address

COUNCIL ON AGING OF WAKE COUNTY, INC.
401 E. Whitaker Mill Rd., Raleigh, NC 27608.
This office publishes an extensive list of discounts available in the Raleigh area, including drug and clothing stores, beauty and barbershops, and over 35 restaurants, some of which are listed below. Send $1 for postage and handling, or stop in for a free copy.

Hotels

BEST WESTERN: *10% discount.*
3901 S. Wilmington St., (919) 772-8900.

DAYS INN: *10%–50% discount with Days Inn September Days Club card.*
6329 Glenwood Ave. (US Hwy. 70 W.), (919) 781-7904.

ECONOLODGE: *10% discount with Econo Senior Class Card.*
3600 Wake Forest Rd., (919) 872-9300.
Oak Park Shopping Center, 5110 Holly Ridge Dr., (919) 782-3201.
309 Hillsborough St., (919) 833-5771.

HOLIDAY INN: *10%–20% discount with Holiday Inn's Travel Venture Club Card.*
Downtown, 320 Hillsborough, (919) 832-0501.
North, US 1 & Rte. 401 N., (919) 872-7666.

HOWARD JOHNSON'S: *15%–50% discount with H.J.'s Road Rally Card.*
North, US 1 & Rte. 401, (919) 872-5000.
West, US 70 & the Beltline, (919) 782-8600.

QUALITY INN: *10% discount for over 60.*
The Plantation Inn, US 1, (919) 876-1411.
Comfort Inn, 4220 Six Forks Rd., (919) 787-2300.
Comfort Inn, 3921 Arrow Dr., (919) 782-7071.

RAMADA INN: *25% discount for over 60.*
Hwy. 55 and US 1 S., (919) 362-8621.

SHERATON: *25% discount for over 60.*
4501 Creedmoor Rd. (US Hwy. 70 W.), (919) 787-7111.
2805 Highwoods Blvd., (919) 872-3500.

Public Transportation

CAPITAL AREA TRANSIT (Raleigh City Bus): *50% discount for over 65. Use Medicare card for ID.*

Transportation

TRANSIT SYSTEMS, INC. (Taxi): *10% discount for holders of Tarheel card.* (919) 790-9846.

Car Rental

AVIS: *5%–25% discount.**
Raleigh-Durham Airport, P.O. Box 1084, Durham, (919) 840-4750.

HERTZ: *5%–25% discount.**
Raleigh-Durham Airport, (919) 787-6112.
1602 Wake Forest Rd., (919) 834-0702.

NATIONAL: *10%–12% discount for over 62.*
Raleigh-Durham Airport, (919) 787-9100.

Restaurants

CHAR-GRILL: *10% discount with Senior Tarheel card.*
616 Hillsborough St., (919) 821-7636.

CIRCUS FAMILY RESTAURANT: *10% discount after 2 p.m. with Senior Tarheel card.*
1600 Wake Forest Road, (919) 834-2213.

CREEKSIDE SEAFOOD: *10% discount and specials for over 60.*
Creekside Dr., (919) 828-8333.

DON MURRAY'S BARBECUE: *Free beverage with meal for 60 and over with Senior Tarheel card.*
2751 N. Boulevard, (919) 872-6270.
2109 Avent Ferry Road, (919) 832-9100.

**An asterisk indicates that the discount is intended for members of senior citizens' organizations that anyone can join. See "Hotel, Transportation, and Sightseeing Discounts."*

FIVE POINTS RESTAURANT: *10% discount to retired persons with Senior Tarheel card.*
1620½ Glenwood Ave., (919) 829-9439.

GOLDEN SKILLET RESTAURANT: *Free small drink with purchase of meal for over 60.*
Several locations.

HARDEE'S: *10% discount with Senior Tarheel card.*
Several locations.

NEWTON'S GRILL AND DELI: *10% discount for over 65 with Senior Tarheel card.*
601 Halifax St., (919) 833-1918.

PIZZA HUT: *10% discount on pizza for over 60.*
Many locations.

PIZZA INN: *10% discount for 60 and over.*
Several locations.
Wednesday, Thursday, Sunday nights.

SIZZLER FAMILY STEAKHOUSE: *20% discount for over 60 on Wednesday and Sunday; 2 p.m. to 5 p.m. daily.*
601 W. Pearce St., (919) 834-0929.
3100 Old Wake Forest Rd., (919) 876-7694.

WENDY'S OLD FASHIONED HAMBURGERS: *10% discount with Senior Tarheel card.*
Several locations.

WESTERN STEER RESTAURANT: *20% discount for over 60 with Senior Tarheel card.*
Hwy. 70, (919) 781-6495.

Theater & Symphony

NORTH CAROLINA SYMPHONY: *$3 discount for over 62.*
P.O. Box 28026, (919) 733-2750.

RALEIGH LITTLE THEATRE: *Discount prices for 65 and over; Musicals—$4 weeknights, $6 weekends, $2 Sunday matinees. Nonmusicals—$3 weeknights, $5 weekends. Reservations required.*
Pogue St., (919) 821-3111.

Movies

CINEMA I AND II: *$2.50 discount price.*
Western Blvd. & Avent Ferry, (919) 834-8520.

IMPERIAL CINEMA IV THEATERS: *$2.50 discount price.*
Cary Village Square Shopping Center, (919) 469-0009.

VALLEY TWIN THEATRES: *$2.50 for matinees during first hour box office opens.*
Crabtree Valley Shopping Center, (919) 782-6948.

Free!

North Carolina Museum of Art, North Carolina Museum of History, North Carolina Museum of Natural History, State Capitol

NORTH DAKOTA

Helpful Addresses

NORTH DAKOTA TOURISM PROMOTION
Capitol Grounds, Bismarck, ND 58505
(701) 224-2525 or (800) 437-2077 (out-of-state);
(800) 472-2100 (North Dakota only)

AGING SERVICES
State Capitol Building, Bismarck, ND 58505
(701) 224-2577

BISMARCK

Hotels

BEST WESTERN: *10% discount.*
122 E. Thayer, (701) 255-1450.
800 S. 3rd St., (701) 258-7700.

HOLIDAY INN: *10%–20% discount with Holiday Inn's Travel Venture Club Card.*
W. Bismarck at Memorial Bridge, (701) 223-9600.

QUALITY INN: *10% discount for over 60.*
Comfort Inn, 1030 Interstate Ave., (701) 223-1911.

RAMADA INN: *25% discount for over 60.*
1400 E. Interchange, (701) 258-7000.

SHERATON: *25% discount for over 60.*
6th & Broadway, (701) 255-6000.

Car Rental

AVIS: *5%–25% discount.**
1801 E. Main St., (701) 255-0707.

HERTZ: *5%–25% discount.**
931 S. 9th St., (701) 223-3977.

NATIONAL: *10%–12% discount for over 62.*
Airport, (701) 223-2380.

Restaurants

COUNTRY KITCHEN: *10% discount for over 65.*
Hwy. 83 N. at Interchange Ave., (701) 258-3470.

MC DOWELL'S BIG BOY: *10% discount with proof of age.*
2511 E. Main St., (701) 223-4125.

Movie Theaters

PLAZA THREE THEATRES: *Discount.*
P.O. Box 1622.

Free!

Camp Hancock State Historic Society, North Dakota State Museum, State Capitol

---

FARGO

Hotels

BEST WESTERN: *10% discount.*
3333 13th Ave. S., (701) 235-3333.

Public Transportation

FARGO CITY BUS SYSTEM: *50% discount for over 60.*
201 N. 4th, (701) 232-7500.

Car Rental

AVIS: *5%–25% discount.**
Hector Airport, (701) 237-6753.

HERTZ: *5%–25% discount.**
Hector Airport, (701) 241-1533.

NATIONAL: *10%–12% discount for over 62.*
Hector Airport, (701) 237-9061.

OHIO

Helpful Addresses

TRAVEL OHIO
P.O. 1001, Columbus, OH 43216
(614) 466-8844, (800) BUCKEYE

DEPARTMENT ON AGING
50 W. Broad St., 9th Fl., Columbus, OH 43215
(614) 466-5500

Golden Buckeye Card/Silver Savers Passport

Thousands of Ohioans aged 60 and over use the Golden Buckeye Card, issued by the Ohio Commission on Aging (address above), to obtain discounts in Ohio. Ramada Inns across the nation honor the Silver Savers Passport (on the reverse side of the Golden Buckeye Card), as do Hertz locations worldwide.

CINCINNATI

Hotels

BEST WESTERN: *10% discount.*
3356 Central Pkwy., (513) 559-1600.
I-75 & Donaldson Rd., (606) 342-6200.

CINCINNATI MARRIOTT: *50% discount for Marriott Leisure Life members.*
11320 Chester Rd., (513) 772-1720.

800 NUMBERS ARE SUPER SAVERS!
See the first two chapters for the 800 numbers of all the major hotel, car rental, tour, and airline companies; 800 numbers are listed where available in the state-by-state listings for the state tourist offices. Use 800 numbers whenever possible to obtain information and make reservations. If no 800 number is provided, be sure to call 800 information at 1 (800) 555-1212, and ask—it's a free call too!

DAYS INN: *10%–50% discount with Days Inn September Days Club card.*
Ft. Wright, 1945 Dixie Hwy., (606) 341-8801.
Monroe, I-75 & Rte. 63, (513) 539-9221.
Richwood, I-75 & Rte. 338, (606) 485-4151.

HARLEY HOTEL: *10% discount.*
8020 Montgomery Rd., (513) 793-4300, (800) 321-2323.

HOLIDAY INN: *10%–20% discount with Holiday Inn's Travel Venture Club Card.*
Downtown, 8th & Linn, (513) 241-8660.
Hamilton-Fairfield, 4670 Dixie Hwy., (513) 829-7000.
Middletown, I-75 & Rte. 122, (513) 424-1201.
North, 2235 Sharon Rd., (513) 771-0700.
Northeast, I-71 & Fields-Ertel Rd., Mason, (513) 721-2634.
Riverfront, 600 W. 3rd St., Covington, KY, (606) 291-4300.
South, 2100 Dixie Hwy., Fort Mitchell, KY, (606) 331-1500.

HOWARD JOHNSON'S: *15%–50% discount with H.J.'s Road Rally Card.*
Airport, 630 Commonwealth Ave., (606) 727-3400.
East, 5410 Ridge Rd., (513) 631-8500.

LA QUINTA: *20% discount.*
11335 Chester Rd., (513) 772-3140.

QUALITY INN: *10% discount for over 60.*
Covington, KY, 666 5th St., (606) 491-1200.
Norwood, 4747 Montgomery Rd., (513) 351-6000.

RADISSON INN: *25% discount.**
11440 Chester Rd., (513) 771-3400.

RAMADA INN: *25% discount for over 60.*
Northeast, 5901 Pfeiffer Rd., (513) 793-4500.
Sharonville, 11029 Dowlin Dr., (513) 771-0300.

RODEWAY INN: *10% discount.*
400 Glensprings Dr., (513) 825-3129.

TRAVELODGE: *Special senior rates for Travelodge's Golden Guest Club.*
3244 Central Pkwy., (513) 559-1800.

Car Rental

AVIS: *5%–25% discount.**
Greater Cincinnati Airport, (606) 283-3764.
Downtown, 212 W. Fourth St., (513) 621-1479.

HERTZ: *5%–25% discount.**
Greater Cincinnati Airport, (606) 283-3535.
Westin Fountain Sq. S., (513) 241-8079.

NATIONAL: *10%–12% discount for over 62.*
Airport, (606) 283-3655.
628 Walnut St., (606) 621-0202.

Sights

CINCINNATI ZOO: *50% discount.*
3400 Vine St., (513) 281-4701.
Memorial Day to Labor Day: daily, 9 a.m. to 6 p.m. Rest of year: 9 a.m. to 5 p.m.

Museums

CINCINNATI ART MUSEUM: *50% discount.*
Eden Park, (513) 721-5204.
Tuesday to Saturday, 10 a.m. to 5 p.m.; Sunday, 1 p.m. to 5 p.m.

CONTEMPORARY ARTS CENTER: *50% discount.*
115 E. 5th St., (513) 721-0390.
Tuesday to Saturday, 10 a.m. to 5 p.m.; Sunday, noon to 5 p.m.

SHARON WOODS VILLAGE: *50% discount.*
Sharonville, Rte. 42, (513) 563-8494.
May to October; closed Monday and Friday. 19th-century restoration.

Free!

Harriet Beecher Stowe Memorial, Taft Museum, William Howard Taft Historical Site, Krohn Conservatory, Mt. Airy Arboretum, Tours of Meier's Wine Cellars

CLEVELAND

Bed & Breakfast Reservation Service

PRIVATE LODGINGS INC.: *10% discount at the Tudor House for* Discount Guide *readers over 60. Write for application.*
P.O. Box 18590, Cleveland, OH 44118, (216) 321-3213.

Hotels

HOLIDAY INN: *10%–20% discount with Holiday Inn's Travel Venture Club Card.*
Airport, 16501 Brookpark, (216) 267–1700.
Beachwood, 3750 Orange Pl., (216) 831-3300.
Independence, 6001 Rockside Rd., (216) 524-8050.
Mayfield, 780 Beta Dr., (216) 461-9200.
North Randall, 4600 Northfield, (216) 663-4100.
Wickliffe, 28500 Euclid Ave., (216) 585-2750.

KNIGHTS INN: *10% discount.*
Broadview Hgts., I-77 at S.R. 82, (216) 526-0640.
Mentor, I-90 at S.R. 306, (216) 953-8835.

QUALITY INN: *10% discount for over 60.*
Airport, 16161 Brookpark Rd., Brookpark, (216) 267-5100.
Wickliffe, 28600 Ridgehills Dr., (216) 585-0600.

RAMADA INN: *25% discount for over 60.*
Aqua Marine Resort, 216 Miller Rd., Avon Lake, (216) 933-2000.
Southeast, 24801 Rockside Rd., (216) 439-2500.

SHERATON: *25% discount for over 60.*
Airport Grounds, 5300 Riverside Dr., (216) 267-1500.

Beachwood, 26300 Chagrin Blvd., (216) 831-5150.
Rocky River, 20375 Center Ridge Rd., (216) 333-6200.

Car Rental

AVIS: *5%–25% discount.**
Airport, (216) 265-3700.
Downtown, 1180 Lakeside Ave., (216) 623-0800.

HERTZ: *5%–25% discount.**
Airport, (216) 267-8900.
Lincoln Parking Garage, 708 St. Clair, (216) 696-6066.

NATIONAL: *10%–12% discount for over 62.*
Airport, (216) 267-0060.

Free!

Cleveland Institute of Art, Cleveland Museum of Art, Howard Dittrick Museum of Historical Medicine, Lake Erie Nature Science Center, NASA Information Center, Rockefeller Park Gardens & Greenhouse, Temple Museum of Religious Art

TOLEDO

Helpful Address

GREATER TOLEDO OFFICE OF TOURISM AND CONVENTIONS
218 Huron St., Toledo, OH 43604, (419) 243-8191

Hotels

HOLIDAY INN: *10%–20% discount with Holiday Inn's Travel Venture Club Card.*
Riverview, Summit & Jefferson, (419) 243-8860.
Southwest, 2429 S. Reynolds Rd. (I-80 & US 20), (419) 381-8765.

QUALITY INN: *10% discount for over 60.*
2426 Oregon Rd., (419) 666-2600.
1821 Manhattan Blvd., (419) 729-3901.

RAMADA INN: *25% discount for over 60.*
2340 S. Reynolds Rd., (419) 865-1361.

SHERATON: *25% discount for over 60.*
Sheraton Westgate Inn, 3536 Secor Rd., (419) 535-7070.

Public Transportation

TOLEDO AREA REGIONAL TRANSIT AUTHORITY: *35¢ discount for 65 and over with Medicare card.*

Car Rental

AVIS: *5%–25% discount.**
Toledo Express Airport, (419) 865-5541.

HERTZ: *5%–25% discount.**
Airport, (419) 865-1286.
505 Jefferson Ave., (419) 243-7193.

NATIONAL: *10%–12% discount for over 62.*
Airport, (419) 865-5513.

Restaurants

FRISCH'S BIG BOY: *Ask about reduced price "Golden Age" dinners.*
Several locations.

Theaters

TOLEDO REPERTOIRE THEATER: *$1 discount off regular season performances.*
16 Tenth St., (419) 243-9277.

WESTGATE DINNER THEATER: *$1 discount.*
Secor & W. Central Ave., (419) 537-1881.

Sights

FORT MEIGS: *20% discount with Golden Buckeye Card.*
State Rte. 65, Perrysburg, (419) 874-4121.
Mid-June to Labor Day: Wednesday to Sunday, 10 a.m. to 6 p.m. April to mid-June, and after Labor Day to October: Wednesday to Sunday, 9:30 a.m. to 5 p.m.

TOLEDO ZOO: *60% discount for over 65.*
2700 Broadway, (419) 385-4040.
April to September: daily, 10 a.m. to 5 p.m. October to March: daily, 10 a.m. to 4 p.m.

Museums

WOLCOTT HOUSE MUSEUM COMPLEX: *10% discount.*
1031 River Rd. S.W., Maumee, (419) 893-9602.
April to December: Wednesday to Sunday, 1 p.m. to 4 p.m.

Free!

Toledo Museum of Art *(Senior discount on guided tours).*

OKLAHOMA

Helpful Addresses

OKLAHOMA DIVISION OF TOURISM PROMOTION
500 Will Rogers Building, 215 N.E. 28th St., Oklahoma City, OK 73105, (405) 521-2409, (800) 652-6552.

OKLAHOMA CITY CONVENTION & TOURISM BUREAU
4 Santa Fe Plaza, Oklahoma City, OK 73102

SPECIAL UNIT ON AGING
P.O. Box 25352, Oklahoma City, OK 73125, (405) 521-2281

OKLAHOMA CITY

Discounts in the Oklahoma Area

The Senior Citizen Discount Directory is available for seniors in Oklahoma City and Tulsa. Contact the Special Unit on Aging (address above) or call (800) 252-6060.

Hotels (National Chains)

BEST WESTERN: *10% discount.*
1800 E. Reno Ave., (405) 235-4531.

DAYS INN: *10%–50% discount with Days Inn September Days Club card.*
4712 W. I-40, (405) 947-8721.

ECONOLODGE: *10% discount with Econo Senior Class Card.*
8217 S. I-35, (405) 632-0807.

HOLIDAY INN: *10%–20% discount with Holiday Inn's Travel Venture Club Card.*
Airport, I-40 at Meridian, (405) 942-8511.
East, 5701 Tinker Diagonal, (405) 737-4481.
North I-35, 120001 N.E. Expwy., (405) 478-0400.
Northwest, 3535 N.W. 39th Expwy., (405) 947-2351.

HOWARD JOHNSON'S: *15%–50% discount with H.J.'s Road Rally Card.*
North, 5301 N. Lincoln, (405) 528-7563.
Airport, 400 S. Meridian Ave., (405) 943-9841.

LA QUINTA: *20% discount.*
Southeast, 8315 S. I-35, (405) 631-8661.

RAMADA INN: *25% discount for over 60.*
Airport West, 800 S. Meridian, (405) 943-8155.
North, 2801 N.W. 39th, (405) 946-0741.
South, 6800 S. I-35, (405) 631-3321.

SHERATON: *25% discount for over 60.*
Sheraton-Century Center, Broadway & Main, (405) 235-2780.

Hotels (Local)

COACHMAN INNS: *10% discount.*
North, 6000 N. Bryant.
South, 1301 S.E. 4th.
West, 820 S. MacArthur.

CROSSWINDS INNS: *$5 off for AARP.*
Airport, 1224 S. Meridian.

DILLON INN: *10% discount.*
1905 S. Meridian.

GUEST HOUSE: *No tax for over 65.*
5200 Classen Blvd.

HAVANA INN: *10% discount for AARP.*
2200 N.W. 39th & Expwy.

MERIDIAN PLAZA HOTEL: *10% discount for AARP.*
2101 S. Meridian.

MYRIAD MOTOR INN: *25% discount for 60 and over.*
1305 Classen Dr.

ROCKWELL INN: *10% for AARP.*
321 S. Rockwell.

SOONER INN: *10% discount for AARP.*
1629 S. Prospect.

SUNDOWN MOTEL: *$5 off.*
I-35 & Wilshire.

TRADEWINDS: *10% discount.*
Central, 1800 E. Reno.

Public Transportation

CITY BUS: *50% discount for Oklahoma residents with Golden Age Bus ID ($1) for 62 and over.*
Call Masstran office, (405) 235-RIDE.

Car Rental

AVIS: *5%–25% discount.**
Will Rogers World Airport, (405) 685-7781.

HERTZ: *5%–25% discount.**
Will Rogers World Airport, (405) 681-2341.

NATIONAL: *10%–12% discount for over 62.*
Airport, (405) 685-7726.

Sights

ENTERPRISE SQUARE, USA: *30% discount.*
2501 E. Memorial Rd., (405) 478-5190, (800) 654-9245. Monday to Thursday, 9 a.m. to 4 p.m.; Friday, Saturday, 9 a.m. to 7 p.m.; Sunday noon to 3:30 p.m. Hands-on exhibits illustrate free enterprise.

FRONTIER CITY AMUSEMENT PARK: *$5 discount for 65 and over.*
11601 N.E. Expwy. (N. I-35 N), (405) 478-2412.

NATIONAL SOFTBALL HALL OF FAME AND MUSEUM: *50% discount.*
2801 N.E. 50th St., (405) 424-5266.

Monday to Friday, 8:30 a.m. to 5 p.m.; Saturday and Sunday, 10 a.m. to 4 p.m. Closed October 15 to March 15.

OKLAHOMA CITY ZOO: *$.50 off for 65 and over.*
N.E. 50 & Martin Luther King Ave., (405) 424-3344.

WHITE WATER: *$1 off for 65 and over.*
3908 West Reno, (405) 943-9687.

Museums

AIR SPACE MUSEUM: *$1 off for 65 and over.*
Kirkpatrick Center, 2100 N.E. 52, (405) 424-1443.

OKLAHOMA MUSEUM OF ART: *$.50 off for 62 and over.*
7316 Nichols Rd., (405) 840-2759.

OMNIPLEX: *$1.25 off for 65 and over.*
Kirkpatrick Center, 2110 N.E. 52nd St., (405) 424-5545.
Monday to Saturday, 10 a.m. to 5 p.m.; Sunday, noon to 5 p.m. Arts and science museum.

Free!

Harn Museum, Kirkpatrick Center, Oklahoma Historical Society, State Capitol, State Museum of Oklahoma, Will Rogers Park Garden Exhibition Building and Garden

OREGON

Helpful Addresses

OREGON STATE TRAVEL INFORMATION
595 Cottage St., N.E., Salem, OR 97310, (503) 378-3451, (800) 547-7842 (except OR), (800) 233-3306.

SENIOR SERVICES DIVISION
313 Public Service Bldg., 772 Commercial St., S.E., Salem, OR 97310, (503) 378-4728

PORTLAND

Hotels

BEST WESTERN: *10% discount.*
420 N.E. Holladay St., (503) 233-6331.
15700 S.W. Upper Boones Fry Rd., (503) 620-2980.

HOLIDAY INN: *10%–20% discount with Holiday Inn's Travel Venture Club Card.*
Airport, 82nd St. & Columbia Blvd., (503) 256-5000.

NENDEL'S: *10% discount for Vagabond's Club 55.*
9900 S.W. Canyon Rd., (503) 297-2551.
Airport, 7101 N.E. 82nd Ave., (503) 255-6722.

RAMADA INN: *25% discount for over 60.*
10 N. Weider St., (503) 239-9900.

RED LION INN: *10% discount for over 50.**
1225 N. Thunderbird Way, (503) 235–8311.
1401 N. Hayden Island Dr., (503) 283-2111.

SHERATON: *25% discount for over 60.*
Airport, 8235 N.E. Airport Way, (503) 281-2500.

TRAVELODGE: *Special senior rates for Travelodge's Golden Guest Club.*
Downtown, 949 E. Burnside St., (503) 234-8411.
Viscount, 1441 N.E. Second Ave., (503) 233-2401.

Car Rental

AVIS: *5%–25% discount.**
Portland Airport, (503) 249-4950.

HERTZ: *5%–25% discount.**
Airport, (503) 249-8216.

NATIONAL: *10%–12% discount for over 62.*
Airport, (503) 249-4900.
620 W. Burnside, (503) 228-6637.

Sights

PITTOCK MANSION: *25% discount.*
3229 N.W. Pittock Dr., (503) 248-4469.
Daily, call for hours. Mansions and gardens; fabulous views.

SANCTUARY OF OUR SORROWFUL MOTHER: *Free.*
N.E. Sandy Blvd. & 85th Ave., (503) 254-7371.
October to April, 10 a.m. to 4 p.m. May to September, 9 a.m. to 7 p.m. Grotto and gardens maintained by Servite Order.

Tours for Seniors
Request information and tour schedules from your national senior citizens' organization and from *Saga International Holidays, Ltd.*, 120 Boylston St., Boston, MA 02116, (800) 343-0273 (except MA); *Grand Circle Travel*, 555 Madison Ave., New York, NY 10022, (800) 221-2610; AARP Travel Service, P.O. Box 92337, Los Angeles, CA 90009, (800) 227-7737; *Passages Unlimited*, 48 Union St., Stamford, CT 06906, (800) 472-7724; 50+ Young at Heart Program, *American Youth Hostels*, Travel Department, P.O. Box 37613, Washington, D.C. 20013, (202) 783-6161; *Interhostel*, Continuing Education, University of New Hampshire, Durham, NH 03824, (603) 862-1147.

WASHINGTON PARK JAPANESE GARDEN: *50% discount for over 65.*
W. Burnside St. to Canyon Rd., (503) 223-1321.
Memorial Day to Labor Day: Tuesday to Saturday, 10 a.m. to 6 p.m.; Sunday, 10 a.m. to 8 p.m. April & May, and after Labor Day to October: Tuesday to Friday, 10 a.m. to 4 p.m.; Saturday & Sunday, noon to 6 p.m.

WASHINGTON PARK ZOO: *50% discount over 65.*
4001 S.W. Canyon Rd., (503) 226-1561.
Summer: daily, 9:30 a.m. to 7 p.m. Winter: daily, 9:30 a.m. to 4 p.m.

WESTERN FORESTRY CENTER: *50% discount.*
4033 S.W. Canyon Rd., (503) 228-1367.
Daily, 10 a.m. to 5 p.m.

Museums

OREGON MUSEUM OF SCIENCE AND INDUSTRY: *30% discount.*
4015 S.W. Canyon Rd., (503) 222-2828.
Mid-June to mid-September: daily, 9 a.m. to 6 p.m. Rest of year: daily, 9 a.m. to 5 p.m.

PORTLAND ART MUSEUM: *Free to 65 and over.*
1219 S.W. Park Ave., (503) 226-2811.
Daily except Monday, noon to 5 p.m.; Friday, noon to 10 p.m.

Package Tour for Seniors

A 16-day van tour that originates in Portland, American Youth Hostels' 50+ "Northwest Borderline" tour moves up the Olympic Peninsula and Puget Sound to Victoria and Vancouver, BC, returning to Portland along the Columbia River ($585 from Portland), (202) 783-6161 for information.

Free

Crystal Springs Rhododendron Gardens, Georgia Pacific Historical Museum, Hoyt Arboretum, Oregon Historical Museum, Pendleton Woolen Mills

PENNSYLVANIA

Helpful Addresses

PENNSYLVANIA BUREAU OF TRAVEL DEVELOPMENT
416 Forum Bldg., Harrisburg, PA 17120
(717) 787-5453 or (800) 847-4872

DEPARTMENT OF AGING
231 State St., Harrisburg, PA 17101
(717) 783-1550

LANCASTER AND PENNSYLVANIA DUTCH COUNTRY

Helpful Address

PENNSYLVANIA DUTCH VISITORS BUREAU
501 Greenfield Rd., Lancaster, PA 17601, (717) 299-8901.

Hotels

BEST WESTERN: *10% discount.*
Carlisle, 1245 Harrisburg Pike, (717) 243-5411.

BRUNSWICK MOTOR INN: *10% discount with advance reservations.*
Chestnut & Queen Sts., P.O. Box 749, Lancaster, PA 17604, (717) 397-4801.

HOLIDAY INN: *10%–20% discount with Holiday Inn's Travel Venture Club Card.*
1492 Lititz Pike, (717) 393-0771.
Rte. 30 & Hempstead Rd., (717) 299-2551.
Ephrata, I-76 & US 272, (215) 267-7541.

HOWARD JOHNSON'S: *15%–50% discount with H.J.'s Road Rally Card.*
Reading, PA 272 at PA Tnpk., Exit 21, (215) 267-7563.

QUALITY INN: *10% discount for over 60.*
500 Centerville Rd., (717) 898-2431.

TRAVELODGE: *Special senior rates for Travelodge's Golden Guest Club.*
2101 Columbia Ave., (717) 397-4201.

TREADWAY RESORT INN: *10% discount.**
222 Eden Rd., (717) 569-6444.

Car Rental

AVIS: *5%–25% discount.**
Lancaster Municipal Airport, (717) 569-3185.

HERTZ: *5%–25% discount.**
229 Queen St., (717) 397-2896.

NATIONAL: *10%–12% discount for over 62.*
121 E. Liberty St., (717) 394-2158.

Theater

FULTON OPERA HOUSE: *Discount available for most performances.*
12 N. Prince St., Lancaster, (717) 397-7425.

Sights

ABE'S BUGGY RIDES: *10% discount for 60 and over.*
Strasburg Rd., Lancaster, (717) 687-0360.

**An asterisk indicates that the discount is intended for members of senior citizens' organizations that anyone can join. See "Hotel, Transportation, and Sightseeing Discounts."*

DUTCH WONDERLAND: *$1.50 to $3.50 discount for over 60.*
2249 Rte. 30 E., Lancaster, (717) 291-1888.

Museums

AMISH VILLAGE: *$.25 discount for 62 and over*
Route 896, Strasburg, (717) 687-8511.
Open daily, 9 a.m. to 7 p.m. in summer; until 5 p.m. spring and fall.

EPHRATA CLOISTER: *$.75 discount.*
632 W. Main St., Ephrata, (717) 733-6600.
Tuesday to Saturday, 9 a.m. to 5 p.m.; Sunday, noon to 5 p.m.

FOLK CRAFT CENTER: *$.50 discount.*
441 Mt. Sidney Rd., Witmer, (717) 397-3609.

HERITAGE CENTER OF LANCASTER COUNTY: *$.25 discount.*
Old City Hall, King & Queen Sts., Lancaster, (717) 299-6440.
Tuesday to Saturday, 10 a.m. to 4 p.m., May to mid-November.

MILL BRIDGE VILLAGE: *$1 discount.*
S. Ronks Rd., Strasburg, (717) 687-8181.
Monday to Saturday, 10 a.m. to 5 p.m., closed January through March. Restored 18th-century village.

PENNSYLVANIA FARM MUSEUM OF LANDIS VALLEY: *$1 discount.*
2451 Kissel Hill Rd., (717) 569-0401.
Tuesday to Saturday: Summer, 9 a.m. to 5 p.m.; rest of year, 10 a.m. to 4:30 p.m.

RAILROAD MUSEUM OF PENNSYLVANIA: *33% discount.*
Strasburg, (717) 687-8628.
Monday to Saturday, 10 a.m. to 5 p.m.; Sunday, 11 a.m. to 5 p.m.

TOY TRAIN MUSEUM: *33% discount.*
Paradise Lane, Strasburg, (717) 687-8976.
Summer, daily, 10 a.m. to 5 p.m.; weekends in spring and fall.

WATCH AND CLOCK MUSEUM: *50% discount.*
514 Poplar St., Columbia, (717) 684-8261.
Monday to Saturday, 9 a.m. to 5 p.m.

Free!

Anderson Pretzel Bakery, Herr's Snack Factory, Mennonite Information Center, Nissley's Vineyards, Phillips Swiss Cheese Company

---

PHILADELPHIA AND VICINITY

Helpful Address

PHILADELPHIA CONVENTION & VISITORS BUREAU
3 Penn Center Plaza, (215) 636-3319.

Hotels

BEST WESTERN: *10% discount.*
4100 Presidential Blvd., (215) 477-0200.

DAYS INN: *10%–50% discount with Days Inn September Days card.*
Airport, 2 Gateway Center, (215) 492-0400.

GEORGE WASHINGTON LODGES: *Discount for AARP.*
King of Prussia, Rte. 202, (215) 265-6100.

HOLIDAY INN: *10%–20% discount with Holiday Inn's Travel Venture Club Card.*
Airport South, 45 Industrial Hwy., Essington, (215) 521-2400.
Center City, 1800 Market, (215) 561-7500.
Independence Mall, 400 Arch St., (215) 923-8660.
Midtown, 1305–11 Walnut St., (215) 735-9300.
Valley Forge, King of Prussia, 260 Goddard Blvd., (215) 265-7500.

HOWARD JOHNSON'S: *15%–50% discount with H.J.'s Road Rally Card.*
Airport South, I-95 at PA-320 and PA-352, (215) 876-7211.
King of Prussia, Rte. 202 N. & S. Guelph Rd., (215) 265-4500.

MARRIOTT: *50% discount for Marriott Leisure Life members.*
Airport, 4509 Island Ave., (215) 365-4150.

RAMADA INN: *25% discount for over 60.*
Fort Washington, 285 Commerce Dr., (215) 542-7930.

SHERATON: *25% discount for over 60.*
Northeast, 9641 Roosevelt Blvd., (215) 671-9600.
University City, 36th & Chestnut Sts., (215) 387-8000.
Valley Forge, Rte. 363, King of Prussia, (215) 337-2000.

TREADWAY INN: *10% discount.**
4200 Roosevelt Blvd., (215) 289-9200.

TREVOSE HILTON: *25% discount subject to advance reservation and availability.*
2400 Old Lincoln Hwy., (215) 638-8300.

Public Transportation

SEPTA: *Free except during rush hours. Show Medicare card.*

FAIRMONT PARK TROLLEY: *33% discount for 65 and over.*
Mailing address: Memorial Hall, West Park, Philadelphia, PA 19131, (215) 879-4044. Wednesday through Sunday, 9:30 a.m. to 4 p.m.

Car Rental

AVIS: *5%–25% discount.**
Airport, (215) 492-0900.
2000 Arch St., (215) 563-8980.

DOLLAR: *10% discount.**
Airport, (800) 421-6868.

HERTZ: *5%–25% discount.**
Airport, (215) 492-7205.
30th St. Station, (215) 492-2958.

NATIONAL: *10%–12% discount for over 62.*
Holiday Inn, 36th & Chestnut, (215) 382-6504.

Restaurants

DICKENS INN: *$5 off one dinner entrée on presentation of* Discount Guide; *available Monday to Thursday evenings except December.*
2nd & Pine Sts., (215) 928-9307.

GOLD STANDARD CAFETERIA AND PALLADIUM RESTAURANT: *15% off with* Discount Guide.
3601 Locust Walk, (215) 387-DINE.

MIDDLE EAST RESTAURANT: *10% discount over 55; 20% over 65; 50% over 80!*
126 Chestnut St., (215) 922-1003.

Theaters

CONCERTO SOLOISTS OF PHILADELPHIA: *$2 discount.*
2136 Locust St., (215) 735-0202.

KOPIA DINNER THEATRE: *$3 discount; call for information on special senior matinee performances.*
4942 Parkside Ave., (215) 877-4426.

PHILADELPHIA DRAMA GUILD: *50% off season tickets; $4 off individual tickets with Medicare card.*
Zellerback Theatre, Annenberg Center, 3680 Walnut St., (215) 563-7530.

Tour Operators

BLACK HISTORY STROLLS & TOURS OF PHILADELPHIA: *20% discount.*
339 S. 2nd St., (215) 923-4136.

CENTIPEDE TOURS: *15% discount.*
1422 Chestnut St., (215) 564-2246.

Sights

LIBERTY BELL RACE TRACK: *$1 discount on Clubhouse or Grandstand admission.*
Knights & Woodhaven Rds., (215) 637-7100.

NEW HOPE MULE BARGE COMPANY: *10% discount.*
S. Main & New Sts., (215) 862-2842.
Daily in summer, 11:30 a.m. to 6 p.m.; call for fall and spring schedule.

PENN MUTUAL TOWER OBSERVATION DECK: *33% discount.*
Independence Square South, (215) 629-0695.
May to October: daily, 10 a.m. to 5 p.m. Rest of year: Tuesday to Saturday, 10 a.m. to 5 p.m.

PENNSBURY MANOR: *$.75 discount.*
400 Pennsbury Memorial La., Morrisville, (215) 946-0400.
Tuesday to Saturday, 9 a.m. to 5 p.m.; Sunday noon to 5 p.m. Re-creation of William Penn's house and gardens.

RAINBOW RIVER TOURS: *25% discount.*
Penns Landing, Delaware Ave., (215) 925-7640.
End of June to mid-September. Two-hour harbor cruise: Monday through Saturday, 11 a.m., 1:30 and 7 p.m.; Friday and Saturday, 9:30 p.m. also. One-hour cruise: noon to 5 p.m., on the hour.

SESAME PLACE: *10% discount.*
100 Sesame Place, Langhorne, (215) 752-4900.

Museums

ACADEMY OF NATURAL SCIENCES: *$.25 discount.*
19th St. & Franklin Pkwy., (215) 299-1000.

AFRO-AMERICAN HISTORICAL AND CULTURAL MUSEUM: *50% discount.*
7th & Arch Sts., (215) 574-0380.
Tuesday to Saturday, 10 a.m. to 5 p.m.

BARTRAM'S HOUSE & GARDENS: *50% discount.*
54th St. & Lindbergh Blvd., (215) 729-5281.
Tuesday to Sunday, 10 a.m. to 4 p.m. Also closed weekends November to March. Restored home and gardens of colonial botanist.

CLIVEDEN: *25% discount.*
6401 Germantown Ave., (215) 848-1777.
April to December: Tuesday to Saturday, 10:30 a.m. to 4:30 p.m. Sunday, 1:30 p.m. to 4:30 p.m. Restored Georgian house.

FRANKLIN INSTITUTE OF SCIENCE MUSEUM AND PLANETARIUM: *33% discount.*
20th St. & Franklin Pkwy., (215) 564-3375.
Monday to Saturday, 10 a.m. to 5 p.m.; Sunday, noon to 5 p.m. Four floors of participatory exhibits.

MORRIS ARBORETUM: *50% discount.*
Hillcrest Ave., Chestnut Hill, (215) 247-5777.
Daily 10 a.m. to 5 p.m. summer; until 4 p.m. in winter.

MUSEUM OF AMERICAN JEWISH HISTORY: *15% discount.*
55 N. 5th St., (215) 923-3811.
Independence Mall East.
Monday to Thursday, 10 a.m. to 5 p.m.; Sunday, 12 noon to 5 p.m.

MUMMERS MUSEUM: *50% discount.*
2nd St. and Washington Ave., (215) 336-3050.
Tuesday to Saturday, 9:30 a.m. to 5 p.m.; Sunday, noon to 5 p.m. Historical exhibits and audio-visual presentations on the famous Philadelphia Mummers.

PENNSYLVANIA ACADEMY OF FINE ARTS: *25% discount.*
Broad & Cherry Sts., (215) 972-7600.
Tuesday to Saturday, 10 a.m. to 4 p.m.; Sunday, 1 to 4 p.m.

PHILADELPHIA MUSEUM OF ART: *50% discount for 62 and over.*
26th St. & Benjamin Franklin Pkwy., (215) 763-8100.
Tuesday to Sunday, 10 a.m. to 5 p.m.

ROSENBACH MUSEUM: *$1 discount.*
2010 DeLancey Pl., (215) 732-1600.
Tuesday to Saturday, 11 a.m. to 4 p.m.
19th-century town house filled with valuable art and manuscripts.

Free!

Atwater Kent Museum, Balch Institute for Ethnic Studies, Betsy Ross House, Christ Church, City Hall Tower, Congress Hall, Elfreth's Alley, Edgar Allan Poe National Historic House, Independence Mall & Liberty Bell, International Coin Museum, Old City Hall, Todd House, U.S. Mint, University Museum.

PITTSBURGH

Helpful Address

GREATER PITTSBURGH CONVENTION & VISITORS BUREAU
4 Gateway Center, Pittsburgh, PA 15222, (412) 281-7711

Hotels

BEST WESTERN: *10% discount.*
Center, 875 Greentree Rd., (412) 922-7070.
West, 3550 William Penn Hwy., (412) 824-6000.

HARLEY HOTEL: *10% discount.*
699 Rodi Rd., (412) 244-1600, (800) 321-2323.

HOLIDAY INN: *10%–20% discount with Holiday Inn's Travel Venture Club Card.*
Airport (Coraopolis), 1406 Beers School Rd., (412) 262-3600.
Airport (Oakdale), Rtes. 22 & 30, (412) 923-2244.
4859 McKnight Rd., (412) 366-5200.

Allegheny Valley, 180 Gamma Dr., (412) 782-4200.
Central, 401 Holiday Dr., (412) 922-8100.
North, 2801 Freeport Rd., (412) 828-9300.
Parkway East, 915 Brinton Rd., (412) 247-2700.

HOWARD JOHNSON'S: *15%–50% discount with H.J.'s Road Rally Card.*
Oakland, 3401 Blvd. of the Allies, (412) 683-6100.
South, 5300 Clairton Blvd., Pleasant Hills, (412) 884-6000.

MARRIOTT/GREENTREE: *50% discount for Marriott Leisure Life members.*
101 Marriott Dr., (412) 922-8400.
Airport, 100 Aten Rd., (412) 788-8800.

QUALITY INN: *10% discount for over 60.*
Airport, 1500 Beers School Rd., (412) 771-5200.

RAMADA INN: *25% discount for over 60.*
Airport, 1412 Beers School Rd., (412) 264-8950.

REDWOOD INN: *10% discount for AARP.*
2898 Bankville Rd., (412) 343-3000.

SHERATON: *25% discount for over 60.*
Airport, Rte. 60 & Thorn Run Rd., Coraopolis, (412) 262-2400.
Station Square, Carson & Smithfield, (412) 261-2000.

UNIVERSITY INN: *10% discount for AARP.*
Forbes Ave. at McKee Pl., (412) 683-6000.

Car Rental

AVIS: *5%–25% discount.**
Airport, (412) 262-5160.
625 Stanwix St., (412) 261-0540.

HERTZ: *5%–25% discount.**
Airport, (412) 262-1705.

NATIONAL: *10%–12% discount for over 62.*
Airport, (412) 262-2312.

THRIFTY RENT-A-CAR: *Discount on daily rate for AARP.*
Airport, (412) 264-1775.

Theaters

HEINZ HALL FOR THE PERFORMING ARTS: *10% to 20% discount for 65 and over; available one hour before performance.*
600 Penn Ave., (412) 392-4800.

PHIPPS CONSERVATORY: *25% discount.*
Schenley Park, (412) 255-2375.

Sights

GATEWAY CLIPPER FLEET: *Discounts on a variety of cruises.*
Station Square Dock, (412) 355-7979.

HARTWOOD ACRES: *50% discount on mansion tours; by reservation.*
215 Saxonburg Blvd., (412) 767-9200.
Tuesday to Saturday, 10 a.m. to 3 p.m.; Sunday noon to 3 p.m.

NATIONALITY CLASSROOMS: *10% discount.*
University of Pittsburgh, (412) 255-2375.
Monday to Friday, 9 a.m. to 5 p.m.; Saturday and Sunday, 12:30 p.m. to 4 p.m.

**An asterisk indicates that the discount is intended for members of senior citizens' organizations that anyone can join. See "Hotel, Transportation, and Sightseeing Discounts."*

Museums

FORT PITT MUSEUM: *Free to seniors.*
Point State Park, Ft. Duquesne & Ft. Pitt Blvds., (412) 281-9284.
Wednesday to Saturday, 10 a.m. to 4:30 p.m.; Sunday, noon to 4:30 p.m. Exhibits on Indian and early American life.

Free!

Frick Art Museum

THE POCONO MOUNTAINS

Helpful Address

POCONO MOUNTAINS VACATION BUREAU CHAMBER OF COMMERCE, Stroudsburg, PA 18360; (717) 421-5791, (800) POCONOS.

Hotels

AUTUMN VIEW LODGE: *10% discount, except holiday weekends.*
R.D. #1, Box 122, Henryville, (717) 629-4388.

BEST WESTERN: *10% discount.*
Stroudsburg, 700 Main St., (717) 421-2200.

HOLIDAY INN: *10%–20% discount with Holiday Inn's Travel Venture Club Card.*
Bartonsville, I-80 & Rte. 611, (717) 424-6100.
Lake Harmony–White Haven, Rte. 940, (717) 443-8417.

HOWARD JOHNSON'S: *15%–50% discount with H.J.'s Road Rally Card.*
Exit 53, I-80, Delaware Water Gap, (412) 372-5500.

QUALITY INN: *10% discount for over 60.*
E. Stroudsburg, Rte. 209 at I-80, (717) 424-1951.

POCONO HERSHEY RESORT: *10% discount for AARP.*
I-80 & PA Tpk., White Haven, (717) 443-8411.

SHERATON-POCONO INN: *25% discount for over 60.*
1220 W. Main St., Stroudsburg, (717) 424-1930.

WHITE BEAUTY VIEW RESORT: *10% discount for 65 and over, except holidays, July, and August. Present Medicare or Medicaid card.*
On Lake Wallenpaupack, Greentown, (717) 857-0234.

Restaurants

WHITE BEAUTY VIEW: *10% discount except holidays, July, and August.*
On Lake Wallenpaupack, Greentown.

RHODE ISLAND

Helpful Addresses

RHODE ISLAND STATE TOURIST PROMOTION DIVISION
Dept. of Economic Development, 7 Jackson Walkway, Providence, RI 02903
(401) 277-2601, (800) 556-2484 (ME to VA, except RI)

DEPARTMENT OF ELDERLY AFFAIRS
79 Washington St., Providence, RI 02903
(401) 277-2858

NEWPORT

Helpful Address

NEWPORT COUNTY CHAMBER OF COMMERCE
P.O. Box 237 MTG, 10 America's Cup Ave., Newport, RI 02840, (401) 847-1600.

Hotels

BEST WESTERN: *10% discount.*
151 Admiral Kalbfus Rd., (401) 849-9880.

HOLIDAY INN: *10%–20% discount with Holiday Inn's Travel Venture Club Card.*
25 America's Cup Ave., (401) 849-1000.

SHERATON: *25% discount for over 60.*
Goat Island 02840, (401) 849-2600.

HARBOR TREADWAY INN: *10% discount.**
49 America's Cup Ave., (406) 847-9000.

Car Rental

AVIS: *5%–25% discount.**
Goat Island, No. 1 Marine Plaza, (401) 846-1843.

HERTZ: *5%–25% discount.**
Foley's Gulf Station, 105 Broadway, (401) 846-1645.

Sights

BELCOURT CASTLE: *30% discount.*
Bellevue Ave., (401) 846-0669.

Daily, 9 a.m. to 5 p.m. Closed February to March. 1891 mansion built in the style of King Louis XIII's palace.

800 NUMBERS ARE SUPER SAVERS!
See the first two chapters for the 800 numbers of all the major hotel, car rental, tour, and airline companies; 800 numbers are listed where available in the state-by-state listings for the state tourist offices. Use 800 numbers whenever possible to obtain information and make reservations. If no 800 number is provided, be sure to call 800 information at 1 (800) 555-1212, and ask—it's a free call too!

HARBOR TOUR: *10% discount.*
Amazing Grace, Oldport Marine, Newport Yachting Center, (401) 849-2111.

NEWPORT ART MUSEUM: *50% discount.*
Bellevue Ave., (401) 847-0179.
Tuesday to Saturday, 10 a.m. to 5 p.m.; Sunday, 1 p.m. to 5 p.m.

NEWPORT AUTOMOBILE MUSEUM: *33% discount.*
Casino Terrace & Bellevue Terrace, (401) 856-6688.
Daily, 10 a.m. to 7 p.m.

Free!

Bowen's Wharf, Newport Historical Society, Ochre Court, Old Colony House, Old Stone Mill, Redwood Library, St. Mary's Church, Second Congregational Church, Touro Synagogue, Trinity Church, United Baptist Church

SOUTH CAROLINA

Helpful Addresses

SOUTH CAROLINA STATE DIVISION OF TOURISM
1205 Pendleton St., Columbia, SC 29202
(803) 758-8735

COMMISSION ON AGING
915 Main St., Columbia, SC 29201
(803) 734-3203

CHARLESTON

Hotels

BEST WESTERN: *10% discount.*
237 Meeting St., (803) 723-7451.

DAYS INN: *10%–50% discount with Days Inn September Days Club card.*
2998 W. Montague Ave., (803) 747-4101.
260 Hwy. 17 Bypass, Mt. Pleasant, (803) 881-1800.
155 Meeting St., (803) 722-8411.

ECONOLODGE: *10% discount with Econo's Senior Class Card.*
4725 Arco Ln., (803) 747-3672.
2237 Savannah Hwy., (803) 571-1880.

HOLIDAY INN: *10%–20% discount with Holiday Inn's Travel Venture Club Card.*
Airport, I-26 & W. Aviation, Box 9427, (803) 744-1621.
Downtown, 115 Meeting & Queen Sts., (803) 577-2400.
Riverview, 201 Savannah Hwy., (803) 556-7100.

HOWARD JOHNSON'S: *15%–50% discount with H.J.'s Road Rally Card.*
Downtown, 250 Spring, (803) 722-4000.

LA QUINTA: *20% discount.*
Airport, 2499 La Quinta La., (803) 797-8181.

QUALITY INN: *10% discount for over 60.*
Downtown Hotel, 125 Calhoun St., (803) 722-3391.

RAMADA INN: *25% discount for over 60.*
Airport, I-26 & W. Montague, (803) 744-8281.

SHERATON: *25% discount for over 60.*
Airport, 5981 Rivers Blvd., (803) 744-2501.
Downtown, 170 Lockwood Blvd., (803) 723-3000.

Car Rental

AVIS: *5%–25% discount.**
Airport, Remount Rd., (803) 767-7030.

HERTZ: *5%–25% discount.**
Airport, (803) 767-7047.

NATIONAL: *10%–12% discount for over 62.*
Airport, (803) 767-3078.

Sights

AIRCRAFT CARRIER *YORKTOWN*—Patriots Point Naval & Maritime Museum: *10% discount.**
Charleston Harbor, Mt. Pleasant, (803) 884-2727. Daily, 9 a.m. to 6 p.m.

SOUTH DAKOTA

Helpful Addresses

SOUTH DAKOTA DIVISION OF TOURISM
Box 1000, 221 S. Central, Pierre, SD 57501
(605) 773-3301, (800) 843-1930

OFFICE OF ADULT SERVICES AND AGING
Kneip Building, 700 N. Illinois St., Pierre, SD 57501
(605) 773-3656

RAPID CITY

Hotels

BEST WESTERN: *10% discount.*
1901 W. Main St., (605) 343-6040.
2505 Mt. Rushmore Rd., (605) 343-5383.

HOLIDAY INN: *10%–20% discount with Holiday Inn's Travel Venture Club Card.*
I-90 at Lacrosse St., (605) 348-1230.

HOWARD JOHNSON'S: *15%–50% discount with H.J.'s Road Rally Card.*
I-90 at 2211 Lacrosse St., (605) 343-8550.

RAMADA INN: *25% discount for over 60.*
1721 Lacrosse St., (605) 342-1300.

Car Rental

AVIS: *5%–25% discount.**
Airport, (605) 393-0740.

HERTZ: *5%–25% discount.**
Airport, Rte. 2, (605) 393-0160.

NATIONAL: *10%–12% discount for over 62.*
Airport, (605) 393-2664.

Tour Operators

GRAY LINE: *5% discount for over 60.*
Gray Line of the Black Hills, P.O. Box 1116, Rapid City, SD 57709, (605) 342-4461.
Bus tours of Mt. Rushmore, the Black Hills, Red Cloud Heritage Center, Custer State Park.

Sights

BEAR COUNTRY U.S.A.: *10% discount.*
SD Rte. 16, (605) 343-2290.
June to mid-October: 8 a.m. to 8 p.m. in summer, 9 a.m. to 5:30 p.m. in fall.

BLACK HILLS CAVERNS: *20% discount.*
S.D. Rte. 44, (605) 343-0542.
Open June through September.

BLACK HILLS PETRIFIED FOREST: *30% discount.*
Elk Creek Rd., (605) 787-4560.
Daily, June through August, 8 a.m. to 7 p.m.

DIAMOND CRYSTAL CAVE: *50¢ discount.*
4553 Wentworth Dr., (605) 342-8008.

MARINE LIFE AQUARIUM: *25% discount for 55 and over.*
US 16 at Keystone, (605) 348-0430.
June to Labor Day: daily, 7:30 a.m. to 8:30 p.m. May, and after Labor Day through September: daily, 8:30 a.m. to 5:30 p.m. October through April: closed.

Free!

Chapel in the Hills, Dinosaur Park, Minnilusa Historical Museum, Museum of Geology, Sioux Indian Museum & Crafts Center

TENNESSEE

Helpful Addresses

TENNESSEE TOURIST DEVELOPMENT
P.O. Box 23170, Nashville, TN 37202
(615) 741-2158

COMMISSION ON AGING
706 Church St., Suite 201, Nashville, TN 37219
(615) 741-2056

TENNE-SENIOR Discount Program

Tennessee residents age 65 and older are eligible to receive a free TENNE-SENIOR card entitling them to discounts at participating merchants throughout the state. Write TENNE-SENIOR Program, 914 Tennessee Bldg., 706 Church St., Suite 201, Nashville, TN 37219, (615) 741-6790.

MEMPHIS

Helpful Address

CONVENTION & VISITORS BUREAU OF MEMPHIS
203 Beale St., Suite 305, Memphis, TN 38103, (901) 526-1919.

Hotels

BEST WESTERN: *10% discount.*
Riverbluff Inn, 340 W. Illinois, (901) 948-9005.

COACH HOUSE: *10% discount.*
1262 Union, (901) 725-1900.

DAYS INN: *10%–50% discount with Days Inn September Days Club card.*
I-55 & Brooks Rd., (901) 345-2470.
I-40 & 5301 Summer Ave., (901) 761-1600.

HOLIDAY INN: *10%–20% discount with Holiday Inn's Travel Venture Club Card.*
I-40 at Macon Rd., 6101 Shelby Oaks Dr., (901) 388-7050.
Convention Ctr., 250 N. Main St., (901) 527-7300.
International Airport, 1441 E. Brooks, (901) 398-9211.
Medical Center, 969 Madison Ave., (901) 522-8300.
Overton Square Area, 1837 Union Ave., (901) 278-4100.
Poplar & I-240, 5679 Poplar Ave., (901) 682-7881.
West Memphis, I-40 & I-55, (901) 735-6480.

HOWARD JOHNSON'S: *15%–50% discount with H.J.'s Road Rally Card.*
3280 Elvis Presley Blvd., (901) 345-1425.

LA QUINTA: *20% discount.*
Airport, 2745 Airways Blvd., (901) 396-1000.
Medical Center, 42 S. Camilla St., (901) 526-1050.

MEMPHIS MARRIOTT: *50% discount for Marriott Leisure Life members.*
2625 Thousand Oaks Blvd., (901) 362-6200.

QUALITY INN: *10% discount for over 60.*
East, 5877 Poplar Ave., (901) 767-6300.

RAMADA INN: *25% discount for over 60.*
Airport, 1471 E. Brooks Rd., (901) 332-3500.
Downtown, 160 Union Ave., (901) 525-5491.
East, 5225 Summer Ave., (901) 682-7691.
2490 Mt. Moriah at I-240, (901) 362-8010.

RODEWAY INN: *10% discount.*
Airport, 2949 Airways Blvd., (901) 345-1250.
271 W. Alston, (901) 946-3301.

SHERATON: *25% discount for over 60.*
Downtown, 300 N. 2nd St., (901) 525-2511.
Sheraton Airport Inn, 2411 Winchester Rd., (901) 332-2370.

TRAVELODGE: *Special senior rates for Travelodge's Golden Guest Club.*
265 Union Ave., (901) 527-4305.

Restaurants

MCDONALD'S: *Free drink with meal for over 60 with a senior citizens' card, available at the restaurant.*
Available at Blytheville, Jonesboro, and W. Memphis only

Car Rental

AVIS: *5%–25% discount.**
Memphis International Airport, P.O. Box 30181, (901) 345-2847.

DOLLAR: *Ask about the "Senior Escape Rate" for 60 and over.*
2031 E. Brooks Rd., (901) 345-3890.

HERTZ: *5%–25% discount.**
Memphis International Airport, (901) 345-5680.

NATIONAL: *10%–12% discount for over 62.*
Memphis International Airport, (901) 345-0070.

Sights

LIBERTYLAND: *45% discount.*
Fairgrounds, E. Pkwy., off I-240, (901) 274-1776.
April to August: daily, 10 a.m. to 10 p.m.; Sunday, 11 a.m. to 10 p.m. Theme park.

MEMPHIS ZOO & AQUARIUM: *65% discount.*
2000 Galloway, Overton Park, (901) 726-4775.
April to October: Daily, 9 a.m. to 6 p.m.; November to March: 9 a.m. to 5 p.m.

MUD ISLAND: *$4.50 for seniors 62 and over.*
Front St. between Poplar and Adam, (901) 576-7241.
Exhibits cover the music, people, and stories of the Mississippi.

PUTT PUTT GOLF: *40% discount for over 60.*
5720 Mt. Moriah Exit.
5484 Summer Ave.

**An asterisk indicates that the discount is intended for members of senior citizens' organizations that anyone can join. See "Hotel, Transportation, and Sightseeing Discounts."*

Museums

DIXON GALLERY AND GARDENS: *50% discount for 65 and over.*
4339 Park Avenue, (901) 761-5250.
Daily except Monday, 11 a.m. to 5 p.m.; Sunday, 1 to 5 p.m. Art collection and 17 acres of gardens.

LICHTERMAN NATURE CENTER: *30% discount for 62 and over.*
5992 Quince Rd., (901) 767-7322.
Tuesday to Saturday, 9:30 a.m. to 5 p.m.; Sunday, 1 p.m. to 5 p.m.

MEMPHIS PINK PALACE MUSEUM: *30% discount for over 62.*
3050 Central Ave., (901) 454-5600.
Tuesday to Friday, 9:30 a.m. to 4 p.m.; Saturday, 9 a.m. to 4 p.m.; Sunday, 1 to 5 p.m. Exhibits on the history of the South. Planetarium.

Free!

Memphis Brooks Museum of Art *(10% discount in museum shop)*, Magevney House, Memphis Botanical Garden, tours of Stroh Brewery

NASHVILLE

Hotels

BEST WESTERN: *10% discount.*
400 5th Ave. N., (615) 254-1651.
I-24 & Bell Rd., (615) 833-8540.
99 Spring St., (615) 259-9160.

CONTINENTAL INNS: *10% discount.*
303 Interstate Dr., (615) 244-6690 or (800) 251-1856.

DAYS INN: *10%–50% discount with Days Inn September Days Club card.*
I-40 & Old Hickory Blvd., (615) 889-8940.
I-65 & Trinity Ln., (615) 226-4500.

ECONOLODGE: *10% discount with Econo Senior Class Card.*
I-24 E & Old Hickory Blvd., (615) 793-7721.
Opryland, 2460 Music Valley Dr., (615) 889-0090.

HOLIDAY INN: *10%–20% discount with Holiday Inn's Travel Venture Club Card.*
I-24 E., 350 Harding Pl., (615) 834-0620.
North, 230 W. Trinity Ln., (615) 226-0111.
Vanderbilt, 2613 West End Ave., (615) 327-4707.

HOWARD JOHNSON'S: *15%–50% discount with H.J.'s Road Rally Card.*
North, 2401 Brick Church Pike, (615) 226-4600.
West, 6834 Charlotte Pike, (615) 352-7080.

LA QUINTA: *20% discount.*
Metro Center, 2001 MetroCenter Blvd., (615) 259-2130.
South, 4311 Sidco Dr., (615) 834-6900.

MISS ANNE'S BED & BREAKFAST: *10% discount on presentation of* Discount Guide.
3033 Windemere Circle, Nashville, TN 37214, (615) 885-1899.

QUALITY INN: *10% discount for over 60.*
10 Interstate Dr., (615) 244-6050.

RAMADA INN: *25% discount for over 60.*
Capitol Hill, 840 James Robertson Pkwy., (615) 244-6130
South, I-24 & Harding Pl., (615) 834-4242.

RODEWAY INN: *10% discount.*
Airport, 797 Briley Pkwy., (615) 361-5900.

SCOTTISH INN: *10% discount with Scottish Identicard.*
1501 Dickerson Rd., (615) 226-6940.

SHERATON: *25% discount for over 60.*
Downtown, 920 Broadway, (615) 244-0150.
South, I-65 & Harding Pl., (615) 834-5000.

TRAVELODGE: *Special senior rates for Travelodge's Golden Guest Club.*
800 James Robertson Pkwy., (615) 244-2630.

Car Rental

AVIS: *5%–25% discount.**
Airport, (615) 361-1838.

HERTZ: *5%–25% discount.**
Airport, P.O. Box 17265, (615) 361-3131.
Hyatt Regency Hotel, 7th Ave. & Union St., (615) 256-8123.

NATIONAL: *10%–12% discount for over 62.*
Airport, (615) 361-7467.
Radisson Plaza, 2 Commerce Pl., (615) 256-2824.

Museums

CUMBERLAND MUSEUM & SCIENCE CENTER: *40% discount.*
800 Ridley Blvd., Ft. Negley Park, (615) 259-6382.

TRAVELLERS' REST HISTORIC HOUSE: *25% discount.*
Farrell Pkwy., (615) 832-2962.
Monday to Saturday, 9 a.m. to 4 p.m.; Sunday, 1 p.m. to 4 p.m.
Historical museum in restored 1799 house.

Free!

Oscar Farris Agricultural Museum, Tennessee State Museum, State Capitol, Upper Room

TEXAS

Helpful Addresses

TEXAS TRAVEL INFORMATION DIVISION, DEPT. MG,
P.O. Box 5064, Austin, TX 78763
(512) 475-5954

DEPARTMENT ON AGING,
P.O. Box 12786
Capitol Station, Austin, TX 78741
(512) 444-2727

CORPUS CHRISTI

Hotels

BEST WESTERN: *10% discount.*
3200 Surfside Blvd., (512) 883-7456.

ECONOLODGE: *10% discount with Econo Senior Class Card.*
Airport, 6033 Leopard St., (512) 289-1116.

HOLIDAY INN: *10%–20% discount with Holiday Inn's Travel Venture Club Card.*
Airport, 5549 Leopard St., (512) 289-5100.
Emerald Beach, 1102 S. Shoreline, (512) 882-5731.
Padre Island, S. Padre Island Dr., (512) 949-8041.

QUALITY INN: *10% discount for over 60.*
411 N. Shoreline Blvd., (512) 884-4815.

LA QUINTA: *20% discount.*
Royale, 601 N. Water, (512) 888-4461.
5155 I-37 N., (512) 888-5721.
6225 S. Padre Island Dr., (512) 991-5730.

RAMADA INN: *25% discount for over 60.*
601 N. Shoreline, (512) 882-7271.

RODEWAY INN: *10% discount.*
2838 S. Padre Island Dr., (512) 854-0005.

SHERATON: *25% discount for over 60.*
300 N. Shoreline Blvd., (512) 883-5111.

Public Transportation

CORPUS CHRISTI REGIONAL TRANSIT AUTHORITY (BUS): *50% discount for over 65; call for other special services for seniors.*
(512) 882-1722

Car Rental

AVIS: *5%–25% discount.**
Airport, (512) 289-0073.
101 N. Shoreline, (512) 883-5108.

HERTZ: *5%–25% discount.**
Airport, (512) 289-0777.

NATIONAL: *10%–12% discount for over 62.*
Airport, (512) 289-0515.

Movie Theaters

30% discount for over 60 at:
AYERS, 3035 Ayers
CENTRE, 408 W. Chaparral
CINE 6, 4701 S. Staples
CINE WEST, 3719 Leopard

FOUR CINEMA, 4543 Padre Isle Dr.
NATIONAL, 3512 S. Staples

Museums

MUSEUM OF ORIENTAL CULTURES: *25% discount for over 60.*
426 S. Staples, (512) 883-1303.
Monday to Friday, 10 a.m. to 4 p.m., closed noon to 1 p.m.; Sunday, noon to 5 p.m.

Free!

Art Museum of South Texas, Corpus Christi Museum, Sidbury House, tours of U.S. Naval Air Station (Thursdays)

DALLAS

Helpful Address

DALLAS CONVENTION & VISITORS BUREAU
1507 Pacific Ave., (214) 954-1111.

Hotels

BEST WESTERN: *10% discount.*
Airport, 4325 W. Hwy. 114, (214) 621-8277.
8051 LBJ Frwy., (214) 234-2431.
2023 N. Industrial Blvd., (214) 741-5041.

DAYS INN: *10%–50% discount with Days Inn September Days Club card.*
I-635 & 2753 Forest Ln., (214) 620-2828.
9386 LBJ Frwy., (214) 690-1220.

DOUBLETREE: *15% discount.*
Campbell Centre, 8250 N. Central Expwy., (214) 691-8700.

HOLIDAY INN: *10%–20% discount with Holiday Inn's Travel Venture Club Card.*

Downtown, 1015 Elm, (214) 748-9951.

Market Center, I-35 & 1955 N. Industrial Blvd., (214) 747-9551.

Six-Flags-Over-Texas area, 903 N. Collins, Hwy. 157, Arlington, (817) 261-3621.

Southwest, 711 E. Camp Wisdom Rd., (214) 298-8911.

Stemmons & Regal Row, 1575 Regal Row-Stemmons Expwy., (214) 638-6100.

Texas Stadium, 1930 E. Airport Frwy., Irving, (214) 438-1313.

HOWARD JOHNSON'S: *15%–50% discount with H.J.'s Road Rally Card.*

North Central, 10333 N. Central Expwy., (214) 363-0221.

LA QUINTA: *20% discount.*

Airport, 4105 W. Airport Frwy., (214) 252-6546.

4440 N. Central Expwy., (214) 821-4220.

10001 N. Central Expwy., (214) 361-8200.

8303 E. Thornton Frwy., (214) 324-3731.

Regal Row, 1625 Regal Row, (214) 630-5701.

MARRIOT HOTELS: *50% discount for Marriott Leisure Life members.*

Market Center, 2101 Stemmons Fwy., (214) 748-8551.

QUALITY INN: *10% discount for over 60.*

2015 Market Center Blvd., (214) 741-7481.

RAMADA INN: *25% discount for over 60.*

Market Center, 1055 Regal Row, (214) 634-8550

Dallas-Ft. Worth Airport, I-35 at Hwy. 121, Lewisville, (214) 221-2525.

Six-Flags-Over-Texas area, 700 E. Lamar, Arlington, (817) 265-7711.

RODEWAY INN: *10% discount.**
Central, 4150 N. Central Expwy., (214) 827-4310.
Dallas-Ft. Worth Airport, 4110 W. Airport Frwy., (214) 339-2005.
Ft. Worth, 1111 W. Lancaster, (817) 332-1951.
Love Field, 3140 W. Mockingbird Ln., (214) 357-1701.
Market Center, 2026 Market Center Blvd., (214) 748-2243.
Six-Flags-Over-Texas area, 833 N. Watson Rd., Arlington, (817) 640-7080.

SHERATON: *25% discount for over 60.*
Sheraton Dallas Hotel, Southland Center, (214) 922-8000.
Sheraton Inn-Mockingbird, 1893 W. Mockingbird Ln., (214) 634-8850.
Sheraton Inn-Northeast, 11350 LBJ Frwy. at Jupiter Rd., (214) 341-5400.

TRAVELODGE: *Special senior rates for Travelodge's Golden Guest Club.*
Viscount, Market Center Tower, 4500 Harry Hines Blvd., (214) 522-6650.

Public Transportation

DALLAS AREA RAPID TRANSIT: *75% discount for Dallas-area residents. Dallas senior citizens can obtain a senior citizens' pass at 101 N. Peak, (214) 828-6700.*

Car Rental

AVIS: *5%–25% discount.**
Dallas-Ft. Worth Airport, P.O. Box 61004, (214) 574-4130.

BUDGET RENT-A-CAR: *10% discount.*
3127 N. Mockingbird, (214) 357-1574.

HERTZ: *5%–25% discount.**
Dallas-Ft. Worth Airport, (214) 453-0370.

NATIONAL: *10%–12% discount for over 62.*
Dallas-Ft. Worth Airport, (214) 574-3400.

Theaters

DALLAS REPERTORY THEATER: *$1 discount for 62 and over.*
North Park Center, (214) 369-8966.

Sights

OBSERVATION DECK, REUNION TOWER, HYATT REGENCY HOTEL: *50% discount.*
300 Reunion Blvd.

OLD CITY PARK: *50% discount*
1717 Gano St., (214) 421-5141.
Tuesday to Friday, 10 a.m. to 4 p.m.; Saturday and Sunday, 1:30 to 4:30 p.m. Last tour starts

Tours for Seniors
Request information and tour schedules from your national senior citizens' organization and from *Saga International Holidays, Ltd.*, 120 Boylston St., Boston, MA 02116, (800) 343-0273 (except MA); *Grand Circle Travel*, 555 Madison Ave., New York, NY 10022, (800) 221-2610; AARP Travel Service, P.O. Box 92337, Los Angeles, CA 90009, (800) 227-7737; *Passages Unlimited*, 48 Union St., Stamford, CT 06906, (800) 472-7724; 50+ Young at Heart Program, *American Youth Hostels*, Travel Department, P.O. Box 37613, Washington, D.C. 20013, (202) 783-6161; *Interhostel*, Continuing Education, University of New Hampshire, Durham, NH 03824, (603) 862-1147.

one hour before closing. Restorations and demonstrations show Dallas history.

Museums

FIRE MUSEUM OF TEXAS: *$1 discount for AARP.*
702 E. Safari Pkwy., Grand Prairie, (214) 263-1047.

THE SCIENCE PLACE: *50% discount.*
1st & M. L. King Jr. Blvd., (214) 428-8351.
Tuesday to Saturday, 9 a.m. to 5 p.m.; Sunday, 1 p.m. to 5 p.m.

SOUTHWEST HISTORICAL WAX MUSEUM: *50% discount for 60 and over.*
601 E. Safari Pkwy., Grand Prairie, (214) 263-2391.
Memorial Day to Labor Day: 9 a.m. to 9 p.m. Rest of the year: Monday to Friday, 10 a.m. to 5 p.m.; Saturday and Sunday, 10 a.m. to 6 p.m.

Free!

Dallas Aquarium, Dallas Museum of Art, Dallas Museum of Natural History, Garden Center, Health and Science Museum.

HOUSTON

Hotels

BEST WESTERN: *10% discount.*
6900 Jetero Blvd., (713) 446-3041.

DAYS INN: *10%–50% discount with Days Inn September Days Club card.*
I-45 & 100 W. Cavalcade, (713) 869-7121.
I-45 & 2200 S. Wayside, (713) 928-2800.

DOUBLETREE: *15% discount.*
Intercontinental Airport, 15747 Drummet Blvd., (713) 442-8000.

EMBASSY SUITES: *10% discount.**
9090 S.W. Frwy., (713) 995-0123.

HOLIDAY INN: *10%–20% discount with Holiday Inn's Travel Venture Club Card.*
Astro Village, 8500 Kirby Dr., (713) 799-1050.
Central, 4640 S. Main St., (713) 526-2811.
Downtown, 801 Calhoun, (713) 659-2222.
Intercontinental Airport, 3702 N. Belt E., (713) 449-2311.
Medical Center, 6701 S. Main, (713) 797-1110.

HOWARD JOHNSON'S: *15%–50% discount with H.J.'s Road Rally Card.*
North, 3939 N. Frwy., (713) 691-3951

LA QUINTA: *20% discount.*
Intercontinental Airport, 6 N. Belt E., (713) 447-6888.
Greenway Plaza, 4015 S.W. Frwy., (713) 623-4750.
11113 Katy Frwy., (713) 932-0808.
11002 N.W. Frwy., (713) 688-2581.
8201 S.W. Frwy., (713) 772-3626.
11999 E. Frwy., (713) 453-5425.
Hobby Airport, 9902 Gulf Frwy., (713) 941-0900.

QUALITY INN: *10% discount for over 60.*
Intercontinental Airport, 6115 Jetero Blvd., (713) 446-9131.
Space Center, 2020 NASA Rd., (713) 332-3551.

RAMADA INN: *25% discount for over 60.*
Greenway Plaza, 2929 S.W. Frwy., (713) 528-6161.
Hobby Airport, 7777 Airport Blvd., (713) 644-1261.
Central, 4225 N. Frwy., (713) 695-6011.
West, 7787 Katy Frwy., (713) 682-1611.

RODEWAY INN: *10% discount.*
Greenway Plaza, 3135 S.W. Frwy., (713) 526-1071.
East, 114 S. Richey St., (713) 477-6871.
West, 5820 Katy Frwy., (713) 869-9211.

SHERATON: *25% discount for over 60.*
Downtown, 777 Polk Ave., (713) 651-9041.
Intercontinental Airport, 15700 Drummet Blvd., (713) 442-5100.
NASA, 1301 NASA Blvd., Clear Lake, (713) 488-0220.

TRAVELODGE: *Special senior rates for Travelodge's Golden Guest Club.*
North, 9025 N. Frwy., (713) 820-1500.
Southwest Tower, 2828 S.W. Frwy., (713) 526-4571.

Car Rental

AVIS: *5%–25% discount.**
Downtown, 2120 Louisiana St., (713) 659-6537.
Galleria, 4825 Richmond Ave., (713) 629-7230.
Hobby Airport, (713) 641-0531.
Houston Intercontinental Airport, (713) 443-5800.

HERTZ: *5%–25% discount.**
Hobby Airport, 7718 Airport Blvd., (713) 941-6821.
Houston Intercontinental Airport, (713) 443-0800.

NATIONAL: *10%–12% discount for over 62.*
Hobby Airport, (713) 641-0533.
Houston Intercontinental Airport, (713) 443-8850.

Sights

BATTLESHIP *TEXAS: 30% discount.*
San Jacinto Battleground, (512) 479-2411.
Daily, 10 a.m. to 5 p.m.

Free!

Contemporary Arts Museum, Houston Arboretum, Houston Festival (March), Houston Museum of Fine Arts, Houston Museum of Natural Science, Houston Zoo, tours of Anheuser-Busch brewery

SAN ANTONIO

Helpful Address

SAN ANTONIO CONVENTION & VISITORS BUREAU
P.O. Box 2277, San Antonio, TX 78298, (512) 299-8123 or (800) 531-5700

Hotels

BEST WESTERN: *10% discount.*
6815 Hwy. 90 W., (512) 675-9690.
2635 N.E. Loop 412, (512) 653-9110.

DAYS INN: *10%–50% discount with Days Inn September Days Club card.*
East, 4100 E. Houston St., (512) 337-6753.
Northeast, 3443 N. Pan Am Hwy., (512) 225-4521.

EMBASSY SUITES: *10% discount.**
7750 Briaridge, (512) 340-5421.

HOLIDAY INN: *10%–20% discount with Holiday Inn's Travel Venture Club Card.*
318 W. Durango, Box 9327, (512) 225-3211.
Coliseum, 3855 Pan Am Hwy., (512) 226-4361.
Northwest, 6023 N.W. Expwy., (512) 732-5141.
Northwest, 3233 N.W. Loop 410, (512) 377-3900.

LA QUINTA: *20% discount.*
Airport East, 333 N.E. Loop 410, (512) 828-0781.
Airport West, 219 N.E. Loop 410, (512) 342-4291.
Downtown, 1001 E. Commerce, (512) 222-9181.
Downtown, 900 Dolorosa, (512) 271-0001.

RAMADA INN: *25% discount for over 60.*
Airport, 1111 N.W. Loop, (512) 828-9031.
Central, 3645 N. Pan Am Expwy., (512) 225-8000.
North, 1131 Austin Hwy., (512) 824-1441.

RODEWAY INN: *10% discount.*
Downtown, 900 N. Main, (512) 223-2951.
Northeast, 1259 Austin Hwy., (512) 824-7321.
Wonderland, 6804 N.W. Expwy., (512) 734-7111.

SHERATON: *25% discount for over 60.*
Airport, 1400 Austin Hwy., (512) 824-5371.

TRAVELODGE: *Special senior rates for Travelodge's Golden Guest Club.*
Alamo, 405 Broadway, (512) 222-9401.
Riverwalk, 100 Villita St., (512) 226-2271.
Northwest, 9806 I-10 W., (512) 696-0810.

Car Rental

AVIS: *5%–25% discount.**
Airport, 9700 Airport Blvd., (512) 826-6332.

HERTZ: *5%–25 discount.**
Airport, 1331 S. Terminal, (512) 826-0651.

NATIONAL: *10%–12% discount for over 62.*
Airport, (512) 824-1841.

Sights

ZOOLOGICAL GARDENS & AQUARIUM: *50% discount.*
3903 N. Mary's St., (512) 734-7183.
May to October: daily, 9:30 a.m. to 6:30 p.m.
November to April: daily, 9:30 a.m. to 5 p.m.

**An asterisk indicates that the discount is intended for members of senior citizens' organizations that anyone can join. See "Hotel, Transportation, and Sightseeing Discounts."*

Museums

SAN ANTONIO MUSEUM OF ART: *50% discount.*
200 W. Jones Ave., (512) 226-5544.
Tuesday to Saturday, 10 a.m. to 5 p.m.; Sunday, noon to 5 p.m. Pre-Columbian, Indian, Mexican, and Spanish colonial art.

SAN ANTONIO MUSEUM OF TRANSPORTATION: *50% discount.*
HemisFair Plaza, (512) 226-5544.
Tuesday to Saturday, 10 a.m. to 5 p.m.; Sunday, noon to 5 p.m.

WITTE MEMORIAL MUSEUM: *50% discount.*
3801 Broadway, (512) 226-5544.
Daily, 10 a.m. to 5 p.m. Exhibits on history, natural history, and art.

Free!

The Alamo, Hertzburg Circus Collection, Institute of Texan Cultures, McNay Art Museum, Missions National Historical Park

UTAH

Helpful Addresses

UTAH STATE TRAVEL COUNCIL
Council Hall, Capitol Hill, Salt Lake City, UT 84114
(801) 533-5681

DIVISION OF AGING AND ADULT SERVICES
150 W. North Temple, Box 45500, Salt Lake City, UT 84145
(801) 533-6422

SALT LAKE CITY

Hotels

HOLIDAY INN: *10%–20% discount with Holiday Inn's Travel Venture Club Card.*
Airport, 1659 W. North Temple, (801) 533-9000.
Downtown, 230 W. 6th St. S., (801) 532-7000.

HOWARD JOHNSON'S: *15%–50% discount with H.J.'s Road Rally Card.*
122 W. South Temple, (801) 521-0130.

QUALITY INN: *10% discount for over 60.*
154 W. 6th St., (801) 521-2930.
4465 Century Dr., (801) 268-2533.

NENDEL'S MOTOR INN: *10% discount for Vagabond's Club 55.*
Airport, 2080 N. Temple, (801) 355-0088.

RODEWAY INN: *10% discount.*
South, 280 W. 7200 South, (801) 566-4141.

SHERATON: *25% discount for over 60.*
255 S.W. Temple St. (801) 328-2000.

TEMPLE SQUARE HOTEL: *10% discount.*
75 W. S. Temple, (801) 355-2961.

TRAVELODGE: *Special senior rates for Travelodge's Golden Guest Club.*
144 W. N. Temple St., (801) 533-8200.
524 S. W. Temple St., (801) 531-7100.
215 W. N. Temple St., (801) 532-1000.

Car Rental

AVIS: *5%–25% discount.**
Airport, AMF Box 22186, (801) 539-1117.

HERTZ: *5%–25% discount.**
Airport, (801) 539-2683.
445 S. Main St., (801) 521-4100.

NATIONAL: *10%–12% discount for over 62.*
Airport, (801) 539-0200.

Sights

HANSEN PLANETARIUM: *15% discount.*
15 S. State St., (801) 535-7007.
Monday to Saturday, 11 a.m., 2, 4:30, and 7 p.m.; Sunday, 2 and 4:30 p.m.

HOGLE ZOOLOGICAL GARDENS: *50% discount.*
2600 Sunnyside Ave., (801) 582-1631.
Summer: daily, 9:30 a.m. to 6 p.m. Winter: daily, 9:30 a.m. to 4:30 p.m.

LAGOON AMUSEMENT PARK AND PIONEER VILLAGE: *Free over 55.*
17 mi. N. on I-15, (801) 451-0101. Daily, in spring and summer.

Free!

Beehive House, Council Hall, Mormon Tabernacle, Pioneer Memorial Museum, Utah Museum of Fine Arts, Wheeler Historic Farm.

VERMONT

Helpful Addresses

VERMONT TRAVEL DIVISION
134 State St., Montpelier, VT 05602
(802) 828-3236

OFFICE ON AGING
103 S. Main, Waterbury, VT 05676
(802) 241-2400

Green Mountain Passport Program

Vermont residents over 62 are eligible to receive a Green Mountain Passport which entitles them to free admission at totally state sponsored parks, museums, and concerts as well as to discounts at many businesses. And the Passport can serve as identification for free tuition at the University of Vermont. The Green Mountain Passport costs $2 and is available from any local town or city clerk's office.

Hotels

ECONOLODGE: *10% discount with Econo Senior Class Card.*
1076 Williston Rd., S. Burlington, (802) 863-1125.

HOLIDAY INN: *10%–20% discount with Holiday Inn's Venture Travel Club Card.*
Burlington, 1068 Williston Rd., (802) 863-6361.
Rutland, US 7, (802) 775-1911.
Waterbury/Stowe, Rte. 100 & I-89, (802) 244-7822.
White River Junction, I-89 & I-91, (802) 295-7537.

HOWARD JOHNSON'S: *15%–50% discount with H.J.'s Road Rally Card.*
Burlington, US 2 & I-89, (802) 863-5541.
White River Junction, I-91 & US 55, (802) 295-3015.

QUALITY INN: *10% discount for over 60.*
Brattleboro, Putney Rd., (802) 254-8701.

RAMADA INN: *25% discount for over 60.*
Bennington, Rte. 7 & Kocher Dr., (802) 442-8145.

SHERATON: *25% discount for over 60.*
Burlington, 870 Williston Rd., (802) 862-6576.

TRAVELODGE: *Special senior rates for Travelodge's Golden Guest Club.*
Rutland, 253 S. Main, (802) 773-3361.
Shelburne, 1907 Shelburne Rd., (802) 985-8037.

Car Rental

AVIS: *5%–25% discount.**
Brattleboro, Quality Inn Putney Rd., (802) 257-1717.
Burlington Airport, (802) 864-0411.
Rutland, Holiday Inn, Rte. 7, (802) 775-2933.

HERTZ: *5%–25% discount.**
Bennington Airport, (802) 442-9640.
Burlington Airport, (802) 864-7409.
Rutland, 137 N. Main St., (802) 773-9301.

Sights

ALPINE SLIDE: *30% to 50% discount.*
Pico Ski Area, (802) 775-4345.
Mt. Mansfield Ski Area, Stowe, (802) 253-7311.
Late May to October.

SHELBURNE FARMS: *10% discount.*
Harbor Rd., Shelburne, (802) 985-3222.
June to September: call for hours. Restored Victorian estate.

Museums

BENNINGTON MUSEUM: *20% discount.*
W. Main St., Old Bennington, (802) 447-1571.
March to November, daily, 9 a.m. to 5 p.m.

NORMAN ROCKWELL MUSEUM: *50% discount.*
U.S. 4, Rutland, (802) 773-6095.
Daily, 9:30 a.m. to 5 p.m.

PARK-MCCULLOUGH HOUSE: *20% discount.*
Rte. 67A, N. Bennington, (802) 442-2747.
May to October: daily, 10 a.m. to 4 p.m. 1865 mansion with Victorian furnishings.

SHELDON ART MUSEUM: *50% discount.*
1 Park St., Middlebury, (802) 388-2117.
June to October: Monday to Saturday, 10 a.m. to 5 p.m. 19th-century Vermont furnishings.

WILSON CASTLE: *35% discount.*
W. Proctor Rd., Rutland, (802) 773-3284.
May to October, 8 a.m. to 6 p.m. 19th-century estate.

WOODSTOCK HISTORICAL SOCIETY: *35% discount.*
Dana House, 26 Elm St., (802) 457-1822.
June to October: Monday to Saturday, 10 a.m. to 5 p.m.; Sunday, 11 a.m. to 2 p.m.

Free!

Bennington: Fairdale Farms. Burlington: Fleming Museum of Art at the University of Vermont. Montpelier: Vermont Historical Society Museum. Rutland: Hubbardton Battlefield & Museum.

Join a National Senior Citizens' Organization
AARP/NRTA, $75.0 yearly, 215 Long Beach Blvd., Long Beach, CA 90801, (800) 453-9600; *National Council of Senior Citizens*, $10 yearly, 925 15th St., NW, Washington, DC 20005, (202) 347-8800; *Mature Outlook*, $7.50 yearly, P.O. Box 1209, Glenview, IL 60025, (800) 336-6226; *Catholic Golden Age*, $7 yearly, 400 Lackawanna Ave., Scranton, PA 18503. Avoid last-minute worry and disappointment by requesting your membership card four to six weeks before your trip.

VIRGINIA

Helpful Addresses

VIRGINIA DIVISION OF TOURISM
101 N. 9th St., Richmond, VA 23219
(804) 786-4484

DEPARTMENT ON AGING
101 N. 14th St., 18th Floor, Richmond, VA 23219
(804) 225-2271

WILLIAMSBURG (with JAMESTOWN and YORKTOWN)

Senior Time

Every September, seniors 55 years and older are saluted in Williamsburg, Jamestown, and Yorktown with special activities and special rates at hotels, guest houses, restaurants, attractions, and retailers. Write to the Williamsburg Area Tourism & Conference Bureau, P.O. Box GB, Williamsburg, VA 23187, for information, or call (804) 253-0192 or (800) 447-8679.

Christmastime in Williamsburg

Low-season rates at most hotels combine with bonfires, Christmas decorations, and candlelight tours of Colonial Williamsburg to make December one of the best and cheapest times to visit. Dates and details of special events are available from the Williamsburg Area Tourism & Conference Bureau.

Hotels

BEST WESTERN: *10% discount. Advance reservation required.*
POD 3108, US 60 W., (804) 565-1000.

COMPARATIVE HOTEL RATES: REGULAR DOUBLE ROOM

HOTEL	SR. DISC.	
B & B	—	$30–70
BEST WESTERN	10%	$53–80
DAYS INN	25%	$29–39
ECONOLODGE	10%	$46–49
HOLIDAY INN	15%	$69–85
HOWARD JOHNSON'S	33%	$23–37
QUALITY INN	10%	$38–66
RAMADA INN	25%	$31–64
SHERATON	25%	$32–62

DAYS INN: *10%–50% discount with Days Inn September Days Club card.*
3074 Richmond Rd. (I-64 & Rte. 60), (804) 565-2700.

ECONOLODGE: *10% discount with Econo Senior Class Card.*
442 Parkway Dr., (804) 229-7564.
Pottery Factory, Rte. 3, (804) 564-3341.
1413 Richmond Rd., (804) 229-8551.
Busch Gardens, 505 York St., (804) 220-3100.

HOLIDAY INN: *10%–20% discount with Holiday Inn's Travel Venture Club Card.*
1776, US 60 (Bypass Rd.), (804) 220-1776.
East, 814 Capitol Landing, (804) 229-0200.

HOWARD JOHNSON'S: *15%–50% discount with H.J.'s Road Rally Card.*
1800 Richmond Rd., (804) 229-2781.

QUALITY INN: *10% discount for over 60.*
Francis Nicholson, US 60 Bypass, P.O. Box CE, (804) 229-6270.

John Yancey, 1900 Richmond Rd., (804) 229-6600.
Colony, Hwys. 60 & 162, (804) 229-1855.
Comfort Inn, 120 Bypass Rd., (804) 229-2000.
Lord Paget, 901 Capitol Landing, (804) 229-4444.

RAMADA INN: *25% discount for over 60.*
351 York St., (804) 229-4100.
West, 5351 Richmond Rd., (804) 565-2000.

SHERATON: *25% discount for over 60.*
Sheraton Patriot, Rte. 60, (804) 565-2600.

Car Rental

AVIS: *5%–25% discount.**
1187 Jamestown Rd., (804) 229-3638.

HERTZ: *5%–25% discount.**
1351 Richmond Rd., (804) 229-5115.

NATIONAL: *10%–12% discount for over 62.*
Hilton, 50 Kingsmill Rd., (804) 220-3856.

Sights

JAMESTOWN ISLAND: *Free with Golden Eagle Passport.*
(804) 898-3400.

Mid-June to Labor Day: daily, 8:30 a.m. to 5:30 p.m. After Labor Day to October, and April to mid-June: 8:30 a.m. to 5 p.m. November to March: 8:30 a.m. to 4:30 p.m. Site of the seventeenth-century settlement. The Old Church Tower is the only standing ruin. Markers, monuments, and recordings explain the history of the town.

JAMESTOWN FESTIVAL PARK: *10% discount.*
(804) 229-1607 and 253-4868.

June to August: daily, 9 a.m. to 5 p.m.

Re-creations of early Jamestown adjacent to the historical site. Powhatan's Lodge, the 1607 fort, and the *Susan Constant*, *Godspeed*, and *Discovery* are shown by costumed guides.

YORKTOWN VICTORY CENTER: *10% discount.*
Rte. 238, (804) 887-1776.

Daily, 9 a.m. to 5 p.m. Virginia's official bicentennial center features exhibits and films tracing the history of the Revolution.

WASHINGTON

Helpful Addresses

WASHINGTON STATE DEPT. OF COMMERCE AND ECONOMIC DEVELOPMENT
Travel Development Division, 101 General Administration Bldg., Olympia, WA 98504.
(206) 753-5600, (800) 541-WASH (except WA), (800) 562-4570 (in WA)

AGING AND ADULT SERVICES ADMINISTRATION
OB-44A, Olympia, WA 98504
(206) 586-3768

SEATTLE

Hotels

BEST WESTERN: *10% discount.*
20717 Pacific Hwy. S., (206) 878-1814.
2500 Aurora Ave. N., (206) 284-1900.
200 Taylor Ave. N., (206) 628-9444.

DOUBLETREE: *15% discount.**
Airport, 205 Strander Blvd., (206) 246-8220.
Airport, 16500 Southcenter Pkwy., (206) 575-8220.

HOLIDAY INN: *10%–20% discount with Holiday Inn's Travel Venture Club Card.*
Boeing Field, 11244 Pacific Hwy. S., (206) 762-0300.
Downtown, 6th & Seneca, (206) 464-1980.
East, 11211 Main St., Bellevue, (206) 455-5240.
International Airport, 17338 Pacific Hwy. S., (206) 248-1000.

NENDEL'S: *10% discount for Vagabond's Club 55.*
International Airport, 16838 Pacific Hwy. S., (206) 248-0901.

QUALITY INN: *10% discount for over 60.*
International Airport, 3000 S. 176th St., (206) 246-9110.

RAMADA INN: *25% discount for over 60.*
2140 N. Northgate Way, (206) 365-0700.

RED LION INN: *10% discount for over 50.**
18740 Pacific Hwy. S., (206) 246-8600.

800 NUMBERS ARE SUPER SAVERS!
See the first two chapters for the 800 numbers of all the major hotel, car rental, tour, and airline companies; 800 numbers are listed where available in the state-by-state listings for the state tourist offices. Use 800 numbers whenever possible to obtain information and make reservations. If no 800 number is provided, be sure to call 800 information at 1 (800) 555-1212, and ask—it's a free call too!

SHERATON: *25% discount for over 60.*
Downtown, 6th & Pike St., (206) 621-9000.
Renton, 800 Rainier Ave. S., Renton, (206) 226-7700.

TRAVELODGE: *Special senior rates for Travelodge's Golden Guest Club.*
Airport, 2900 S. 192nd, (206) 241-9292.
Aurora Ave., 1911 Aurora Ave., (206) 283-6070.
Downtown, 2213 8th Ave., (206) 624-6300.
Space Needle, 200 6th Ave., N., (206) 441-7878.
University, 4725 25th Ave., (206) 525-4612.

Car Rental

AVIS: *5%–25% discount.**
1919 Fifth Ave., (206) 448-1700.
Seattle-Tacoma International Airport, (206) 433-5231.

HERTZ: 5%–25% discount.*
722 Pike St., (206) 682-5050.
Seattle-Tacoma International Airport, (206) 433-5264.

NATIONAL: *10%–12 discount for over 62.*
Airport, (206) 433-5501.
1942 Westlake Ave., (206) 448-7368.

Sights

BILL SPEIDELS'S UNDERGROUND TOURS: *30% discount.*
610 1st Ave., (206) 682-4646.
Daily, hours vary. Guided tour of five blocks where the street level was raised 10 feet after the 1889 fire. Storefronts and interiors remain intact underground.

**An asterisk indicates that the discount is intended for members of senior citizens' organizations that anyone can join. See "Hotel, Transportation, and Sightseeing Discounts."*

KINGDOME: *50% discount on tours for over 65.*
201 S. King St., (206) 628-3331.
Tours daily, except when there are midday events. January to May, 1 p.m. and 3 p.m.; June to December: 11 a.m., 1 p.m., and 3 p.m.

MONORAIL: *60% discount.*
Seattle Center (site of 1962 World's Fair) to Westlake Mall.
Daily, every 15 min.

SEATTLE AQUARIUM: *60% discount over 65.*
Pier 59, Waterfront Park, (206) 625-4357.
Summer: daily, 10 a.m. to 9 p.m. Winter: daily, 10 a.m. to 5 p.m.; Friday, 10 a.m. to 9 p.m.

SEATTLE HARBOR TOUR: *25% discount.*
Pier 55, Seneca St., (206) 623-1445.
May to October: daily, 11 a.m. to 5:30 p.m.

TILLICUM VILLAGE: *10% discount.*
Blake Island State Park, (206) 329-5700.
Cruise leaves from Pier 56, Seneca St., mid-May to mid-October. Indian dinner featuring baked salmon and dancing. Reservations required.

WOODLAND PARK ZOO: *85% discount.*
Phinney Ave., N., (206) 789-7919.
Opens daily at 8:30. Closing varies with season.

Museums

MUSEUM OF FLIGHT: *35% discount.*
"Red Barn," King County Int'l. Airport, (206) 767-7373.
Daily, 9 a.m. to 5 p.m. Aviation history.

MUSEUM OF HISTORY & INDUSTRY: *50% discount.*

2161 E. Hamlin St., McCurdy Park, (206) 324-1125.
Monday to Saturday, 10 a.m. to 5 p.m.; Sunday, noon to 5 p.m. History of Seattle.

PACIFIC SCIENCE CENTER: *40% discount.*
200 2nd Ave. N., (206) 728-2886.
Winter: Monday to Friday, 10 a.m. to 5 p.m.; Saturday, Sunday, 10 a.m. to 6 p.m.

SEATTLE ART MUSEUM: *50% discount.*
14th Ave. E. & E. Prospect St., (206) 443-4670.
Tuesday to Saturday, 10 a.m. to 5 p.m.; Thursday, 10 a.m. to 9 p.m.; Sunday, noon to 5 p.m.

Free!

Alki Beach Park, Frye Art Museum, Klondike Gold Rush National Historical Park, Museum of History and Industry, Pike Place Market, Schmitz Park, Washington Park Arboretum, Wing Luke Memorial Museum

WEST VIRGINIA

Helpful Addresses

WEST VIRGINIA TRAVEL DEVELOPMENT DIVISION
State Capitol, 1900 Washington St. E., Charleston, WV 25305
(304) 348-2286, (800) 624-9110

COMMISSION ON AGING
State Capitol, Charleston, WV 25305
(304) 348-3317

CHARLESTON

Hotels

HOLIDAY INN: *10%–20% discount with Holiday Inn's Travel Venture Club Card.*
Broad St., 1000 Washington St. E., (304) 343-4661.
Downtown, 600 Kanawha Blvd. E., (304) 344-4092.

KNIGHTS INN: *10% discount.*
South, I-77 at MacCorkle Ave., (304) 925-0451.

RAMADA INN: *25% discount for over 60.*
2nd Ave. & B St., (304) 744-4641.

Car Rental

AVIS: *5%–25% discount**
416 Capitol St., (304) 343-9446.

HERTZ: *5%–25% discount.**
Airport, (304) 346-0573.

NATIONAL: *10%–12% discount for over 62.*
Airport, (304) 344-2563.

Rules for Savings on Car Rentals

1. Join a national senior citizens' organization and use its discount identification number.
2. Make advance reservations with the toll-free national reservation service.
3. Renting mid-week? A senior-citizen rate can save you money.
4. Renting for seven days or for the weekend? Senior discounts can save you another 5% to 10%.
5. Always ask, "Is this the cheapest rate you offer?"

See pages 32–34 for more information.

Free!

The Cultural Center, Museums at Sunrise (Art Gallery, Children's Museum, Garden Center), State Capitol.

WISCONSIN

Helpful Addresses

WISCONSIN STATE DIVISION OF TOURISM
123 W. Washington Ave., P.O. Box 7606, Madison, WI 53707
(608) 266-2161, (800) ESCAPES (No. IL, MI, MN, WI only)

BUREAU OF AGING
1 W. Wilson St., Rm. 480, Madison, WI 53702
(608) 266-2536

Bicycle Tour

Participants in American Youth Hostels' 50+ "Big Cheese" tour spend 9 days exploring the Wisconsin Bikeway ($230 from Madison). Call (202) 783-6161 for information.

MILWAUKEE

Hotels

BEST WESTERN: *10% discount.*
251 N. Mayfair Rd., (414) 774-3600.
5501 W. National Ave., (414) 671-6400.

HOLIDAY INN: *10%–20% discount with Holiday Inn's Travel Venture Club Card.*
Airport, 6331 S. 13th St. & College Ave., (414) 764-1500.

Northeast, 5423 N. Port Washington Rd., (414) 962-9410.
West, 201 N. Mayfair Rd., (414) 771-4400.

HOWARD JOHNSON'S: *15%–50% discount with H.J.'s Road Rally Card.*
Airport, 1716 W. Layton Ave., (414) 282-7000.
Downtown, 611 W. Wisconsin Ave., (414) 273-2950.
North, 2275 Mayfair Rd., Wauwatosa, (414) 771-4800.

QUALITY INN: *10% discount for over 60.*
Airport, 5311 S. Howell Ave., (414) 481-2400.

RAMADA INN: *25% discount for over 60.*
Downtown, 633 W. Michigan, (414) 272-8410.
West, 11811 W. Bluemound Rd., (414) 771-4500.

SHERATON: *25% discount for over 60.*
2303 N. Mayfair Rd., Wauwatosa, (414) 257-3400.

Car Rental

AVIS: *5%–25% discount.**
Airport, (414) 744-2266.

HERTZ: *5%–25% discount.**
Airport, 5300 S. Howell, (414) 747-5200.

NATIONAL: *10%–12% discount for over 62.*
Airport, (414) 483-9800.

Museums

MILWAUKEE ART MUSEUM: *50% discount.*
750 N. Lincoln Memorial Dr., (414) 271-9508.
Tuesday, Wednesday, Friday, Saturday, 10 a.m. to 5 p.m.; Thursday, noon to 5 p.m.; Sunday, 1 to 6 p.m.

PABST MANSION: *40% discount.*
2000 W. Wisconsin Ave., (414) 931-0808.

Monday to Saturday, 10 a.m. to 3:30 p.m.; Sunday, noon to 3:30 p.m. Built in 1893, the restored mansion of Captain Pabst.

Free!

Allis Art Museum, Milwaukee County Historical Center, Villa Terrace Museum of Decorative Arts, tours of Miller, Pabst, and Schlitz breweries.

WYOMING

Helpful Addresses

WYOMING TRAVEL COMMISSION
Frank Norris Jr. Travel Center, I-25 at College Dr., Cheyenne, WY 82002
(307) 777-7777

COMMISSION ON AGING
Hathaway Bldg., Rm. 139, Cheyenne, WY 82002
(307) 777-7986

Package Tour for Seniors

Covering six states, Saga's 14-night National Park Holiday includes Yellowstone, Mt. Rushmore, Grand Teton National Park, as well as Rocky Mountain State Park, Zion National Park, and the Black Hills of South Dakota (from $1300). See pages 7–10 for more information on package tours.

YELLOWSTONE AREA

Hotels

HOLIDAY INN: *10%–20% discount with Holiday Inn's Travel Venture Club Card.*
Cody, 1701 Sheridan Ave., (307) 587-5555.

Car Rental

AVIS: *5%–25% discount.**
Cody Airport, (307) 587-5792.
Jackson Airport, (307) 733-3422.

HERTZ: *5%–25% discount.**
Cody Airport, (307) 587-2914.
Jackson Airport, (307) 733-2272.

NATIONAL: *10%–12% discount for over 62.*
Jackson Airport, (307) 733-4132.

Sights

BUFFALO BILL HISTORICAL CENTER: *15% discount.*
Sheridan Ave., Cody, (307) 587-4771.
Daily, March to November. Extended hours in summer. 4-museum complex.

CANADA

Helpful Addresses

CANADIAN TOURIST OFFICE
Exxon Building, 16th Fl.,
1251 Ave. of the Americas, New York, NY 10020
(212) 757-4917

510 W. 6th St.,
Los Angeles, CA 90014
(213) 622-4292

**An asterisk indicates that the discount is intended for members of senior citizens' organizations that anyone can join. See "Hotel, Transportation, and Sightseeing Discounts."*

PLANE, TRAIN, AND BUS TRAVEL

AIRFARE DISCOUNTS

Air Canada and Canadian Airlines International offer 20% to 30% discounts to travelers over 65 on full-fare flights within Canada. Canadian air travel is currently being deregulated, so be sure to shop around for the best deal.

DISCOUNT TRAIN TRAVEL

Via Rail, Canada's national rail system, offers discounts of 33% off regular coach fares to travelers over 60. Information is available from travel agents, from Amtrak (call 800-USA-RAIL), or from Via Rail Canada, P.O. Box 1358, Montreal, PQ, H5A 1H2, Canada. Always be sure to check; promotional fares may be cheaper than the discounted coach fare. Also, be sure you understand whether the price quoted is in Canadian or U.S. dollars; in 1987, $1 U.S. equaled $1.33 in Canadian currency.

DISCOUNT BUS TRAVEL

Greyhound offers the same 10% discount to travelers over 65 on its routes in Canada as it does in the U.S. Gray Coach, which serves primarily Ontario, also offers a 10% discount on its one-way and round-trip fares, while Voyageur, serving both Ontario and Quebec, offers a 33% senior discount.

BRITISH COLUMBIA

Helpful Address

MINISTRY OF TOURISM
Province of British Columbia, 1117 Wharf St.,
Victoria V8W 2Z2

VANCOUVER

Helpful Address

GREATER VANCOUVER CONVENTION & VISITORS BUREAU
1055 W. Georgia St., Suite 1625, P.O. Box 11142, Vancouver, V6E 4C8, (604) 682-2222.

Hotels

AUSTIN MOTOR HOTEL: *10% discount.*
1221 Granville St., V6Z 1M6, (604) 685-7235.

BEST WESTERN: *10% discount.*
1100 Granville St., (604) 669-7070.
1755 Davie St., (604) 682-1831.
5411 Kingsway, (604) 438-1383.

HOLIDAY INN: *10%–20% discount with Holiday Inn's Travel Venture Club Card.*
Broadway, 711 W. Broadway & Heather St., (604) 879-0511.
City Centre, 1133 W. Hastings St., (604) 689-9211.

SHERATON: *25% discount for over 60.*
Plaza 500, 500 W. 12th Ave., (604) 873-1811.
Burnaby, 4331 Dominion St., (604) 430-2828.
Downtown, 1400 Robson St., (604) 687-0511.

TRAVELODGE: *Special senior rates for Travelodge's Golden Guest Club.*
Centre, 1304 Howe St., (604) 682-2767.
Kingsway, 2075 Kingsway, (604) 876-5531.
Lions Gate, 2060 Marine Dr., (604) 985-5311.

Car Rental

AVIS: *20% discount.**
757 Hornby St., (604) 682-1621.

HERTZ: *15% discount.**
Airport, (604) 278-4001.
666 Seymour St., (604) 688-2411.

TILDEN RENT-A-CAR: *10%–20% discount.**
Airport, 1140 Alberni St., (604) 685-6111.

Tours

HARBOUR TOURS: *$2 off ticket price.*
Denman St., (604) 687-9558.
Sternwheeler cruises. Call for times and prices.

Package Tour for Seniors

A 16-day van tour that originates in Portland, American Youth Hostels' 50+ "Northwest Borderline" tour moves up the Olympic Peninsula and Puget Sound to Victoria and Vancouver, BC, returning to Portland along the Columbia River ($585 from Portland). Call (202) 783-6161 for information.

Sights

BLOEDEL CONSERVATORY: *50% discount for over 65.*
Queen Elizabeth Park, Cambie St. & W. 33rd. (604) 873-1133.
Summer: 10 a.m. to 9:30 p.m. Rest of year: 10 a.m. to 5:30 p.m.

FORT LANGLEY NATIONAL HISTORIC PARK: *Free for seniors over 65.*
Off Trans-Canada Hwy., (604) 888-4424.
Mid-June to Labor Day: daily, 10 a.m. to 9 p.m.
Rest of year: 10 a.m. to 5 p.m.

GROUSE MOUNTAIN TRAMWAY: *40% discount for over 65.*
5100 Capilano Rd., (604) 984-0661.
April to October: Monday to Friday, 11 a.m. to 10 p.m.; weekends, 10 a.m. to 10 p.m.

STANLEY PARK AQUARIUM: *55% discount.*
Stanley Park, (604) 685-3364.
Daily, 10 a.m. to dusk.

VANDUSEN BOTANICAL DISPLAY GARDEN: *50% discount.*
5151 Oak St., (604) 266-7194.
October to March: daily, 10 a.m. to 4 p.m. September, and April to June: daily, 10 a.m. to 8 p.m. July, August: daily, 10 a.m. to 9 p.m.

Museums

ARTS, SCIENCE & TECHNOLOGY MUSEUM: *50% discount.*
600 Granville St., (604) 687-8414.

Join a National Senior Citizens' Organization *AARP/NRTA*, $7.50 yearly, 215 Long Beach Blvd., Long Beach, CA 90801, (800) 453-9600; *National Council of Senior Citizens*, $10 yearly, 925 15th St., NW, Washington, DC 20005, (202) 347-8800; *Mature Outlook*, $7.50 yearly, P.O. Box 1209, Glenview, IL 60025, (800) 336-6226; *Catholic Golden Age*, $7 yearly, 400 Lackawanna Ave., Scranton, PA 18503. Avoid last-minute worry and disappointment by requesting your membership card four to six weeks before your trip.

BURNABY VILLAGE MUSEUM: *50% discount.*
4900 Deer Lake, Burnaby, (604) 294-1233
March to December: Tuesday to Sunday, 11 a.m. to 4:30 p.m. 1890 to 1925 thirty-building village. Craft demonstrations. Miniature steam train.

MARITIME MUSEUM: *50% discount. Seniors free on Tuesday.*
Foot of Cypress St., (604) 736-7736.
June to August: daily, 10 a.m. to 9 p.m.
September to May: daily, 10 a.m. to 5 p.m.

MUSEUM OF ANTHROPOLOGY: *50% discount.*
N. W. Marine Dr., U. of B.C., (604) 228-3825.

VANCOUVER MUSEUM: *50% discount. Seniors free on Tuesday.*
1100 Chestnut St., (604) 736-4431.
Tuesday to Saturday, 10 a.m. to 8 p.m.; Monday, Sunday, 10 a.m. to 5 p.m.

Free!

Burnaby Art Gallery, Capilano Salmon Hatchery, Old Hasting Mill Store Museum, Stanley Park, Tilford Gardens, Transportation Museum

---

VICTORIA

Helpful Address

GREATER VICTORIA VISITORS & CONVENTION BUREAU
812 Wharf St., (604) 382-2127

Hotels

COLONY INN: *10% discount upon presentation of health-care card.*
2852 Douglas St., (604) 385-2441.

RODEWAY INN: *10% discount.*
2915 Douglas St., (604) 385-6731.

TRAVELODGE: *Special senior rates for Travelodge's Golden Guest Club.*
Airport, 2280 Beacon Ave., Sidney, (604) 656-1176.
Tally Ho Inn, 3020 Douglas St., (604) 386-6141.

Car Rental

AVIS: *20% discount.**
3200 Douglas St., (604) 386-8468.

HERTZ: *15% discount (except Class A cars).**
990 Blanchard St., (604) 388-4411.

TILDEN RENT-A-CAR: *10%–20% discount.**
767 Douglas St., (604) 386-1213.

Package Tours for Seniors

A 16-day van tour that originates in Portland, American Youth Hostels' 50+ "Northwest Borderline" tour moves up the Olympic Peninsula and Puget Sound to Victoria and Vancouver, BC, returning to Portland along the Columbia River ($585 from Portland). Call (202) 783-6161 for information.

Sights

CRYSTAL GARDEN: *50% discount.*
713 Douglas St., (604) 381-1213.
Daily, 10 a.m. to 5:30 p.m.; until 8 p.m. in summer.

PACIFIC UNDERSEA GARDENS: *25% discount.*
490 Belleville St., (604) 382-5717.
May to October: 9 a.m. to 9 p.m. Rest of year, 10 a.m. to 5 p.m.

Museums

ART GALLERY OF GREATER VICTORIA: *50% discount over 65.*
1040 Moss St., (604) 384-4101.
Tuesday to Saturday, 10 a.m. to 5 p.m.; Sunday, 1 to 5 p.m.; Thursday, 10 a.m. to 9 p.m.

BC FOREST MUSEUM: *$1 discount.*
Rte. 1, Duncan, (604) 746-1251.
Mid-May to mid-September: daily, 10 a.m. to 5:30 p.m. Logging museum and steam train.

MARITIME MUSEUM: *$1 discount over 65.*
28 Bastion Sq., (604) 385-4222.
July to Labor Day: daily, 10 a.m. to 5 p.m.; Sunday, 1 p.m. to 5 p.m.; closed Monday in winter.

Free!

Carr House, Emily Carr Gallery, Craigflower Manor National Historic Site, Dominion Astrological Observatory, Hatley Castle, Helmcken House, Point Ellice House Museum.

ONTARIO

OTTAWA

Helpful Address

CANADA'S CAPITAL VISITORS & CONVENTION BUREAU
222 Queen St., Ottawa K1P 5V9
(613) 237-5158

Hotels

HOLIDAY INN: *10%–20% discount with Holiday Inn's Travel Venture Club Card.*
Centre, 100 Kent St., (613) 238-1122.
Downtown, 350 Dalhousie St., (613) 236-0201.

HOWARD JOHNSON'S: *15%–50% discount with H.J.'s Road Rally Card.*
140 Slater St., (613) 238-2888.

Car Rental

AVIS: *20% discount.**
Airport, (613) 731-8427.
Place de Ville, 320 Queen St., (613) 238-3421.

HERTZ: *15% discount.**
Airport, (613) 521-3332.
881 St. Laurent Blvd., (613) 746-6683.

TILDEN RENT-A-CAR: *10%–20% discount.**
199 Slater St., (613) 232-3536.

Free!

Canadian Ski Museum, Canadian War Museum, Agriculture Museum, Canadian Currency Museum, Central Experimental Farm, Laurier House, National Aeronautical Collection, National Gallery of Canada, Canadian Museum of Civilization, National Museum of Natural Science, National Museum of Science and Technology, National Postal Museum, Parliament Buildings, Governor General's Grounds, Public Archives of Canada, Royal Canadian Mint

**An asterisk indicates that the discount is intended for members of senior citizens' organizations that anyone can join. See "Hotel, Transportation, and Sightseeing Discounts."*

TORONTO

Helpful Address

METROPOLITAN TORONTO CONVENTION & VISITORS ASSOCIATION
Toronto Eaton Center, Suite 110, Box 510, 220 Yonge St., Toronto M5B 2H1
(416) 979-3143

Hotels

HOLIDAY INN: *10%–20% discount with Holiday Inn's Travel Venture Club Card.*
Airport, 970 Dixon Rd., Rexdale, (416) 675-7611.
Don Valley, 1250 Eglinton Ave. E., (416) 449-4111.
Downtown, Armoury & Chestnut St., (416) 977-0707.
East, Hwy. 401 at Warden Ave., Scarborough, (416) 293-8171.
West, Hwy. 427, Etobicoke, (416) 621-2121.
Yorkdate, 3450 Dufferin St., (416) 789-5161.

HOWARD JOHNSON'S: *15%–50% discount with H.J.'s Road Rally Card.*
Airport, 801 Dixon Rd., (416) 675-6100.
East, 40 Progress St., (416) 439-6200.
West, 590 Argus Rd., Oakville, (416) 842-4780.

QUALITY INN: *10% discount for over 60.*
300 Jarvis St., (416) 977-4823.

RAMADA INN: *25% discount for over 60.*
Downtown, 111 Carlton, (416) 977-8000.

SHERATON: *25% discount for over 60.*
Sheraton Centre, 123 Queen St., (416) 361-1000.

TRAVELODGE: *Special senior rates for Travelodge's Golden Guest Club.*
Viscount, 55 Hallcrown Pl., (416) 493-7000.

Car Rental

AVIS: *20% discount.**
Airport, (416) 676-3844.
Downtown, Hudson Bay Centre, (416) 964-2410.

HERTZ: *15% discount.**
Airport, (416) 676-3241.
Downtown, Hudson Bay Centre, (416) 961-3320.

TILDEN RENT-A-CAR: *10%–20% discount.**
Airport, (416) 676-2647.
930 Yonge St., (416) 925-4551.

Sights

BLACK CREEK PIONEER VILLAGE: *50% discount.*
Jane & Steeles, (416) 661-6610.
Weekends, 10 a.m. to 6 p.m.; Monday to Friday: 9:30 a.m. to 5. Closed January to mid-March. Restored village with 30 buildings.

C. N. TOWER: *20% discount.*
301 Front St., (416) 360-8500.
Daily, 10 a.m. to 10 p.m.

HISTORIC FORT YORK: *50% discount.*
Garrison Rd., S.E., (416) 392-6907.
May to Labor Day: daily, 9:30 a.m. to 5 p.m. Rest of year: Monday to Saturday, 9:30 a.m. to 5 p.m.; Sunday, noon to 5:30 p.m. Restored fort from War of 1812.

METRO TORONTO ZOO: *50% discount.*
Meadowvale Rd., Scarborough, (416) 392-5900.
Daily, 9:30 a.m. to 7 p.m. Last admission 6 p.m.

ONTARIO PLACE: *Free to seniors over 65.*
955 Lakeshore Blvd. W., (416) 965-7711.
Open daily in summer, 10 a.m. to 1 a.m.; Sunday

until 11 p.m. Entertainment and recreation complex.

Museums

ART GALLERY OF ONTARIO: *$1.50 admission. Seniors free on Friday.*
317 Dundas St., (416) 977-0414.
Tuesday, Friday to Sunday, 11 a.m. to 5 p.m.; Wednesday & Thursday, 11 a.m. to 9 p.m. Free to all, Thursdays, 5:30 p.m. to 9 p.m.

CASA LOMA: *66% discount.*
1 Austin Terrace, (416) 923-1171.
Open 10 a.m. to 4 p.m. Enormous medieval-style castle (1911).

COLBORNE LODGE: *33% discount.*
Colborne Lodge Dr. & The Queensway in High Pk., (416) 595-1567.
Monday to Saturday, 9:30 a.m. to 5 p.m.; Sunday, noon to 5 p.m. 1836 restored house & art gallery.

GARDINER MUSEUM OF CERAMIC ART: *50% discount.*
111 Queen's Park, (416) 593-9300.
Tuesday to Sunday, 10 a.m. to 5 p.m.

GIBSON HOUSE MUSEUM: *50% discount.*
5172 Yonge St., N. York. (416) 225-0146.
Monday to Saturday, 9:30 a.m. to 5 p.m.; Sunday, noon to 5 p.m. Restored 1850s house. Craft demonstrations.

MACKENZIE HOUSE: *33% discount.*
82 Bond St., (416) 595-1567.
Monday to Saturday, 9:30 a.m. to 5 p.m.; Sunday, noon to 5 p.m. Restored nineteenth-century house of first mayor of Toronto. Tea is served daily from 2 to 4 p.m.

MARINE MUSEUM OF UPPER CANADA: *35% discount.*
Exhibition Place, (416) 595-1567.
Mid-August to Labor Day: Monday to Saturday, 9:30 a.m. to 10 p.m.; Sunday, noon to 10 p.m. Rest of year: Monday to Saturday, 9:30 a.m. to 5 p.m.; Sunday, noon to 5 p.m.

MCLAUGHLIN PLANETARIUM: *40% discount. Seniors free on Tuesday.*
In Royal Ontario Museum, 100 Queen's Park, (416) 586-5736.
September to June: Tuesday to Friday, 3 to 7:30 p.m. Rest of year, and Saturday and Sunday: 12:30 to 1:45, 3 to 7:30 p.m.

ONTARIO SCIENCE CENTER: *Free for seniors.*
770 Don Mills Rd., (416) 429-4100.
Daily, 10 a.m. to 6 p.m. Science exhibits and demonstrations in which visitors can participate.

ROYAL ONTARIO MUSEUM: *65% discount. Seniors free on Tuesday.*
100 Queen's Park, (416) 586-5549.
Monday, Wednesday, Saturday, 10 a.m. to 6 p.m.; Tuesday, 10 a.m. to 9 p.m.; Sunday, noon to 8 p.m.

TODMORDEN MILLS MUSEUM: *33% discount.*
67 Pottery Rd., E. York, (416) 425-2250.
May to October: Tuesday to Friday, 10 a.m. to 5:30 p.m.; Saturday and Sunday, 11 a.m. to 6 p.m. November and December: Tuesday to Friday, 10 a.m. to 4 p.m.; Saturday and Sunday, 11 a.m. to 4:30 p.m. Two restored houses (1798 and 1838) and museum in restored railroad station (1899).

Free!

McMichael Canadian Collection, Toronto Stock Exchange, Ontario Place, Tours of City Hall

QUEBEC

Helpful Address

TOURISME QUÉBEC
P.O. Box 20,000, Québec G1K 7X2
Written requests only. Information on Québec Province.

MONTREAL

Helpful Addresses

TOURISME QUÉBEC
2 Place Ville-Marie, Suite 70, Montreal, (514) 873-2015.

Hotels

HOLIDAY INN: *10%–20% discount with Holiday Inn's Travel Venture Club Card.*
Downtown, 420 Sherbrooke W., (514) 824-6111.
Longueuil, 999 De Serigny, (514) 670-3030.
Place Dupuis, 1415 St. Hubert, (514) 842-4881.
Pointe Claire, 6700 Trans-Canada Hwy., (514) 697-7110.
Richelieu, 505 Sherbrooke St. E., (514) 842-8581.
Seigneurie, 7300 Cote de Liesse, (514) 731-7751.
Le Seville, 4545 Cote Vertu W., (514) 332-2720.

QUALITY INN: *10% discount for over 60.*
475 Sherbrooke St. W., (514) 842-3961.

RAMADA INN: *25% discount for over 60.*
Downtown, 1005 Guy St., (514) 866-4611.
Olympic Park, 5500 Sherbrooke E., (514) 256-9011.

SHERATON: *25% discount for over 60.*
Charron Island, 2405 Ile Charron, Longueuil, (514) 651-6510.
Downtown, 1201 Dorchester West, (514) 878-2000.
Laval, 2440 Autoroutes des Laurentides, (514) 687-2440.

Car Rental

AVIS: *20% discount.**
Airport, (514) 636-1902.
1225 Metcalf St., (514) 866-7906.

HERTZ: *15% Discount.**
Airport, (514) 636-9530.
1475 Alymer St., (514) 842-8537.

TILDEN: *10%–20% discount.**
1200 Stanley St., (514) 878-2771.

Sights

MONTREAL AQUARIUM: *50% discount.*
Ile Ste. Helene, (514) 872-4656.

MONTREAL BOTANICAL GARDEN: *50% discount.*
4110 Sherbrooke St. E., (514) 872-1400. Daily, 9 a.m. to 6 p.m.

Museums

CENTRE D'HISTOIRE DE MONTREAL: *50% discount.*
335, rue Saint-Pierre, (514) 872-3207.
Tuesday to Sunday, 10 a.m. to 4:30 p.m.

CHATEAU RAMEZAY: *50% discount.*
280 Notre Dame E., (514) 861-7182. Tuesday to Sunday, 10 a.m. to 4:30 p.m. History of 17th- and 18th-century Montreal.

McCORD MUSEUM: *60% discount.*
690 Sherbrooke St. W., (514) 392-4778.
Wednesday to Sunday, 11 a.m. to 5 p.m.
Canadian social history.

MUSÉE MARC-AURÉLÈ FORTIN: *50% discount.*
118, rue Saint-Pierre, (514) 845-6108.
Tuesday to Sunday, 11 a.m. to 4:30 p.m.

MUSEUM OF DECORATIVE ARTS: *50% discount.*
Sherbrooke St. & Pie IX, (514) 259-2575.
Wednesday to Sunday, noon to 5 p.m.

MUSEUM OF FINE ARTS: *Free for seniors.*
1379 Sherbrooke St. W., (514) 285-1600.
Tuesday to Sunday, 11 a.m. to 5 p.m.

PLANETARIUM DE MONTRÉAL: *50% discount.*
1000, rue Saint-Jacques ouest, (514) 872-4530.
Daily.

Free!

Bank of Montreal Museum, Maison de Radio-Canada, Man and His World, Museum of Contemporary Art, St. Joseph's Oratory

QUEBEC CITY

Helpful Addresses

QUEBEC MINISTRY OF TOURISM
12 Sainte-Anne St., Quebec
(418) 643-2280

QUEBEC CITY REGION TOURISM & CONVENTION BUREAU
60 Rue d'Auteuil, (418) 692-2471

Hotels

HOLIDAY INN: *10%–20% discount with Holiday Inn's Travel Venture Club Card.*
Downtown, 395 Rue de la Couronne, (418) 647-2611.
Ste. Foy, 3225 Hochelaga, (418) 653-4901.

QUALITY INN: *10% discount for over 60.*
Ste. Foy, 3115 Blvd. Wilfrid Laurier, (418) 658-5120.

Car Rental

HERTZ: *15% discount.**
44 Cote du Palais, (418) 694-1224.

TILDEN: *10%–20% discount.**
295 St. Paul St., (418) 871-1224.

Sights

QUEBEC AQUARIUM: *50% discount.*
1675 Parc Ave., Ste. Foy, (418) 659-5264.
Daily, 9 a.m. to 5 p.m.; to 7 p.m. in summer.

QUEBEC ZOO: *50% discount.*
8191 Ave. du Zoo, Charlesbourg, (418) 622-0312.
Daily, 9:30 a.m. to 6 p.m.; later in summer.

Free!

Fort No. 1 del la pointe Levis, Fortifications of Quebec, Hotel du parlement, Maison Chevalier, Martello Towers, Musee du Quebec, Parc Carter-Brebeuf, Parc de l'Artillerie, Place Royale, Port de Quebec au XIXe siècle.

**An asterisk indicates that the discount is intended for members of senior citizens' organizations that anyone can join. See "Hotel, Transportation, and Sightseeing Discounts."*

EUROPE

Many countries maintain tourist offices in Chicago and Dallas. Call information to see if there is one near you.

AUSTRIA

Helpful Addresses

AUSTRIAN NATIONAL TOURIST OFFICES
500 Fifth Ave., 20th Fl., New York, NY 10110
(212) 944-6880

11601 Wilshire Blvd., Suite 480, Los Angeles, CA 90025
(213) 477-3332

1010 Sherbrooke St. W., Suite 1410-W,
Montreal H3A 2R7
(514) 849-3709

Transportation

RAIL TRAVEL: *50% discount with senior citizens' railroad ID. Men over 65 and women over 60 can buy an ID card for about $10 at railroad stations and major post offices in Austria. A passport-size photo and proof of age are required.*

Package Tours for Seniors

Both Saga and Grand Circle Travel offer Austrian vacations for seniors. For a two- or three-week tour, expect to pay $1200 to $1800 and up depending on whether you want to tour Austria or spend your holiday in one place. See "Package Tours for Seniors" for more information.

Museums

Many Austrian museums give a 50% discount to men over 65 and women over 60.

INNSBRUCK

Helpful Address

TOURIST INFORMATION
Verkehrsverein, Burggraben 3
tel. 05222 26 771

Car Rental

AVIS: *10% discount.**
Salurnerstrasse 15, tel. 05222 31 754.

EUROPCAR: *10%–20% discount.**
Salurnerstrasse 16, tel. 05222 32 151.

HERTZ: *5%–25% discount.**
Suedtirolerplatz 4, tel. 05222 20 901.

SALZBURG

Helpful Address

CITY TOURIST SERVICE
Auerspergstrasse 7, tel. (0662) 7 46 20

Hotels

SHERATON: *25% discount for over 60.*
Auerspergstrasse 4, (662) 3 14 29.

Car Rental

AVIS: *10% discount.**
Ferdinand Porschestrasse 7, tel. (662) 7 72 78.

EUROPCAR: *10%–20% discount.**
Neutorstrasse/Bayernstrasse 1, tel. (662) 4 37 21.

HERTZ: *5%–25% discount.**
Ferdinand Porschestrasse 7, tel. (662) 7 66 74.

VIENNA

Helpful Addresses

U.S. EMBASSY
Boltzmanngasse 16, tel. 31 55 11

CANADIAN EMBASSY
Dr.-Karl-Lueger-Ring 10, tel. 533 36 91

TOURIST INFORMATION
Kinderspitalgasse 5, tel. (0222) 43 16 08

Car Rental

AVIS: *10% discount.**
Opernring 1, tel. 57 35 95
Schwechat Airport, tel. 7770 27 00.

EUROPCAR: *10%–20% discount.**
Schwechat Airport, tel. 7770 26 99.
Mollardgasse 15, tel. 597 16 75.

HERTZ: *5%–25% discount.**
Kaerntnerring 17, tel. 52 86 77.
Schwechat Airport, tel. 7770 26 61.

BELGIUM

Helpful Address

BELGIAN NATIONAL TOURIST OFFICE
745 Fifth Ave., New York, NY 10151
(212) 758-8130

Transportation

SABENA: *Discovery Fare for seniors 60 and over saves $150 round trip off regular APEX fare. Just book the $169 one-way fare no more than 72 hours before departure. Contact the airline's local ticket office.*

BRUSSELS

Helpful Addresses

U.S. EMBASSY
blvd. du Regent 27, tel. 513 38 30

CANADIAN EMBASSY
rue de Loxum 6, tel. 513 79 40

TOURIST OFFICE
rue Marche aux Herbes 61, tel. 513 90 90

WELCOME TO BRUSSELS—CENTRE D'ACCUEIL
Gare du Midi, tel. 522 58 66

Hotels

RAMADA INN: *25% discount for over 60.*
Chausse de Charleroi 38, tel. (2) 539 30 00.

SHERATON: *25% discount for over 60.*
Place Rogier 3, tel. 219 34 00.

Car Rental

AVIS: *10% discount.**
Airport, Arrivals Hall, 720 09 44.
Manhattan Centre, place Rogier, tel. 217 25 48.

EUROPCAR: *10%–20% discount.**
Airport, tel. 721 05 92.
Louise, rue de l'Abbaye, 640 01 95.

HERTZ: *5%–25% discount.**
Airport, Tel. 751 50 59.
8 blvd. Maurice Lemonnier, tel. 513 28 86.

DENMARK

Helpful Addresses

DANISH TOURIST BOARD
655 Third Ave., New York, NY 10017
(212) 949-2333

150 N. Michigan Ave., Chicago, IL 60601
(312) 899-1121

8929 Wilshire Blvd., Beverly Hills, CA 90211
(213) 854-1549

P.O. Box 115, Station N., Toronto M8V 3S4
(416) 823-9620

Transportation

SAS: *Airlines discount for over 60.*
Standby travel from Copenhagen to any city in Denmark is only $32 one way. Must be arranged with SAS in Denmark.

RAIL TRAVEL: *30% discount for seniors over 65.*
On trips over 30 km each way, seniors can receive a 50% discount when they present identification showing their age at the train station.

COPENHAGEN

Helpful Addresses

U.S. EMBASSY
24 Dag Hammarskjoldsalle, tel. 01 12 31 44

CANADIAN EMBASSY
Kr. Bernikowsgade 1, tel. 01 12 22 99

DANMARKS TURISTRAAD (Tourist Information Center)
H. C. Andersens Boulevard 22 (opposite City Hall), tel. 01 11 1325.

Hotels

SHERATON: *25% discount.**
6 Vester Sogade, tel. 01 14 35 35.

Public Transportation

Seniors traveling during off-peak hours receive a discount when traveling on Copenhagen's trams and buses.

Car Rental

AVIS: *10% discount.**
Kastrup Airport, tel. 01 51 22 99.

EUROPCAR: *10%–20% discount.**
Kastrup Airport, tel. 01 50 66 66.
Gammel Kongevej 70, tel. 01 24 66 77.

HERTZ: *10% discount.**
Kastrup Airport, tel. 01 50 93 00.

Incredible Deals

The "Copenhagen Card" gets you unlimited travel on city bus and rail, free admission to museums and sights, and discounted ferry crossings to Sweden. Approximately $10 for one day, $17 for two days, $21 for three days from the Tourist Information Center listed above.

FINLAND

Helpful Address

FINNISH TOURIST BOARD
655 Third Ave., New York, NY 10017
(212) 949-2333

Transportation

FINNAIR: *50% discount on domestic flights for over 65. Not valid from Friday noon to Monday noon. Seniors over 65 can book flights from the United States to Helsinki at special rates if reservations are made no more than three days in advance. Fares from New York are $250 one way; $500 round trip.*
10 E. 40th St., New York, NY 10016, (212) 689-9300, (800) 223-5700.

RAIL TRAVEL: *50% discount on round trips for over 65 with railroad ID. Men and women over 65 can buy a senior citizen's ID card at any train station for about $4.*

BUS TRAVEL: *30% discount for over 65 with bus card. For approximately $3, seniors can buy a discount card at the bus station which entitles them to a 30% discount on rides of more than 50 miles each way.*

SHIPPING LINES: 50% discount for over 65. Silja Line and Viking Line ships traveling between Helsinki and Stockholm or Turku and Stockholm give a 50% discount.

Museums

Many museums in Finland give a 30% discount to seniors over 65.

HELSINKI

Helpful Addresses

U.S. Embassy
Itainen Puistotie 14A, tel. (90) 171 931

CANADIAN EMBASSY
Pohjoisesplanadi 25B, tel. (90) 171 141

FINNISH TOURIST BOARD
Unioninkatu 26, tel. (90) 144 511

HELSINKI CITY TOURIST OFFICE
Pohjoisesplanadi 19, tel. (90) 169 3757

Car Rental

AVIS: *10% discount.**
Fredrikinkatur 36, tel. (90) 694 400.
Helsinki-Lento Airport, tel. (90) 821 380.

EUROPCAR: *10%-20% discount.**
Helsinki-Lento Airport, tel. (90) 821 699.
Miriankatu 24, tel. (90) 177 588.

HERTZ: *5%–25% discount.**
Helsinki Airport, tel. (90) 821 052.
Hotel Intercontinental, Mannerheimintie 46-48, tel. (90) 446 910.

Incredible Deals

The "Helsinki Card" gets you unlimited travel on city buses and trams, free sightseeing tours, free entrance to museums and attractions, and discounts on recreation. $12 for 1 day, $7 for 2 days, $20 for 3 days from Helsinki Tourist Office.

FRANCE

Helpful Addresses

FRENCH GOVERNMENT TOURIST OFFICE
610 Fifth Ave., New York, NY 10020
(212) 757-1125

9401 Wilshire Blvd., Beverly Hills, CA 90212
(213) 272-2661

372 Bay St., Suite 610, Toronto, M5H 2W9
(416) 361-1605

1840 W. Sherbrooke, Montreal H3H 1E4
(514) 931-3855

FRENCH NATIONAL RAILROADS
610 Fifth Ave., New York, NY 10020
(212) 582-2110

Rail Travel

CARTE VERMEIL: *50% discount. Men over 62 and women over 60 can buy a discount card for 85 francs (approximately $14), good for one year, entitling them to buy first- or second-class tickets at a 50% discount. Discounts are available only for domestic travel on nonholiday weekdays ("blue tickets"). Discounts for SNCF rail tourist services and bus excursions are also available. The Carte Vermeil may be purchased in person only at major train stations in France. For more information, contact the French National Railroads office in New York.*

Package Tours for Seniors

Grand Circle offers an 18-day tour of France, from $2200, a 17-day tour of the French countryside from $1500, plus a two-week Riviera stay for $1200, with the option of an additional week in Paris for $400 extra. Saga offers a four-week tour of France and Spain from $1700 to $2200. See pages 7–10 for more about tours for seniors.

PARIS

Helpful Addresses

U.S. EMBASSY
2 ave. Gabriel, tel. 296-12-02

CANADIAN EMBASSY
35 ave. Montaigne, tel. 225-99-55

ACCUEIL DE FRANCE (Tourist Office)
127 ave. des Champs-Elysees, tel. 723-72-11

Hotels

HOLIDAY INN: *10%–20% discount with Holiday Inn's Travel Venture Club Card.*
Orly Airport, 4 ave. Lindbergh, tel. 687-26-66.
Roissy Airport, 1 allee du Verge, tel. 988-00-22.
10 place de la Republique, tel. 355-44-34.

MARRIOTT: *50% Leisurelife discount over 62.*
33 ave. Georges V, tel. 723-55-11.

Car Rental

AVIS: *10% discount.**
78 ave. Pierre Grenier, Boulogne, tel. 609-04-30.
Charles de Gaulle Airport, tel. 862-34-34.
Orly Airport, tel. 884-44-91.

EUROPCAR: *10%–20% discount.**
48 rue de Berri, tel. 563-0427
Charles de Gaulle Airport, tel. 862-33-33.
Orly Ouest Terminal, tel. 884-47-47.

HERTZ: *5%–25% discount.**
27 place St. Ferdinand, tel. 574-97-39.
Charles de Gaulle Airport, tel. 862-29-00.
Orly Airport, tel. 687-10-44.

GERMANY

Helpful Addresses

GERMAN NATIONAL TOURIST OFFICE
747 3rd Ave., New York, NY 10017
(212) 308-3300

444 S. Flower St., Los Angeles, CA 90071
(213) 688-7332

P.O. Box 417, 2 Fundy, Place Bonaventure, Montreal H5A 1B8
(514) 878-9885

GERMAN INFORMATION CENTER
950 Third Ave., New York, NY 10022
(212) 888-9840

Transportation

GERMAN FEDERAL RAILWAY: *50% discount with purchase of Senioren-Pass.*
950 Third Ave., New York, NY 10022, (212) 308-3100. *Men over 65 and women over 60 can buy either* Senioren-Pass A *for about $35 or* Senioren-Pass B *for about $55. Pass A entitles holder to 50% discount on Tuesdays, Wednesdays, and Thursdays only; Pass B is good for 50% discount travel any day of the week. Both passes are valid for one year. Neither pass is valid for Maundy Thursday, Good Friday, Tuesday and Wednesday after Easter, or December 23 and 24.* Senioren-Pass *can only be bought at GermanRail ticket offices in Germany.*

Package Tours for Seniors

Interhostel sponsors a two-week study holiday at the university in Trier, the oldest city in Germany. Current price: $1600 from Boston. See page 13 for more about Interhostel. Saga offers an 18-night Rhine cruise from $1900. Grand Circle Travel offers two weeks in the Black Forest from $1300 and includes Germany in several package tours. A 16-day Oktoberfest tour is offered by American Youth Hostels' 50+ program. See pages 7–10 for more information on package tours.

MUNICH

Helpful Address

TOURIST OFFICE OF THE CITY OF MUNICH
2 Sendlingerstrasse, D8000 Munich 2, tel. (089) 2 39 11.

Hotels

SHERATON: *25% discount for over 60.*
Arabellastrasse 6, tel. (089) 92 40 11.

Car Rental

AVIS: *10% discount.**
Airport, tel. (089) 90 74 11.
Nymphenburgerstrasse 61, tel. (089) 18 50 11.
Sheraton Hotel, Arabellastrasse 6, tel. (089) 91 80 04.

EUROPCAR: *10%–20% discount.**
Airport, tel. (089) 90 81 08.
Schwanthalerstrasse 10A, tel. (089) 59 47 23.

HERTZ: *5%–25% discount.**
Airport, tel. (089) 90 87 44
Nymphenburgerstrasse 81, tel. (089) 12 950 01.

GREAT BRITAIN

Helpful Addresses

BRITISH TOURIST AUTHORITY
40 W. 57th St., New York, NY 10019
(212) 581-4700

John Hancock Center, 875 N. Michigan Ave., Suite 3320, Chicago, IL 60611, (312) 787-0490.

2305 Cedar Springs Rd., Dallas, TX 75201, (214) 720-4040.

World Trade Center,
350 S. Figueroa St., Suite 450, Los Angeles, CA 90071, (213) 628-3525.

BRITRAIL TRAVEL INTERNATIONAL
630 Third Ave., New York, NY 10017, (212) 599-5400.

333 N. Michigan Ave., Chicago, IL 60601, (312) 263-1910.

2305 Cedar Springs Rd., Dallas, TX 75201, (214) 720-4040.

World Trade Center,
350 S. Figueroa St., Suite 450, Los Angeles, CA 90071, (213) 628-3525.

Transportation

BRITRAIL SENIOR CITIZENS PASS: *First-class travel at economy-class rates. Available to seniors over 60 from BritRail offices in New York, Chicago, Los Angeles, Toronto, and Vancouver. Not available in Britain. BritRail passes are issued for 8, 15, 22 days, or one month.*

British Tour Operators

Several British tour operators offer vacation packages in resort towns for senior citizens, usually in the spring and fall when prices are low. These packages are very reasonable, and while you probably would not want to plan your whole British vacation around one, a week at a resort town would be an ideal way to relax either before or after a concentrated period of sightseeing. Be sure to ask the tour operators for their definition of "senior citizen," usually 60 years old for women and 65 for men.

CO-OP TRAVEL: *Senior citizen holidays in April, May, June, and September.*
P.O. Box 53, Corporation St., Manchester M60 4ES, England, tel. (061) 832-8248.

SAGA (SENIOR CITIZENS) HOLIDAYS: *Senior citizens' holidays all year.*
Department E/SC, 119 Sandgate Rd., Folkestone, Kent, England, tel. Folkestone 30311. (See also pages 7–8).

SUNWIN TOURS: *Senior citizens' holidays in May, June, August, September, and October.*
Dept. 7, Sunwin House, 65 Sunbridge Rd., Bradford BD1 2AP, England, tel. Bradford 34277.

WALLACE ARNOLD TOURS LTD.: *Senior citizens' holidays available September to November and February to June.*
53 Corn Exchange, Leeds, England, tel. Leeds 30691.

Package Tours for Seniors

Saga Tours (which is British based) offers a variety of British tours ranging from seven nights in London ($900–1200) to a 17-day coach tour ($1900) to a 24-day holiday where travelers stay in universities in England, Scotland, Wales, and Ireland ($1600–$2100). Grand Circle Travel tours include a two-week stay in London (from $1200) and a two-week British tour (from $1900 with the option of an extra week in London). Interhostel sponsors two-week educational programs in Bristol, Lancaster, Leeds, London, Yorkshire, Scotland, and Wales for about $1700 from New York or Boston. See pages 7–10 for more about package tours.

LONDON

Helpful Addresses

U.S. EMBASSY
24 Grosvenor Square
tel. (01) 499-9000

CANADA HOUSE
Trafalgar Square
tel. (01) 629-9492

Hotels

MARRIOTT: *50% Leisurelife over 62.*
Grosvenor Square, (01) 493-1232.

RODEWAY INN: *10% discount.*
11 Kensington High St., (01) 603-3333.

SHERATON: *25% discount for over 60.*
Sheraton Park Tower Hotel, 101 Knightsbridge, (01) 235-8050.
Belgravia, 20 Chesham Place, SW1, (01) 235-6040.
Sheraton-Heathrow Hotel, at Heathrow Airport, (01) 759-2424.

Car Rental

AVIS: *10% discount.**
35 Headfort Pl., SW1, (01) 235-3235.
Heathrow Airport, (01) 897-9321.

EUROPCAR: *10%–20% discount.**
Gatwick Airport, tel. (0293) 310 624.
Heathrow Airport, tel. (01) 897-0811.
Victoria Station, tel. (01) 834-8484.

HERTZ: *5%–25% discount.**
35 Edgware Rd., Marble Arch, tel. (01) 402-4242.
Gatwick Airport, tel. (0293) 30555.
Heathrow Airport, tel. (01) 897-3347.

Theater

Senior discounts and tickets for nine London theaters can be obtained at the Queens Theatre on Shaftsbury Avenue.

Senior Discounts

Guinness World of Records, London Experience, Westminster Abbey, Wimbledon Lawn Tennis Museum, London Banqueting House, Light Fantastic, Royal Ballet School, Royal Mews, Tower Bridge Walkway, Whitechapel Art Gallery.

GREECE

Helpful Addresses

GREEK NATIONAL TOURIST ORGANIZATION
645 Fifth Ave., New York, NY 10022
(212) 421-5777

168 N. Michigan Ave., Chicago, IL 60601
(312) 782-1084

611 W. 6th St., Los Angeles, CA 90017
(213) 626-6696

Package Tours for Seniors

Interhostel sponsors a two-week study holiday based at the American College of Greece near Athens ($1900 from Boston or NY). More about Interhostel on page 13. Saga Tours offers a 17-night Aegean cruise and stay ($2100–2300) and a 15-night tour of classical Greece ($1350–1450).

ATHENS

Helpful Addresses

U.S. EMBASSY
91 Vassilissis Sofias Ave., tel. (01) 721 2951.

CANADIAN EMBASSY
411 Ioannou Genadiou St., tel. (01) 723 9511.

NATIONAL TOURIST ORGANIZATION OF GREECE
2 Amerikis St., tel. (01) 322 3111.
2 Karagiorgi Servias St., tel. (01) 322 2545.

Hotel

MARRIOTT: *50% Leisurelife over 62.*
115 Syngrov Ave., tel. 934 7711.

Car Rental

AVIS: *10% discount.**
Airport, tel. (01) 322 4951.
48 Queen Amalia Ave., tel. (01) 322-4951.

EUROPCAR: *10%–20% discount.**
148 Syngrou Ave., tel. (01) 923 5353.

HERTZ: *5%–25% discount.*
East Airport, tel. (01) 961 3625.
West Airport, tel. (01) 981 3701.
12 Syngrou Ave., tel. (01) 922 0102.
71 Vassilissis Sofias Ave., tel. (01) 724 7071.

IRELAND

Helpful Addresses

IRISH TOURIST BOARD
757 Third Ave., New York, NY 10017
(212) 418-0800

10 King St., E., Toronto, Ontario, M5C 1C3
(416) 364-1301

Springtime in Ireland

Ireland comes to life in the spring when everything turns green and discounts can be found everywhere. Get a copy of the booklet "Springtime in Ireland" from the tourist board before you go. It lists savings at restaurants, hotels, and stores participating in the springtime promotion. Also ask for the "tourist menu," a listing of hotels and restaurants offering "prix fixe" three-course meals throughout Ireland—a money-saving way to enjoy your stay.

Package Tours for Seniors

Interhostel sponsors a two-week learning experience in Galway and the Aran Islands, the home of archeological sites. University College hosts the program, and the cost is $1700 from Boston. Saga Holidays offers a 10-night tour of Ireland, starting at $1300. See pages 7–10 for more about tours.

Incredible Deals

You can purchase the "Rambler Pass" for unlimited travel on the Irish national bus and rail systems. Passes are for 8 or 15 days and you can choose either rail or bus travel (8 days: $66; 15 days: $99) or both (8 days: $84; 15 days $122). Write to C.I.E., 122 E. 42nd St., New York, NY 10168, or ask your travel agent.

DUBLIN

Helpful Addresses

U.S. Embassy
42 Elgin Rd., tel. 68-87-77

CANADIAN EMBASSY
65-68 Stephen's Green, tel. 78-19-88

TOURIST OFFICE
14 Upper O'Connell St., tel. 74-77-33

Hotels

QUALITY INN: *10% discount for over 60.*
Downtown, 2 Anglesea St., tel. (01) 715622.
Sutton 13, Dublin Rd., tel. (01) 322613.

Car Rental

AVIS: *10% discount.**
Airport, tel. 372369.
One Hanover Sq., E., tel. 776971

EUROPCAR: *10%–20% discount.**
Airport, tel. 378179
Baggott St. Bridge, tel. 681777.

HERTZ: *5%–25% discount.**
Airport, tel. 371693.
12 Upper O'Connell St., tel. 788322.

Free

Guinness Brewery, Trinity College, Bank of Ireland, Phoenix Park, St. Patrick.

ITALY

Helpful Addresses

ITALIAN GOVERNMENT TRAVEL OFFICE (ENIT)
630 Fifth Ave., New York, NY 10111
(212) 245-4822

360 Post St., Suite 801, San Francisco, CA 94108
(415) 392-6206

1 Place Ville Marie, Plaza 56, Montreal H3B 3M9
(514) 866-7667

Package Tours for Seniors

Interhostel sponsors a two-week studio arts experience in Florence (from $1900) based at the Studio Arts Center International. Passages Unlimited's "At Home" program offers private apartment vacations in Florence and Rome (from $300 per week). Saga offers an 18-day tour of "Romantic Italy" (from $1500). See pages 7–10 for more about package tours for seniors.

ROME

Helpful Addresses

U.S. EMBASSY
Via Vittorio Veneto 119a, tel. (06) 4674

CANADIAN EMBASSY
Via Zara 30, tel. (06) 854825 or 865004

EPT (Tourist Office)
Termini Station

Hotels

HOLIDAY INN: *10%–20% discount with Holiday Inn's Travel Venture Club Card.*
Parco dei Medici, Viale Castello della Magliana 65, tel. (06) 5475.
St. Peters, Via Aurelia Antica 415, tel. (06) 5872.

SHERATON: *25% discount for over 60.*
Viale del Pattinaggio, tel. (06) 5453.

Car Rental

AVIS: *10% discount.**
Ciampino Airport, tel. 60 0195.
Fiumicino Airport, tel. 60 1579.
Piazza Esquilino 1c, tel. (06) 4701.

EUROPCAR: *10%–20% discount.**
Ciampino Airport, tel. 60 0387.
Fiumicino Airport, tel. 60 1977.
Via Lombardia 7, tel. (06) 465 802.

HERTZ: *5%–25% discount.**
Ciampino Airport, tel. 60 0095.
Fiumicino Airport, tel. 60 1448.
Via Sallustiana 28, tel. (06) 51713.

THE NETHERLANDS

Helpful Addresses

NETHERLANDS NATIONAL TOURIST OFFICE
355 Lexington Ave., New York, NY 10017
(212) 370-7367

605 Market St., Room 401, San Francisco, CA 94105
(415) 543-6772

25 Adelaide St., Suite 710, Toronto, Ontario M5C 1Y2
(416) 363-1577

Transportation

RAIL: *Senior discounts vary by route. Check at local train stations.*

Incredible Deals

The Museum Year Card and the Holland Culture Card are both terrific values. The Museum Year Card costs about $8 for those up to age 64 and $5 for those 65 and over. It gets you free entry to museums throughout Holland and is available from VVV tourist offices throughout the country. The Holland Culture Card costs $17.50 (no discount for seniors) and provides free admission to museums, monuments, and galleries, plus discounts on car rentals and public transportation. It is available only from NNTO offices in the U.S. and Canada.

AMSTERDAM

Helpful Addresses

U.S. CONSULATE
Museumplein 19, tel. (020) 79-03-21.

VVV TOURIST INFORMATION
Centraal Stationsplein 10; Leidseplein 15.

Hotels

SONESTA: *15% discount.**
Downtown, 1 Kattengat, (020) 21-22-23.

Car Rental

AVIS: *10% discount.**
Schiphol Airport, (020) 17-67-54.

EUROPCAR: *10%–20% discount.**
Schiphol Airport, (020) 17-54-47.
51–53 Overtoom, (020) 18-45-95.

HERTZ: *5%–25% discount.**
Schiphol Airport, (020) 17-08-66.
Overtoom 333, (020) 12-24-41.

NORWAY

Helpful Addresses

NORWEGIAN TOURIST BOARD
655 3rd Ave., New York, NY 10017
(212) 949-2333

NORWEGIAN INFORMATION SERVICE
825 3rd Ave., New York, NY 10022
(212) 421-7333

Transportation

RAIL: *50% discount for seniors over 67.*

Package Tours for Seniors

Grand Circle Travel and Saga Holidays offers a variety of Scandinavian tours which include Norway. See pages 7–10 for information about package tours for seniors.

OSLO

Helpful Addresses

U.S. EMBASSY
Drammensveien 18, tel. (02) 44-85-50

CANADIAN EMBASSY
Oscargate 20, tel. (02) 46-69-55

Car Rental

AVIS: *10% discount.**
Airport, tel. (02) 53-05-47.
Munkendamsveien 27, tel. (02) 41-00-60.

EUROPCAR: *10%–20% discount.**
Airport, tel. (02) 53-09-39.
Storgata 55, tel. (02) 42-69-20.

HERTZ: *5%–25% discount.**
Airport, tel. (02) 53-36-47.
General Birchagt 16, tel. (02) 69-60-10.

Incredible Deals

The Oslo Card provides free admission to major attractions, free travel on public transportation, and discounts on tours, recreational activities, at restaurants, and car-rental firms. Cards are available for one- to three-day periods, starting at $10, and can be purchased from the Oslo Tourist Information Office at City Hall and from most hotels in Oslo.

PORTUGAL

Helpful Addresses

PORTUGAL NATIONAL TOURIST OFFICE
548 Fifth Ave., New York, NY 10036
(212) 354-4403

2180 Yonge St., Toronto, Ontario

Transportation

TAP AIR PORTUGAL: *Offers seasonal savings for seniors over 60 on airfare between New York and Boston to Lisbon, Porto, and Faro. One-way fare is $218.*

RAIL: *Portuguese National Railroads gives a 50% discount to travelers over 65 on trips of over 50 kilometers in either 1st or 2nd class. Show your passport when purchasing your ticket to get the discount.*

Package Tour for Seniors

Interhostel offers a two-week stay in Cascais, Portugal, for $1700 from Boston or New York. See page 13 for more on Interhostel.

LISBON

Helpful Addresses

U.S. EMBASSY
Avda. des Forcas Armadas, tel. 72 56 00

CANADIAN EMBASSY
Rua Rosa Aranjo 2, tel. 56 25 47

LISBON TOURIST OFFICE
Rua Jardim do Regedor

Car Rentals

AVIS: *10% discount.**
Airport, tel. 89 48 36.
Avda. Praia de Victoria, tel. 54 51 17.

EUROPCAR: *10%–20% discount.**
Airport, tel. 80 11 76.
Avda. de Aguiar 24, tel. 53 51 15.

HERTZ: *5%–25% discount.**
Airport, tel. 89 27 22.
Avda. 5 Outubro, tel. 57 90 77.

**An asterisk indicates that the discount is intended for members of senior citizens' organizations that anyone can join. See "Hotel, Transportation, and Sightseeing Discounts."*

SPAIN

Helpful Addresses

NATIONAL TOURIST OFFICE OF SPAIN
665 Fifth Ave., New York, NY 10022
(212) 759-8822

San Vicente Plaza Bldg., 8383 Wilshire Blvd., Suite 960, Beverly Hills, CA 90211
(213) 658-7188

4800 The Galleria, 5085 Westheimer, Houston, TX 77056
(713) 840-7411

Casa del Hidalgo, Hypolita and St. George Sts., St. Augustine, FL 32084
(904) 829-6460

60 Bloor St., Toronto, Ontario
(416) 961-3131

Rail Travel

RENFE (Spanish National Railroad): *50% discount for Spanish residents over 65 with purchase of card. Purchase of senior citizen ID card (approx. 50¢) from Spanish railroad stations entitles travelers over 65 to 50% discount on domestic journeys exceeding 100 kilometers (about 60 miles).*

Package Tours for Seniors

Interhostel's two-week study holiday in Malaga or Toledo depart from New York (from $1700). See page 13 for more on Interhostel. Saga Tours offers a 17-night coach tour of southern Spain ($1200–$1700), and a month-long apartment stay ($1100–$1400). AARP offers two weeks in the Costa del Sol (from $675) and a 15-day tour of the Costa del Sol and Andalusia (from $1000). More about package tours on pages 7–10.

MADRID

Helpful Addresses

U.S. EMBASSY
Serrano 75, tel. 276 34 00

CANADIAN EMBASSY
Nunez de Balboa, 34, tel. 225 91 19

TOURIST OFFICE
Princesa 1, Plaza de Espana, tel. 241 23 25

Hotels

HOLIDAY INN: *10%–20% discount with Holiday Inn's Travel Venture Club Card.*
Plaza Carlos Trias Bertran, tel. 456 70 14.

Car Rental

AVIS: *10% discount.**
Airport, tel. 205 85 32.
Gran Via 60, tel. 247 20 48.

EUROPCAR: *10%–20% discount.**
Airport, tel. 205 51 63.
Orense 29, tel. 455 99 30.

HERTZ: *5%–25% Discount.**
Airport, tel. 952 318740.
Edificio España Local 18, tel. 248 58 05.

SWEDEN

Helpful Addresses

SWEDISH TOURIST BOARD
655 3rd Ave., New York, NY 10017
(212) 949-2333

8929 Wilshire Blvd., Beverly Hills, CA 90211
(213) 854-1549

Transportation

SAS SCANDINAVIAN AIRLINES SYSTEM:
Variable discount for seniors over 65 on domestic flights.
For details, call SAS, (800) 221-2350 or your travel agent.

RAIL: *30% discount for seniors over 65.*

Package Tours for Seniors

Grand Circle Travel offers a 19-day tour of Scandinavia (from $3000). Passages Unlimited offers a 17-day "Magnificent Fjords" tour starting at $2200. See pages 7–10 for more on tours.

STOCKHOLM

Helpful Addresses

U.S. EMBASSY
Strandvagen 101, tel. 783 5300.

CANADIAN EMBASSY
Tegelbacken 4, 7th Floor, tel. 23 79 20.

SVERIGEHUSET TOURIST INFORMATION DESK
Hamngatan 27, tel. 789 2000.

Hotels

SHERATON: *25% discount for over 60.*
Tegelbacken 6, tel. (08) 14 26 00.

Car Rental

AVIS: *10% discount.**
Arlanda Airport, tel. 0760.

Sveavgen 61, tel. (08) 34 99 10.
Sheraton Hotel, tel. (08) 20 20 60.

EUROPCAR: *10%–20% discount.**
Arlanda Airport, tel. (0760) 61013.
Birger Jarlsgatan 59, tel. (08) 23 10 70.

HERTZ: *5%–25% discount.**
Arlanda Airport, tel. (0760) 60555.
Master Samuelsgatan 67, tel. (08) 240 720.

SWITZERLAND

Helpful Addresses

SWISS NATIONAL TOURIST OFFICE
608 Fifth Ave., New York, NY 10020
(212) 757-5944

250 Stockton St., San Francisco, CA 94108
(415) 362-2260

Commerce Ct., P.O. Box 215, Toronto M5L 1E8
(416) 868-0584

Package Tours for Seniors

Swissair's Golden Age Tours feature three two-week packages, two in the Lucerne area and one in Interlacken/Lugano. Expect to pay between $1150 and $1400 for land costs. Contact Swissair for brochure.

Incredible Deals

You can buy money-saving discount rail cards from any Swiss National Tourist Office. Half-Fare Travel Cards, Regional Holiday Season Tickets, and the Swiss Holiday Card are three ways to save money on rail travel.

Hotels

SAISON FÜR SENIOREN (Season for Senior Citizens); *Discount hotel rates. All senior citizens qualify for reduced all-inclusive hotel rates based on double-occupancy room, breakfast, taxes, and service charge. If a couple checks in at a participating hotel, only one spouse has to be in possession of a Half-Fare Card in order to qualify for reduced rates. Because over 350 participating Swiss hotels offer the discount at varying times of the year, careful planning is needed to take advantage of the program. Contact your travel agent or the Swiss National Tourist Office for further information and a directory of hotels.*

SHERATON: *25% discount for over 60.*
Zurich, Doltschiweg 234, tel. 463 00 00.

Car Rental

AVIS; *10% discount.**
Geneva Reservation Center, 44 rue de Lausanne, (022) 31 90 00.
Zurich Reservation Center, Flughofstrasse 61, (01) 810 20 20.

EUROPCAR: *10%–20% discount.**
Geneva Airport, (022) 981 110.
Zurich Airport, (01) 813 20 44.

HERTZ: *5%–25% discount.**
Geneva Prestige Car Service; 60 rue de Berne, (022) 982 202.
Zurich Prestige Car Service, Lagerstrasse 33, (01) 242 84 84.

**An asterisk indicates that the discount is intended for members of senior citizens' organizations that anyone can join. See "Hotel, Transportation, and Sightseeing Discounts."*

YUGOSLAVIA

Helpful Address

YUGOSLAV NATIONAL TOURIST OFFICE
630 Fifth Ave., New York, NY 10111
(212) 757-2801

Transportation

JAT-YUGOSLAVAIKLINES: *Offers senior citizen discount fares from New York, Chicago, and Cleveland to six Yugoslavian cities. Round-trip fares range from $610–$660.*

Package Tours for Seniors

Yugoslavia is a popular destination for senior tours because of the low prices and good weather. Grand Circle offers extended-stay vacations in and of four different cities, starting at $1,000 for two weeks including airfare. Saga Holidays offers a 17-night tour starting at $1450, while Yugotours and European Travel Center are both promoting two-week trips for about $1000 from New York, including meals, accommodations, and sightseeing. For more information on Grand Circle and Saga, see pages 7–8; for details on Yugotours and European Travel Center, ask your travel agent.

MEXICO & THE CARIBBEAN

Incredible Deals

SEASON OF SWEET SAVINGS: April 15–December 15 is bargain time in the Caribbean. Hotel prices are cut from 30% to 50%, airfares decrease, and numerous gifts and bonuses are offered. The only thing that doesn't change much is the temperature, which increases only 5 degrees from winter to summer. Contact the Caribbean Tourism Association, 20 E. 46th St., New York, NY 10017, (212) 682-0435 for details.

MEXICO

Helpful Addresses

MEXICAN GOVERNMENT TOURISM OFFICE
405 Park Ave., New York, NY
(212) 838-2949

10100 Santa Monica Blvd., Suite 224,
Los Angeles, CA 90067
(213) 203-8191

1 Place Ville Marie, Suite 2409, Montreal
(514) 871-1052

Package Tours for Seniors

AARP sponsors a 15-day hosted holiday in Mexico City and Guadalajara (from $530) and a 15-day "Archaeological Wonders" tour (from $1170). Prices do not include airfare. See pages 7–10 for more about tours.

GUADALAJARA

Helpful Address

MEXICAN NATIONAL TOURIST COUNCIL
Avenida Juarez 638, tel. (9136) 22-41-30

Hotels

HOLIDAY INN: *10%–20% discount with Holiday Inn's Travel Venture Club Card.*
Lopez Mateos 2500, tel. 31-55-66.

QUALITY INN: *10% discount for over 60.*
Avda. Arienda Juarez, 170, tel. 14-86-50.

SHERATON: *25% discount for over 60.*
Ave. Niños Heroes & 16 de Septiembre, tel. 14-72-72.

Car Rental

AVIS: *10% discount.**
Airport, tel. 89-02-21.
Ave. Vallarta y Calle, tel. 15-48-25.

HERTZ: *10% discount.**
Airport, tel. 35-89-39.
Ave. Niños Heroes 9, tel. 14-61-39.

NATIONAL: *20% discount.**
Airport, tel. 35-8405.
Ave. Niños Heroes 631-C, tel. 13-62-49 or 14-71-75.

MEXICO CITY

Helpful Address

MEXICAN NATIONAL TOURIST COUNCIL
Mariano Escobedo, 726, tel. 250-8555.

Hotels

HOLIDAY INN: *10%–20% discount with Holiday Inn's Travel Venture Club Card.*
Airport, Blvd. Pto. Aereo 502, (905) 762-40-88.
Paseo de la Reforma 80, (905) 566-7777.

QUALITY INN: *10% discount for over 60.*
Londres 130, (905) 211-0071.

SHERATON: *25% discount for over 60.*
Paseo de la Reforma 325, (905) 211-0001.

Car Rental

AVIS: *10% discount.**
Airport, (905) 762-8111.
Dr. Velasco 138, (905) 761-3300.

HERTZ: *10% discount.**
Airport, (905) 784-7547.
Versailles 6, (905) 592-6082.

NATIONAL: *20% discount.**
Airport, (905) 571-8710.
Mexicana Gate, (905) 762-8426.

PUERTO VALLARTA

Hotels

HOLIDAY INN: *10%–20% discount with Holiday Inn's Travel Venture Club Card.*
Ave. de las Garzas, tel. 2-17-00.

QUALITY INN: *10% discount for over 60.*
Plaza las Glorias and Plaza Vallarta, Ave. de las Garzas, tel. 2-22-24.

SHERATON: *25% discount for over 60.*
Carretera Aeropuerto 999, tel. 2-30-00.

Car Rental

AVIS: *10% discount.**
Airport, tel. 2-11-12.

HERTZ: *10% discount.**
Airport, tel. 2-04-73.
Hotel Oceano, Av. Presidente Diaz Ordaz 16 & 18, tel. 2-00-04.

NATIONAL: *20% discount.**
Airport, tel. 2-11-07.

ARUBA (Netherlands Antilles)

Helpful Addresses

ARUBA TOURIST BUREAU
1270 Sixth Ave., New York, NY 10020
(212) 246-3030

A. Shuttestraat 2, Oranjestad, Aruba, tel. 23777

Hotels

BEST WESTERN: *10% discount.*
LG Smith Blvd. 55, tel. 2-3444.

HOLIDAY INN: *10%–20% discount with Holiday Inn's Travel Venture Club Card.*
Palm Beach, tel. 011-599-8-23600.

Car Rental

AVIS: *10% discount.**
Airport, 25496.
Sheraton, Smith Blvd., Palm Beach, 23900.

HERTZ: *10% discount.**
Airport, (364) 4800.
142 Smith Blvd., Palm Beach, (364) 4545.

NATIONAL: *20% discount.**
Airport, 24641.

BERMUDA

Helpful Address

BERMUDA DEPARTMENT OF TOURISM
310 Madison Ave., Suite 201, New York, NY 10017
(212) 818-9800

Package Tours for Seniors

Both AARP and Saga Holidays offer 7-day cruises to Bermuda ($800–$1200). See pages 7–10 for more on package tours.

Hotels

SONESTA: *15% discount.**
Sonesta Beach Hotel, Southampton, (809) 298-8122.

JAMAICA

Helpful Addresses

JAMAICA TOURIST BOARD
866 Second Ave., New York, NY 10017
(212) 688-7650

36 S. Wabash Ave., Suite 1210, Chicago, IL 60603
(312) 346-1546

3440 Wilshire Blvd., Suite 1207, Los Angeles, CA 90010
(213) 384-1123

20 Knudsford Blvd., Kingston, Jamaica
(809) 929-9200

Hotels

HOLIDAY INN: *10%–20% discount with Holiday Inn's Travel Venture Club Card.*
Rose Hall, Montego Bay, (809) 953-2485.

SHERATON: *25% discount for over 60.*
Ochos Rios Sheraton, St. Ann, (809) 974-2201.

Car Rental

AVIS: *10% discount.**
Kingston, 2 Haining Rd., (809) 926-1560.
Montego Bay Airport, (809) 952-4543.

HERTZ: *10% discount.**
Kingston Airport, (809) 924-8028.
Montego Bay Airport, (809) 952-4472.

NATIONAL: *20% discount.**
Kingston Airport, (809) 928-9775.
Montego Bay Airport, (809) 952-2769.

PUERTO RICO

Helpful Addresses

COMMONWEALTH OF PUERTO RICO TOURISM COMPANY
1290 Ave. of the Americas, New York, NY 10104
(212) 541-6630

3575 W. Cahuenga Blvd., Suite 248, Los Angeles, CA 90068
(213) 874-5991

10 King St. E., Suite 501, Toronto, Ontario M5C 1C3
(416) 367-0190

301 San Justo St., San Juan, Puerto Rico 00903
(809) 721-2400

GERICULTURE COMMISSION
Dept. of Social Services, P.O. Box 11398, Santurce, P.R. 00910
(809) 721-3141

Package Tours for Seniors

Interhostel sponsors a two-week opportunity to study culture at the University of Puerto Rico, with departures from Boston and New York (from $1350). Saga Holidays offers a seven-day Caribbean Cruise that starts off in San Juan. Prices start at $850. For more about tours, see pages 7–10.

SAN JUAN

Hotels

HOWARD JOHNSON'S: *15%–50% discount with H.J.'s Road Rally Card.*
Condado, 1369 Ashford Ave., (809) 721-7300.

Car Rental

HERTZ: *30% discount.**
Airport, (809) 791-0085.
Condado, 1365 Ashford Ave., (809) 725-2027.

AVIS: *10% discount.**
Airport, (809) 791-2500.
Condado, 52 Aguadilla St., (809) 721-8605.

NATIONAL: *20% discount.**
Airport, (809) 791-1805.

Rules for Savings on Car Rentals

1. Join a national senior citizens' organization and use its discount identification number.
2. Make advance reservations with the toll-free national reservation service.
3. Renting mid-week? A senior-citizen rate can save you money.
4. Renting for seven days or for the weekend? Senior discounts can save you another 5% to 10%.
5. Always ask, "Is this the cheapest rate you offer?"

See paged 32–34 for more information.

PLEASE HELP US TO HELP YOU

When the next revised, updated edition of *The Discount Guide for Travelers Over 55* is published, we'd like to serve you and other future readers better by incorporating your suggestions and information you'd care to pass along. If you've discovered a restaurant, hotel, or some other place that isn't in the book but *ought* to be, we'd be grateful if you would take a moment to let us know about it by writing to *The Discount Guide for Travelers Over 55*, E. P. Dutton, 2 Park Avenue, New York, NY 10016.

I would like to recommend the following establishments or places for inclusion in the next revised, updated edition of *The Discount Guide for Travelers Over 55:*

Name of Establishment or Place____________________
Address____
City________________State______________Zip______
Senior Discount__________________________________

Name of Establishment or Place____________________
Address____
City________________State______________Zip______
Senior Discount__________________________________

Name of Establishment or Place____________________
Address____
City________________State______________Zip______
Senior Discount__________________________________

If any of these places are included in future editions of *The Discount Guide for Travelers Over 55*, we'd like to acknowledge your assistance and cite you by name as a contributor. If you'd like us to do so, please print your name clearly in this space:

____

____

(over)

Can you spare a moment to tell us what you thought of *The Discount Guide for Travelers Over 55?*

Were there sections in the book that you thought should be longer or more detailed? (Please be specific if possible.)___

Was there any information omitted that you felt *should* be included?___

Were there any establishments listed in the *Discount Guide* that were reluctant—or refused—to offer you a senior citizens' discount, or gave poor service, or disappointed you for some other reason? (Please be specific.)___

Please feel free to offer additional comments, criticisms, or suggestions in this space:___

Your Name___

City___ State___ Zip___

NOTE: Unless we are asked not to, we shall assume that we may publish your name as a contributor of new travel ideas and information.

PLEASE DETACH THIS PAGE, FOLD, AND MAIL TO:
The Discount Guide for Travelers Over 55, E. P. Dutton, 2 Park Ave., New York, NY 10016.